GEOGRAPHIES OF THE UNITED STATES

Ingolf Vogeler, General Editor

Texas: A Geography

Terry G. Jordan with

John L. Bean, Jr., and William M. Holmes

Texas—largest of the forty-eight contiguous states and perhaps the object of more stereotyping than any of the others—is the subject of this systematic geography. Far from being populated strictly by cattle ranchers and oil magnates, Texas is characterized by a rich internal diversity, reflected in its pronounced regionalism. The state exhibits an enormous variety in its environmental and cultural assets, with pecans, oranges, and symphony orchestras as evident as chili, armadillos, and the Superdome; and Texas cities are just as likely to be bustling centers of commerce, like Houston and Dallas/Fort Worth, as sleepy cowtowns. Midland and Odessa—barely wide spots in the road 30 years ago— now are boom towns thriving on the riches of oil. The Gulf determines the character of Galveston and Corpus Christi. The Alamo and the charm of the deep South entice people to San Antonio. Austin, in the hill country, is the home of political machinations so complex that Yale University offers a course on Texas politics. El Paso and Laredo exemplify the important Hispanic influence on Texas's culture. Indeed, the only stereotype that holds true of Texas is its size—no matter how you look at it, Texas *is big*.

This topical geography, the first published on Texas, looks at the state's bountiful variety; at its environmental and demographic patterns; cultural, religious, and ethnic groups; dialects and languages; agriculture; industry; and rural and urban configurations. It reveals Texas to be many instead of one, celebrates its diversity, and points to a multitude of reasons why the Lone Star State is one of the fastest rising stars in the nation's Sun Belt.

Dr. Terry G. Jordan is Walter Prescott Webb Professor in the Department of Geography at the University of Texas at Austin. Dr. John L. Bean, Jr., is associate professor of geography at North Texas State University, where Dr. William M. Holmes is an assistant professor in the same department.

TEXAS

A GEOGRAPHY

**Terry G. Jordan with
John L. Bean, Jr., and
William M. Holmes**

Westview Press / Boulder and London

Geographies of the United States

Jacket photo: State capital, Austin (photo courtesy of Austin–Travis County Collection of the Austin Public Library).

Copyright © 1984 by Westview Press, Inc.

Published in 1984 in the United States of America by Westview Press, Inc., 5500 Central Avenue, Boulder, Colorado 80301; Frederick A. Praeger, President and Publisher

Library of Congress Cataloging in Publication Data
Jordan, Terry G.
  Texas, a geography.
  (Geographies of the United States)
  Includes bibliographies and index.
  1. Texas—Description and travel. I. Bean, John L.
II. Holmes, William M. III. Title. IV. Series.
F386.J7 1983   976.4   83-6642
ISBN 0-86531-088-2
ISBN 0-86531-481-0 (pbk.)

Printed and bound in the United States of America

10   9   8   7   6   5   4   3   2   1

CONTENTS

TABLES

ILLUSTRATIONS

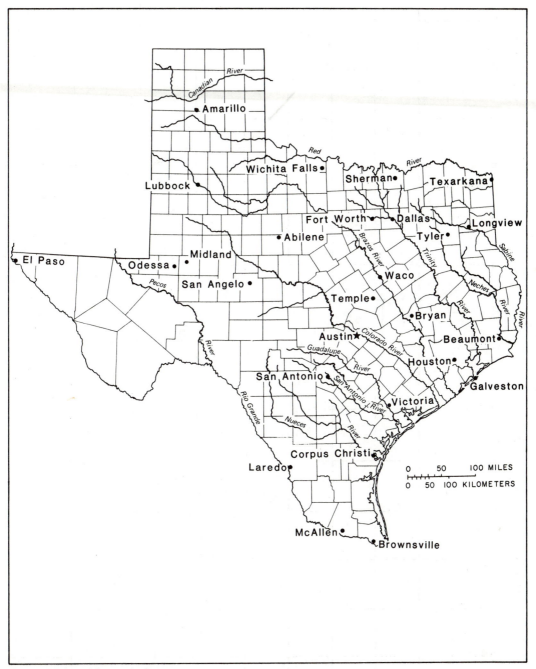

Texas: Major cities and rivers.

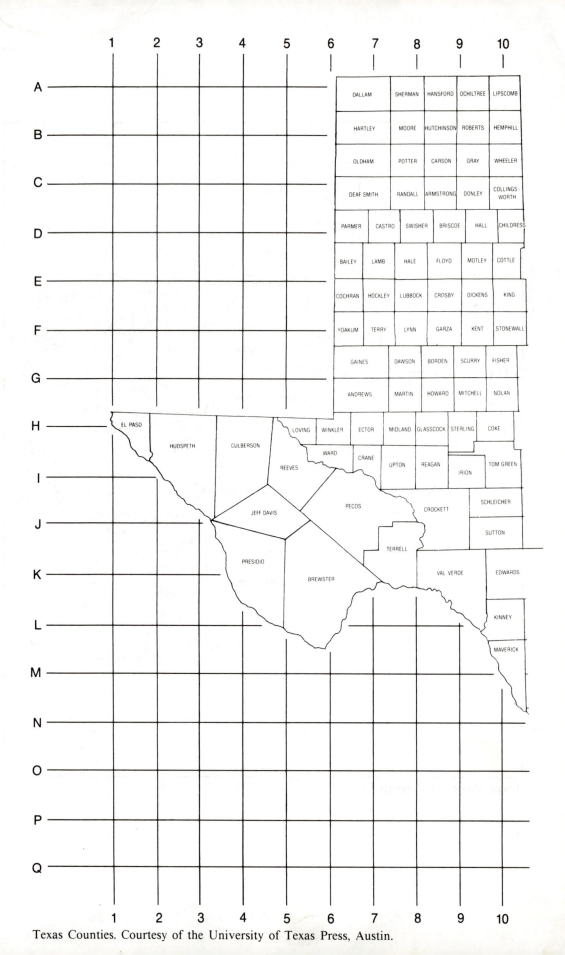

Texas Counties. Courtesy of the University of Texas Press, Austin.

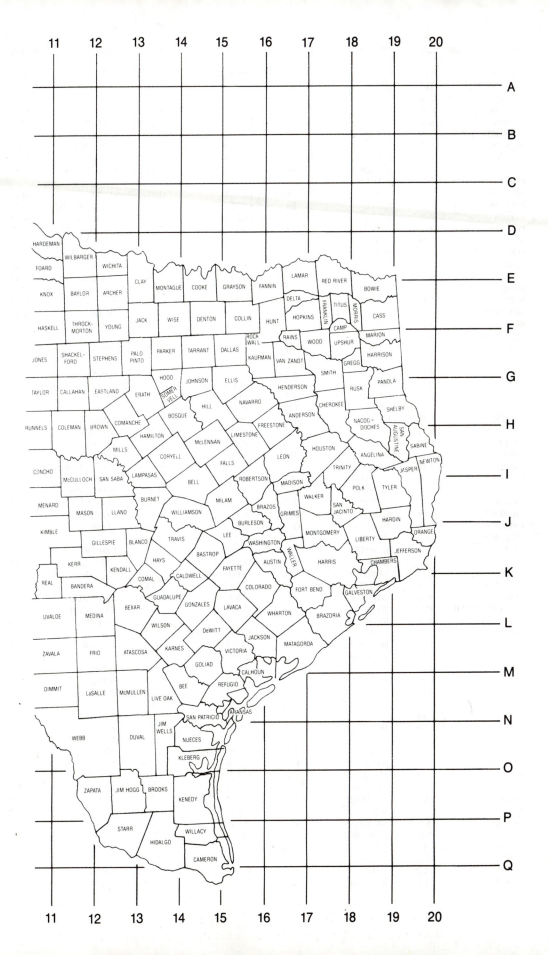

COUNTY	LOCATION	COUNTY	LOCATION	COUNTY	LOCATION	COUNTY	LOCATION
ANDERSON	H-17	EASTLAND	G-12	KENDALL	K-13	REAL	K-11
ANDREWS	G-7	ECTOR	H-7	KENEDY	P-15	RED RIVER	E-18
ANGELINA	H-19	EDWARDS	K-10	KENT	F-9	REEVES	I-5
ARANSAS	N-16	ELLIS	G-15	KERR	K-12	REFUGIO	M-15
ARCHER	E-12	EL PASO	H-1	KIMBLE	J-11	ROBERTS	B-9
ARMSTRONG	C-9	ERATH	G-13	KING	E-10	ROBERTSON	I-16
ATASCOSA	M-13			KINNEY	L-10	ROCKWALL	F-16
AUSTIN	K-16	FALLS	I-15	KLEBERG	O-15	RUNNELS	H-11
		FANNIN	E-16	KNOX	E-11	RUSK	G-18
BAILEY	E-6	FAYETTE	K-15				
BANDERA	K-12	FISHER	G-10	LAMAR	E-17	SABINE	H-20
BASTROP	K-15	FLOYD	E-9	LAMB	E-7	SAN AUGUSTINE	H-20
BAYLOR	E-12	FOARD	E-11	LAMPASAS	I-13	SAN JACINTO	J-18
BEE	M-14	FORT BEND	L-17	LaSALLE	N-12	SAN PATRICIO	N-15
BELL	I-14	FRANKLIN	F-17	LAVACA	L-16	SAN SABA	I-12
BEXAR	L-13	FREESTONE	H-16	LEE	J-15	SCHLEICHER	J-10
BLANCO	K-13	FRIO	M-12	LEON	I-17	SCURRY	G-9
BORDEN	G-8			LIBERTY	J-19	SHACKELFORD	G-12
BOSQUE	H-14	GAINES	G-7	LIMESTONE	H-16	SHELBY	H-20
BOWIE	E-19	GALVESTON	L-18	LIPSCOMB	A-10	SHERMAN	A-8
BRAZORIA	L-18	GARZA	F-9	LIVE OAK	N-14	SMITH	G-18
BRAZOS	J-16	GILLESPIE	K-12	LLANO	J-13	SOMERVELL	H-14
BREWSTER	K-6	GLASSCOCK	H-8	LOVING	H-5	STARR	Q-13
BRISCOE	D-9	GOLIAD	M-15	LUBBOCK	E-8	STEPHENS	G-12
BROOKS	P-14	GONZALES	L-15	LYNN	F-8	STERLING	H-9
BROWN	H-12	GRAY	C-9			STONEWALL	F-10
BURLESON	J-16	GRAYSON	E-15	McCULLOCH	I-12	SUTTON	J-10
BURNET	J-13	GREGG	G-18	McLENNAN	H-15	SWISHER	D-8
		GRIMES	J-17	McMULLEN	N-13		
CALDWELL	K-14	GUADALUPE	L-14	MADISON	I-17	TARRANT	G-15
CALHOUN	M-16			MARION	F-19	TAYLOR	G-11
CALLAHAN	G-12	HALE	E-8	MARTIN	G-8	TERRELL	K-7
CAMERON	Q-15	HALL	D-9	MASON	J-12	TERRY	F-7
CAMP	F-18	HAMILTON	H-13	MATAGORDA	M-17	THROCKMORTON	F-12
CARSON	B-8	HANSFORD	A-8	MAVERICK	M-10	TITUS	F-18
CASS	F-19	HARDEMAN	D-11	MEDINA	L-12	TOM GREEN	I-10
CASTRO	D-7	HARDIN	J-19	MENARD	J-11	TRAVIS	K-14
CHAMBERS	K-19	HARRIS	K-18	MIDLAND	H-8	TRINITY	I-18
CHEROKEE	H-18	HARRISON	G-19	MILAM	J-15	TYLER	I-19
CHILDRESS	D-10	HARTLEY	B-7	MILLS	I-13		
CLAY	E-13	HASKELL	F-11	MITCHELL	H-9	UPSHUR	F-18
COCHRAN	E-6	HAYS	K-14	MONTAGUE	E-14	UPTON	I-8
COKE	H-10	HEMPHILL	B-10	MONTGOMERY	J-18	UVALDE	L-11
COLEMAN	H-11	HENDERSON	G-17	MOORE	B-8		
COLLIN	F-16	HIDALGO	Q-14	MORRIS	F-18	VAL VERDE	K-9
COLLINGSWORTH	C-10	HILL	H-15	MOTLEY	E-9	VAN ZANDT	G-17
COLORADO	K-16	HOCKLEY	E-7			VICTORIA	M-16
COMAL	K-13	HOOD	G-14	NACOGDOCHES	H-19		
COMANCHE	H-13	HOPKINS	F-17	NAVARRO	H-16	WALKER	J-18
CONCHO	I-11	HOUSTON	I-18	NEWTON	I-20	WALLER	K-17
COOKE	E-15	HOWARD	G-8	NOLAN	G-10	WARD	I-6
CORYELL	I-14	HUDSPETH	H-2	NUECES	O-15	WASHINGTON	K-16
COTTLE	E-10	HUNT	F-16			WEBB	O-12
CRANE	I-7	HUTCHINSON	B-8	OCHILTREE	A-9	WHARTON	L-17
CROCKETT	J-8			OLDHAM	C-7	WHEELER	C-10
CROSBY	E-9	IRION	I-9	ORANGE	J-20	WICHITA	E-12
CULBERSON	I-4					WILBARGER	D-12
		JACK	F-13	PALO PINTO	G-13	WILLACY	P-15
DALLAM	A-7	JACKSON	M-16	PANOLA	G-19	WILLIAMSON	J-14
DALLAS	G-15	JASPER	I-20	PARKER	G-14	WILSON	L-14
DAWSON	G-8	JEFF DAVIS	J-4	PARMER	D-6	WINKLER	H-6
DEAF SMITH	C-7	JEFFERSON	K-20	PECOS	J-6	WISE	F-14
DELTA	F-17	JIM HOGG	P-13	POLK	I-19	WOOD	F-18
DENTON	F-15	JIM WELLS	O-14	POTTER	C-8		
DeWITT	L-15	JOHNSON	G-15	PRESIDIO	K-4	YOAKUM	F-6
DICKENS	E-9	JONES	G-11			YOUNG	F-12
DIMMIT	M-11			RAINS	F-17		
DONLEY	C-9	KARNES	M-14	RANDALL	C-8	ZAPATA	P-12
DUVAL	O-13	KAUFMAN	G-16	REAGAN	I-8	ZAVALA	M-11

CHAPTER 1

EMPIRE OR BORDER PROVINCE?

The essential geographical question concerning Texas can be easily stated: Is it one or many? Culturally, economically, and environmentally is Texas empire or border province, core or periphery, unity or diversity? Does the functional cohesiveness provided by the political framework or the diversity of land and people prevail? The essence of the answer is spatial and thus inherently geographical, providing an appropriate theme for this book.

A great variety of writers, lay and scholar alike, have sought to provide an answer to the question, without reaching agreement. Proponents of the "Texas is one" viewpoint are legion. From diverse quarters one hears of "typically Texan" characteristics of phenomena as varied as terrain, speech, weather, and politics. Many outsiders, as well as some natives and residents of the state, stereotype Texas and Texans. In this image, perhaps fostered and nurtured mainly by Hollywood and television but not lacking scholarly support, Texas is a flat, hot, dry, and very nearly treeless place inhabited by proud, wealthy, boastful, bigoted, violent, ambitious, and anti-intellectual people speaking a distinctive, twangy, nasal dialect and concerned mainly with cattle, oil, football, marital infidelity, and power politics. Popular regional terms dear to the news media, particularly Sun Belt and Bible Belt, reinforce the image of environmental and cultural oneness, as do best-selling books such as Edna Ferber's *Giant* and the television series "Dallas." Even John Steinbeck, whose acute perception of microregionalism, or place, shines so brightly in most of his works, succumbs to the concept of unity when confronted with Texas, describing it as "a state of mind, . . . an obsession, . . . a nation in every sense of the word."

The writers of movies, television shows, and novels are not alone in championing the unitary image of Texas. Anthropologist Evon Z. Vogt writes of a "Texan subculture" encompassing a stretch of territory "from the Southern Appalachians to California," including, "undoubtedly," outliers in Detroit and other northern industrial cities. In a series of astounding generalizations, Vogt informs his learned readers that members of this subculture speak a "Texan dialect," do not "have much to do with Negroes," enjoy "hillbilly" music, favor "individual independence and competition" to the detriment of group cooperation, argue and feud a lot, dislike Mexicans, adhere to Protestantism, and look to the "cattle and oil millionaires" as their "cultural heroes." Vogt no doubt represents an extreme viewpoint, but even scholars who clearly do not subscribe to the unitary concept of Texas sometimes foster it in titles such as *Imperial Texas*, "Land of

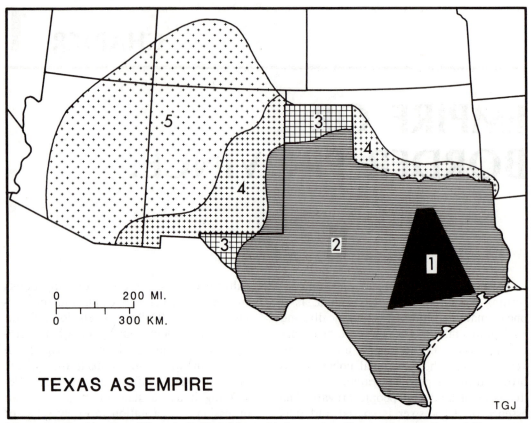

Figure 1.1. In this view, "Texanity" diminishes with increasing distance from a Central Texas core, but its influence is felt far to the west. (Based on Donald W. Meinig, *Imperial Texas* [Austin: University of Texas Press, 1969], Map 17.)
Key: 1 = core; 2 = primary domain; 3 = secondary domain; 4 = sphere; 5 = zone of penetration.

the Monied 'Establishment,'" and *A Nation Within a Nation* (Figure 1.1).

Many other observers of the Texas scene are more impressed by the internal contrasts than by the mystique of unity. The state's own official tourist guidebook, issued by the Travel and Information Division of the Highway Department, bears the title *Texas: Land of Contrast* and advises prospective visitors that "there's enough variety so you can pick just what appeals to you." Ten regions, given names such as "ranch and hill country," "vibrant gateway," and "border tropics," form the basic outline of the guidebook. Diversity, both human and environmental, is the theme throughout.

A favorite concept of those who emphasize internal regionality is the contrast

between east and west within Texas, a contrast perhaps most concisely (two sentences and nine hyphens) captured by the southern writer Robert Penn Warren in his novel *All the King's Men*. East Texas, in Warren's words, is "the part where the flat-footed, bilious, frog-sticker-toting Baptist biscuit-eaters live," very different from West Texas, where dwell "the crook-legged, high-heeled, gun-wearing, spick-killing, callous-rumped sons of the range." The famous historian Walter Prescott Webb, who in the formative years of boyhood lived in both East and West Texas, became the greatest champion of the east-west division. He presents the contrast as, essentially, an environmental one, with profound secondary implications for society, culture, and econ-

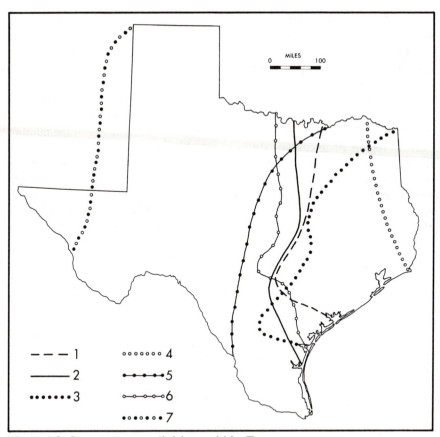

Figure 1.2. Some east-west divisions within Texas.
Key: 1 = Webb's eastern border of the Great Plains; 2 = Zelinsky's border between the South and West; 3 = Jordan's border between Upper South and Lower South; 4 = Gastil's border between eastern South and western South; 5 = Lane's border between quasi-South and non-South; 6 = isohyet for 30 inches (76 cm) annual average precipitation; 7 = Gastil's border between the South and the Interior Southwest.

omy. "The dividing line between the East and West cuts the state of Texas into two almost equal parts," writes Webb, running from "near Sherman" on the Red River southward, "passing near Waco, Austin, and San Antonio" and on to "Indianola, on the Gulf of Mexico" (Figure 1.2). East of this environmental and "institutional fault line" lies a "forested and well-watered country" occupied by people accustomed by experience and ancestry to the dewy greenness of humid woodlands. To the west stretches the dry, flat, treeless expanse of the Great Plains, an environment that, Webb argues, drastically reshaped the economy, society,

and culture of those who entered the area.

Certain other scholars, particularly cultural geographers, downplay the environmental contrasts and focus instead on the human aspects of the east-west division. Their viewpoint derives from the realization that, from pre-Columbian times to the present, Texas has housed a multicultural population, arranged spatially in such a way as to present contrasts between east and west. Immigration to Texas involved a confluence of cultures, with many groups from diverse backgrounds coming to people the state. When the first Europeans penetrated Texas, they observed the fundamental contrast between the relatively advanced farming Indians of the east and the primitive hunter-gatherers living to the west. European settlement of the state reinforced this ancient cultural division, as Robert Penn Warren accurately and irreverently perceives.

Geographer Wilbur Zelinsky, though labeling Texas a "region of uncertain status or affiliation," draws a "first order cultural boundary" directly through the state, pretty much following Webb's environmental line. In this manner, he separates the South from the West. Similarly, Charles Lane designates an arched line from Laredo to Sherman as the divide between the quasi-South and

the non-South. Jordan, too, stresses an east-west contrast, though his dividing line between Upper South and Lower South lies considerably east of Lane's, Zelinsky's, or Webb's, running from Texarkana in the northeast corner of Texas to San Antonio. East of that boundary the traditional rural culture and economy of the plantation South holds sway, with roots in the Chesapeake Bay and Carolina Tidewater regions, while to the west the influence of the hill South, derived from the Middle Atlantic colonies, prevails. This contrast of planter and yeoman, of family farm and landed estate, though implanted before the Civil War remains vivid yet today, he maintains. Ray-

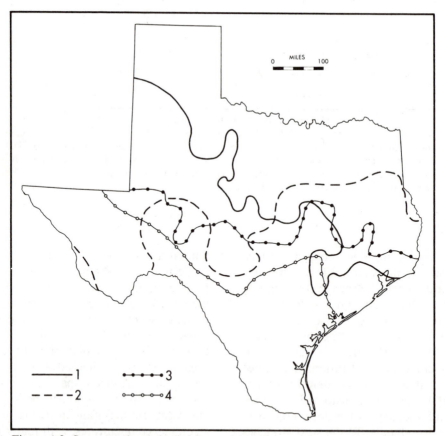

Figure 1.3. Some north-south divisions within Texas.
Key: 1 = Nostrand's northern boundary of the Hispanic borderland in 1960; 2 = isotherm for 66° F (19° C) mean annual temperature; 3 = "wet-dry" legal border for alcoholic beverages, 1971; 4 = Sopher's major religious border in 1950.

mond Gastil, while regarding all of Texas except the transmontane portion as a part of the South, also favors an east-west division. His proposed border runs from near Clarksville to Port Arthur, leaving a narrow strip several counties wide along the Louisiana border in the eastern South, while the much larger remainder forms the bulk of the western South.

Others profess to see north-south contrasts as a key to understanding Texas (Figure 1.3). Richard Nostrand's definition of a Hispanic borderland divides the state almost evenly between a Latin South and an Anglo North. His boundary is inherently mobile, shifting northward with the massive migration of the Spanish-surnamed population. Deanna Dooley concurs, noting that the pattern of legal status of alcoholic beverages displays a similar north-south contrast. That "wet-dry" border in turn parallels the major religious divide, described by David Sopher and others, separating the Baptist/Methodist northern half of Texas from the Catholic/Lutheran southern part. Some environmental features, particularly temperature, reinforce the concept of a north-south contrast.

One or many? We choose in this book to emphasize the formal plurality of Texas rather than its functional unity. Perhaps as geographers, by definition and inclination concerned with areal variation, with *places*, we are simply following our academic instincts. In any case, Texas in our view is a border province, where are joined Anglo-America and Latin America; the Bible Belt and Roman Catholicism; South, West, and Midwest; plains and mountains; forest and prairie; farmer and rancher; urban and rural; humid subtropics and desert. Texan chauvinism and statehood pale in significance before these fundamental spatial contrasts of land and culture.

A logical and traditional point of departure for our celebration of Texas's geographical diversity is the physical environment. Accordingly, Chapter 2 is devoted to the terrain, climate, soils, and vegetation of the state.

Figure 1.4. Political location of Texas.

SOURCES AND SUGGESTED READINGS

Arbingast, Stanley A., et al. *Atlas of Texas.* 5th ed. Austin: University of Texas, Bureau of Business Research, 1976.

Dooley, Deanna D. "The Decision to Drink: An Explanation of the Wet/Dry Boundary in Texas." M.A. thesis, Department of Geography, Ohio University, Athens, 1974.

Ferber, Edna. *Giant.* Garden City, N.Y.: Doubleday, 1952.

Gastil, Raymond D. *Cultural Regions of the United States.* Seattle: University of Washington Press, 1975.

Jordan, Terry G. "The Imprint of the Upper and Lower South on Mid-Nineteenth-Century Texas." *Annals of the Association of American Geographers* 57 (1967), 667–690.

Lane, Charles F. "Southern and Quasi-Southern Cultural Landscapes." In Francis B. Simkins, ed., *The South in Perspective.* Farmville, Va.: Institute of Southern Culture, Longwood College, 1959, pp. 93–107.

Mangus, A. R. *Rural Regions of the United States*. Washington, D.C.: Works Progress Administration, 1940.

Meinig, Donald W. *Imperial Texas: An Interpretive Essay in Cultural Geography*. Austin: University of Texas Press, 1969.

Nackman, Mark E. *A Nation Within a Nation: The Rise of Texas Nationalism*. Port Washington, N.Y.: Kinnikat Press, 1976.

Nostrand, Richard L. "The Hispanic-American Borderland: Delimitation of an American Culture Region." *Annals of the Association of American Geographers* 60 (1970), 638–661.

Peirce, Neal R. "Texas: Land of the Monied 'Establishment.'" In *The Megastates of America: People, Politics, and Power in the Ten Great States*, pp. 495–563. New York: W. W. Norton, 1972.

Pluta, Joseph E.; Wright, Rita J.; and Anderson, Mildred C. *Texas Fact Book: 1981*. Austin: University of Texas, Bureau of Business Research, 1981.

Sopher, David E. *Geography of Religions*. Englewood Cliffs, N.J.: Prentice-Hall, 1967.

Texas Almanac and State Industrial Guide. Dallas: *Dallas Morning News*, A. H. Belo Corp., published semiannually, latest edition is 1982–1983.

Texas: Land of Contrast. Austin: Texas Highway Department, Travel and Information Division, ca. 1975.

Vogt, Evon Z. "American Subcultural Continua as Exemplified by the Mormons and Texans." *American Anthropologist* 57 (1955), 1163–1172.

Webb, Walter P. *The Great Plains*. Boston: Ginn and Co., 1931.

Webb, Walter P.; Carroll, H. Bailey; and Branda, Eldon S., eds. *The Handbook of Texas*. 3 vols. Austin: Texas State Historical Association, 1952–1976.

SOURCES OF QUOTATIONS

Steinbeck, John, *Travels with Charley: In Search of America* (New York: Viking Press, 1962).

Warren, Robert Penn, *All the King's Men* (New York: Harcourt, Brace, 1946).

Zelinsky, Wilbur, *The Cultural Geography of the United States* (Englewood Cliffs, N.J.: Prentice-Hall, 1973).

CHAPTER 2

THE PHYSICAL ENVIRONMENT

Consisting of 267,338 sq mi (692,405 sq km), the state of Texas possesses an astounding physical versatility. Virtually all known weather phenomena frequent the state, resulting in climatic variation and vegetational striation unsurpassed by most other regions of comparable size in the world. These factors, coupled with a complex geologic background, produce more than 800 recognized soil series in the state.

TERRAIN

Terrain, too, reflects the environmental variety of Texas, in spite of the popular image of the state as an unbroken plain. Landforms range from offshore bars and barrier beaches to formidable mountains, from rugged canyons, gorges, and badlands to totally flat plains. Four major physiographic provinces of the United States extend into Texas, including the Gulf and Atlantic Coastal Plain, Interior Lowlands, Great Plains, and Basin and Range, or Intermontane Plateaus (Figure 2.1).

The Gulf Coastal Plain extends into Texas from the east, occupies the eastern and southern portions of the state, and is one of the largest physiographic provinces in Texas. Formerly a portion of the floor of the Gulf of Mexico, the Gulf Coastal Plain reaches north to the Red River and west to the Rio Grande. The interior bound-ary is distinguished by the Balcones fault zone, including its conspicuous escarpment roughly along a line from Del Rio (Val Verde County) on the Rio Grande through San Antonio, Austin, and Temple (Figure 2.2). Escarpment relief at Del Rio is nearly 1,000 ft (305 m), decreasing to about 450 ft (137 m) at Austin and to an undulating plain before it reaches the Brazos River at Waco. North of the Brazos River the interior boundary is marked by the contact between the harder, Lower Cretaceous rock to the west and softer, Upper Cretaceous materials to the east (Figures 2.3 and 2.4).

Generally, the plain's elevation above sea level along its interior boundary is less than 1,000 ft (305 m) and declines south-eastward toward the Gulf of Mexico at a gradient of about 10 ft per mi (1.9 mpk). The monotony of this slope is interrupted by less prominent, inward-facing escarpments such as the White Rock, Nacog-doches, and Kisatchie and by the outward-facing Hockley Escarpment, which lies about 50 mi (80 km) from the coast. The coast of Texas has emerged from the Gulf of Mexico in relatively recent geologic time and is characterized by ill-drained marsh-land and a large number of shallow bays and lagoons, fringed by offshore bars and elongated barrier beaches like Galveston, Matagorda, and Padre.

One of the largest of the physiographic

8

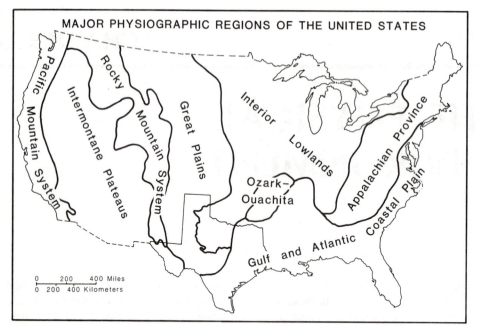

Figure 2.1. The four major physiographic regions that extend into Texas are the (1) Gulf and Atlantic Coastal Plain, (2) Interior (Central) Lowlands, (3) Great Plains, and (4) Basin and Range Province (Intermontane Plateaus).

Figure 2.2. A portion of the Balcones fault zone west of San Antonio. (Photo: Texas Highway Department.)

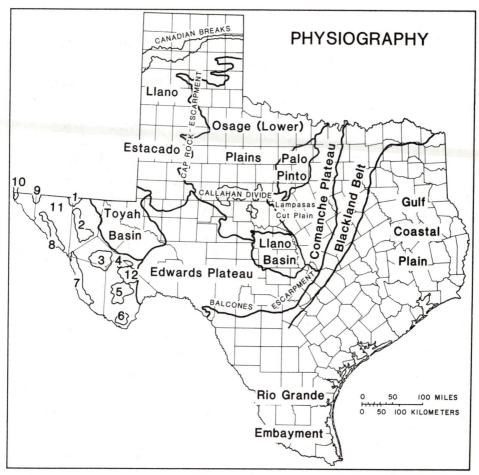

Figure 2.3.
Features of the Basin and Range section of Texas: 1 = Guadalupe Mountains; 2 = Delaware and Apache mountains; 3 = Davis Mountains; 4 = Ord and Glass mountains; 5 = Santiago, Chalk, and Christmas mountains; 6 = Chisos Mountains; 7 = Chinati Mountains and Sierra Vieja; 8 = Finlay, Quitman, and Van Horn mountains; 9 = Hueco Mountains; 10 = Franklin Mountains; 11 = Diablo Plateau; 12 = Marathon Basin.

provinces of the United States is the Interior (or Central) Lowlands, reaching south and west from the Great Lakes. This vast interior plain protrudes to the southwest, crossing the Red River and terminating in North Central Texas, where it is known by such names as Rolling Plains, Lower Plains, North Central Plains, and Osage Plains. Elevations in the eastern margins of this region are slightly less than 1,000 ft (305 m) and range upward to about 2,200 ft (671 m) at the base of the Cap Rock Escarpment in the west. Most of the terrain

of the North Central Plains is gently undulating to rolling, rather thoroughly eroded by the numerous rivers and streams that cross it. Occasionally, however, the local relief is sufficiently strong that the landscape appears hilly. In the southern portion of the region an erosional remnant, the Callahan Divide, appears. The divide lies between the Colorado and Brazos rivers and is characterized by numerous flat-topped mesas and buttes.

The physiographic province of the United States lying immediately east of the Rocky

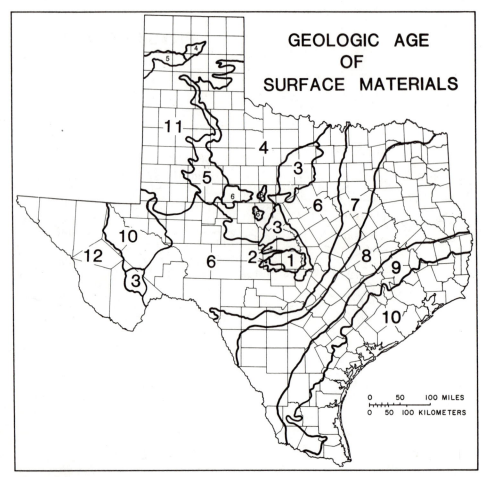

Figure 2.4.
Key: 1 = Pre-Cambrian Llano region; 2 = Older Paleozoics of Llano region and Marathon Basin; 3 = Mississippian Llano Basin and Pennsylvanian Palo Pinto section; 4 = Permian Osage Plain; 5 = Triassic and Jurassic Cap Rock Escarpment; 6 = Lower Cretaceous Edwards Plateau, Lampasas Cut Plain, and Comanche Plateau; 7 = Upper Cretaceous Blackland Prairie; 8 = Early Tertiary Gulf Coastal Plain; 9 = Later Tertiary Gulf Coastal Plain; 10 = Pleistocene Gulf Coastal Plain and Quaternary Pecos Valley; 11 = Late Cenozoic High Plains alluvium; 12 = Trans-Pecos basins and ranges, including a confusion of numerous outcrops of older and younger Paleozoics, Cretaceous, and undated igneous intrusive and extrusive.

Mountains is the Great Plains, an extensive upland plain stretching from the central part of Canada to northern Mexico. This province is so diverse that it is partitioned into ten subdivisions or sections, five of which are found in the western half of Texas.

The High Plains section occupies most of northwestern Texas, or the Texas Panhandle. With an area of about 40,000 sq mi (103,600 sq km), this region is bordered by New Mexico on the west, the Cap Rock Escarpment on the east, and Oklahoma on the north and extends as a large tableland to the south for some 350 mi (563 km). Elevations range from about 2,500 ft (762 m) on the eastern and southern margins to more than 4,500 ft (1,372 m) in the vicinity of the northwestern corner of the Panhandle. Midland and Odessa, in the south, are slightly less than 3,000 ft (915 m); Lubbock is 3,241 ft (988 m); Amarillo,

Figure 2.5. Palo Duro Canyon. (Photo: Texas Highway Department.)

3,676 ft (1,121 m); and Dalhart, the county seat of Dallam County in the north, about 4,000 ft (1,220 m) above sea level.

The most conspicuous feature of the High Plains is the Cap Rock Escarpment, which serves as the boundary with the Lower Plains. With a maximum local relief of about 1,100 ft (336 m), the Cap Rock represents one of the more spectacular landforms in Texas. Badlands topography, sheer cliffs, and colorful canyons have been created through the erosion of Triassic and Jurassic rocks by the intermittent tributaries of the Red River. The most striking of these numerous canyons is Palo Duro, located east of the town of Canyon in Randall County (Figure 2.5).

The most common characteristic of the High Plains section, by contrast, is the absence of obvious landforms. Geologically

the region is an upland plain of older, almost undisturbed alluvium that represents the finest example of level terrain found within the entire Great Plains system. Local relief is insignificant, but the portion north of the Canadian River is even more level than that to the south. The term *Llano Estacado* (Staked Plain) is used to identify the southern portion of the High Plains. Although it is very flat for the most part, occasional solution sinks (buffalo wallows), isolated canyons, mesas and buttes, and badlands interrupt the monotony. To the north of the Canadian River, extending north into eastern Colorado, are the flats, a portion of the Great Plains that may be the flattest upland feature in the world. The breaks of the Canadian River and its tributaries represent a startling departure from the flatness that occurs on either side.

To the south of the High Plains is the Edwards Plateau, the northern boundary of which is common with the High Plains alluvium. The plateau is often regarded as an outstanding example of a stripped plain, even though there is nothing to suggest that it ever had an alluvial cover. Generally, it is composed of a massive accumulation of extremely durable Lower Cretaceous limestone that is almost indestructible in an environment such as that of this semiarid portion of Texas. Bounded on the south and east by the Balcones Escarpment, this limestone mass extends west beyond the Pecos River to the mountains of West Texas and north to the High Plains and North Central (Osage) Plains. The section west of the Pecos River sometimes is called the Stockton Plateau even though this area is geologically identical with the rest of the Edwards Plateau.

The elevation of the Edwards Plateau ranges from about 850 ft (259 m) in the eastern margin to about 4,000 ft (1,220 m) at the foot of the mountains in the west. Throughout most of the region, the character of the terrain is level to gently rolling, but along the southern and eastern extremities, in the uplands of the Balcones fault zone where springs, creeks, and rivers have effectively dissected limestone materials through erosion and solution work, the landscape is especially rugged. Gradational activity is sufficiently thorough that local relief frequently exceeds 500 ft (153 m), with as much as 1,000 ft (305 m) found occasionally. Here the plateau loses its identity and often is referred to as the Hill Country of Central Texas. As the plateau extends to the north, the sculpturing becomes so severe that the Lampasas Cut Plain emerges as a separate entity. This region is typical of plateau surfaces developed from a durable limestone material but subjected to a comparatively humid environment, supporting numerous rivers and streams on the surface and attacked from within by solution work of groundwater.

The Llano Basin, which occupies about 4,000 sq mi (10,360 sq km) of the geographic center of the state, is one of the more interesting physiographic sections in Texas (Figure 2.6). Structurally the basin is the product of a local uplift the overlying limestone materials of which were eroded away by the Colorado River and its antecedent tributaries as vertical diastrophic movement progressed. The result is an erosional basin, some 1,000 ft (305 m) deep, where the greatest expanse of Lower Paleozoic and pre-Cambrian rock found in Texas is exposed at the surface. Generally, the terrain is hilly in the southwestern portion of the basin, where the bedrock is mainly composed of pre-Cambrian granite, gneiss, schist, and diorite, but becomes more rolling toward the northeast and the valley of the Colorado River. The limestone rim of the basin represents its most rugged portion and has an elevation of about 2,000 ft (610 m) where it blends into the Hill Country and Lampasas Cut Plain to the south, east, and northeast (Figure 2.7).

The Pecos River rises in northern New Mexico and flows southward for about 500 mi (805 km) before becoming the major U.S. tributary of the Rio Grande. Through much of its length, the river sluggishly flows across a broad, shallow, alluvium-filled valley that is considered a section of the Great Plains. The southern portion of this valley, lying between the Edwards Plateau and the thirty-second parallel, is the Texas portion of the valley and is referred to as the Pecos section or Toyah Basin. Toward the southern end of the Toyah Basin, the Pecos River encounters the resistant limestone of the Edwards Plateau, and the character of the river's valley abruptly changes. Since the river maintained its position while the remainder of the plateau was being uplifted, the valley becomes deeper, with steep-sided walls approaching 900 ft (274 m) near the confluence with the Rio Grande.

The Great Basin, or Basin and Range Province, of the United States is centered in Nevada and northern Utah and includes southeastern California, southern Arizona, southern New Mexico, and northern Mex-

Figure 2.6. Llano Basin in San Saba County. (Photo: Texas Highway Department.)

Figure 2.7. Outcrop of Lower Paleozoic rocks in Llano County. (Photo: William M. Holmes, 1981.)

Figure 2.8. Landscape of the Marathon Basin. (Photo: Texas Highway Department.)

ico, as well as the western extremity of Texas (Figure 2.8). Some geomorphologists consider its higher Texas ranges, especially the volcanic Davis Mountains, to be southern portions of the Rocky Mountain complex. Such a presumption is not unreasonable, but the greater part of Trans-Pecos is made up of numerous small mountain clusters interspersed with larger expanses of level-floored interior drainage basins and playas (Figure 2.9). Each mountain cluster has its own identity, mode of origin, and geologic character. For example, the Van Horn and Franklin mountains are Lower Paleozoic to pre-Cambrian in age, while the Glass Mountains are Permian, and the Chalk Mountains Cretaceous. Some are the product of diastrophism, and others are erosional remnants. The only characteristic they have in common is that all are surrounded by extensive desert flats that encroach their slopes to an elevation of about 5,000 ft (1,524 m). The highest elevation in Texas is Guadalupe Peak, a Permian coral reef in the Guadalupe Mountains,

with an elevation of 8,751 ft (2,668 m), but there are only six additional peaks in Texas with elevations exceeding 8,000 ft (2,439 m) (Figure 2.10).

Perception of Terrain

Many environmental decisions made by Texans, early settlers as well as later ones, rested on how the people *perceived* their physical surroundings. Early guidebooks and travel diaries provide some suggestion of how the settlers viewed the land and how these views may have influenced choice of settlement site, decisions to modify the habitat, and the like.

Perception of terrain by the early settlers seems to have been basically accurate, although the pioneers recognized a somewhat different series of regions than those described above. Almost all early Anglo-American observers of Texas divided the province into three distinct terrain zones. Nearest the coast was the level region, a belt of almost completely flat land—described by D. Edward in 1835 as "dead

Figure 2.9. Desert flat south of the Guadalupe Mountains. (Photo: Texas Highway Department.)

Figure 2.10. Guadalupe Peak, the highest point in Texas, with El Capitan to the left. (Photo: Texas Highway Department.)

level"—which supposedly broadened from a width of 30 mi (48 km) at the Sabine River to 80 or 100 mi (128 or 160 km) at the Colorado, then narrowed to the west and south beyond the Guadalupe River. At the mouth of the Brazos, the anonymous author of *A Visit to Texas* noted in 1831 that the country was "so perfectly flat that the eye embraced an extent of many miles towards the interior." The only notable variety was provided by a few widely scattered salt domes and hills, including the famous Damons Mound in Brazoria County described by Mary Holley in 1836 as "a remarkable elevation rising from the level surface of the prairie," 100 ft (30 m) high and visible from 20 or 30 mi (32 or 48 km) away.

To the interior and adjacent to the level area, lay the rolling plains or undulating region, which was felt to be the largest terrain zone, supposedly some 150–200 mi (240–320 km) in width. Representative of the area was Robertson County, described in 1858 in J. DeCordova's handbook: "The ascent to the divide between the two rivers [Navasota and Brazos] is an almost imperceptible rise through a succession of beautiful sweeps or long slopes of country, gradual in rise and declivity till you reach the ridge that separates their waters." Holley, in the 1830s, described it as "a perpetually varying surface" with round-topped eminences. The large majority of observers found the landscape in this region much more pleasing to the eye than that of the level coastal area, and Stephen F. Austin located the capital of his colony, San Felipe, on the Brazos River just about 2 mi (3.2 km) into the undulating region.

Still further inland, in the settler's view, was the hilly or mountainous region, which was reported to enter Texas at the headwaters of the Nueces River and end at the Brazos. This account fairly accurately described the location of the Balcones Escarpment, and part of the area west and north of it is still today called the Hill Country. The High Plains of West Texas were not explored by Americans until the

1840s, but a map drawn by Stephen F. Austin in the mid-1830s correctly locates not only the hill region, but also a large "level prairie" beyond to the west.

The pioneers who settled Texas often evaluated the various terrain regions, such as the Hill Country, in terms of the characteristics of the area from which they came. A good example is the settlers who came from the Appalachian South, where a distinctive subculture had arisen by the early 1800s, typified mainly by a preservation of archaic traits including the persistence of a frontier way of life. This subculture, spawned in the isolation of remote hills, hollows, and coves, was outside the mainstream of southern life, and within it archaic elements such as Elizabethan speech and British folk songs survived. In the middle third of the nineteenth century, emigrants from the southern Appalachians crossed the Mississippi River to colonize another, almost identical, mountain area—the Ozark-Ouachita district of Arkansas and southern Missouri. A few decades later, other highland southern pioneers, from both the Appalachians and the Ozarks, pushed on still further to settle much of the Texas Hill Country beyond the Balcones Escarpment (Figure 2.11).

The Texas hills do not have the areal dimensions of the Ozarks or the Appalachians, and the natural vegetation cover is less impressive than that of the eastern mountain regions of the South, but there was enough that was familiar about the Texas hills to make them an attractive home for the southern mountain folk. The hillbillies passed through and rejected the splendid rolling lands east of the Texas Hill Country and deliberately chose the areas of broken terrain—areas inferior in quality but familiar in appearance.

That the mountaineers recognized the environmental similarity between the Central Texas hills and their former homelands in Arkansas, Missouri, and Tennessee is evident from a study of placenames. They applied the same descriptive suffixes to the topographic features that their ancestors

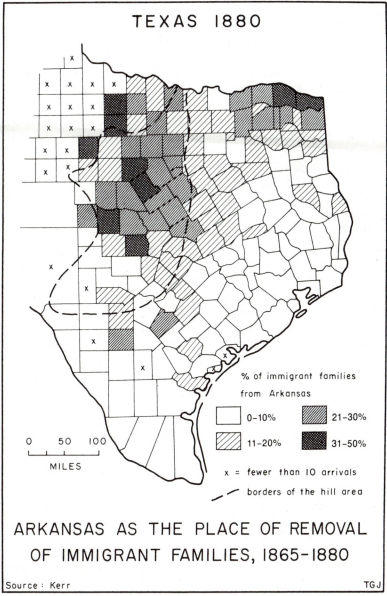

Figure 2.11. The concentration of hill folk from the Ouachita and Ozark mountains of Arkansas in the hills of Central Texas is quite striking. (Reprinted, by permission, from Terry G. Jordan, "The Texan Appalachia," *Annals of the Association of American Geographers* 60 [1970], 412.)

had used in the Ozark-Ouachita area and the Appalachians. In particular, there are extraordinary areal correlations between the zone occupied by hill southerners in Central Texas and the suffixes *gap*, *cove*, and *hollow*, all of which are quite common in the mountains of the South (see Chapter 5). *Cove*, used to describe a small flat area wholly or partially enclosed by hills, ap-

pears almost exclusively in the Anglo-American hill area.

The threefold divisions described by early writers depicted rather accurately, then, the reality of terrain in the eastern half of Texas, and the pioneers evaluated the terrain in terms of the lands from which they had come. One can find errors in dimensions, but the general pattern was accurate.

WEATHER

If the state's terrain can be described as varied, weather and climate are even more deserving of that title. The tropics and polar regions compete for dominion over Texas, as do desert and rain forest. To understand the capricious and diverse natures of the atmospheric phenomena that occur in Texas, one must consider location, air-mass characteristics, and jet-stream behavior. These controls, in addition to the substantial area, are responsible for Texas having such a wide range of weather activity. Virtually every known atmospheric condition occurs and may drastically change from one form to another without warning. So widely known is the fickle character of Texas weather that stories, tales, puns, and jokes are told concerning its character.

The location of Texas on the continent of North America is certainly an important climatological factor (Figure 2.12). The eastern half of Texas is exposed to the Gulf of Mexico, which serves as the major source of the maritime tropical air masses that seasonally move unrestricted over the plains of the eastern portion of the continent. On the other hand, the western half of Texas, bordered by Mexico, has no access to the sea and is seasonally confronted with hot, dry continental air masses spawned in the north-central part of Mexico. In a typical summer, these two air masses not only influence Texas, but dominate weather activity for much of the remainder of the United States as well. Normally during the summer, a series of semipermanent cyclonic systems migrate sluggishly from west to east across the northern half of the United States, pulling tropical air masses across Texas. As a result, the eastern half of Texas is hot and humid while the western half is hot and dry, and the warm seasons persist from early in the spring until late in the fall.

It is also important to consider the latitudinal position of Texas. The middle-latitude zones of the world are located between thirty and sixty degrees north and south. They are bordered by tropical conditions on one side and polar conditions on the other, both of which expand and contract to influence the character of the middle latitudes as the seasons change. The thirtieth parallel passes through the southern portion of Texas, establishing a subtropical influence for almost the entire state. A dry, subtropical condition exists in the west, and a humid, subtropical condition in the east. Regardless of where they might be located, however, virtually all weather stations receive more precipitation during the warm six months than during the cold months. Warm-season precipitation is the rule, but as one progresses eastward across the state, the cold six months receive an increasingly greater percentage of moisture so the extreme eastern parts of the state receive almost equal portions of their precipitation during the warm and cold periods (Figures 2.13 and 2.14).

The position of the jet stream is also a vital factor in controlling Texas weather. Although much remains to be learned about

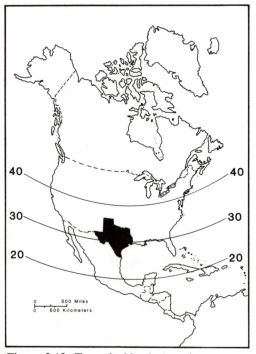

Figure 2.12. Texas in North America.

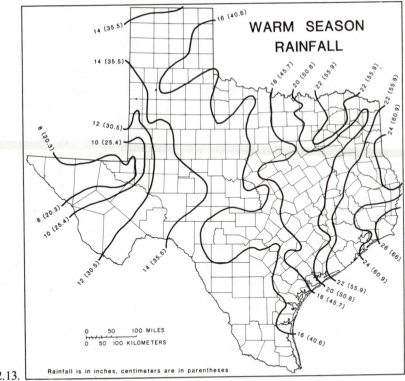

Figure 2.13.

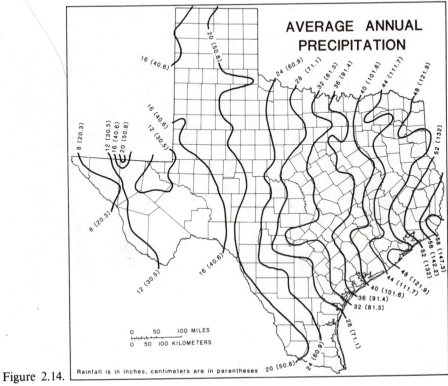

Figure 2.14.

these erratic, strong high-altitude winds, it is clear that certain weather activity in Texas is directly linked to the jet streams and their relationship to semipermanent middle-latitude cyclones and anticyclones. During periods of excessive dryness, such as 1954–1956 and 1979–1980, the western United States was dominated by weak jet-stream patterns, which permitted the growth of impenetrable semipermanent anticyclones that retarded the atmospheric instability mandatory for precipitation production. The summer of 1980 was both dry and hot, and heat records were broken while most of Texas was under the influence of this massive high-pressure system. By contrast, severe winters occurred in Texas in 1978 and 1979 when the jet streams made periodic sharp dips south from the central part of Canada to the Gulf of Mexico during the months of December, January, and February, following a path that paralleled the eastern edge of the Rocky Mountains (Figure 2.15).

During most of the years through the 1960s and 1970s, however, the precipitation pattern across Texas was more consistent. The jet streams were stronger and situated in such a position that alternating cyclones and anticyclones migrated across the continent, following customary paths of movement and creating what might be regarded as more-typical precipitation activity. During the years 1965 through 1969 and 1971 through 1976, all portions of Texas received at least 75 percent of their normal precipitation, a condition attributed to the fact that the jet-stream patterns assumed a more typical position.

Precipitation extremes reflect the diversity of Texas weather. Records indicate that in 1956 Wink, in West Texas, received only 1.56 inches (3.96 cm) of precipitation, but Clarksville, in Northeast Texas, received 109.38 inches (277.8 cm) in 1873. On September 9–10, 1921, Thrall in Williamson County received an astounding 38.2 inches (97 cm). Large amounts of snowfall are not

Figure 2.15. Snowstorm in Dallas, 1979. (Photo: Texas Highway Department.)

common to Texas, but the western and northwestern portions of the state receive some snow nearly every winter. The largest accumulation of snow at any one time occurred during the blizzard of February 1956, when the High Plains was covered with more than 30 inches (76.8 cm). The average annual precipitation map illustrates the striking contrast between the eastern and western extremes of the state. The isohyets, which range from 58 inches (147.3 cm) in the east to 8 inches (20.3 cm) near El Paso, create distinct belts that trend in a north-south alignment.

By contrast, the distribution of temperature zones conforms largely to latitude and reveals east-west belts. Such controls as increased altitude to the west and increased distance from the Gulf Coast tend to alter the impact of latitude, but winter temperatures rapidly decrease from south to north across the state. The extremes are such that weather stations in the Rio Grande Valley often experience tropical winters while their counterparts in Dallam County, in the northwest corner of the state, experience microthermal (cold) winters. Geographer R. J. Russell, in his early work on climatic years in Texas, suggests that tropical winters occasionally occur in the region around Brownsville and that microthermal winters are experienced more than one-half the time in Dalhart. Twenty-two counties in the northwestern portion of the state experience a frost-free period of fewer than 200 days per year, and there are three—Dallam, Sherman, and Hartley—in which the frost-free period is less than half the year. On the other extreme, there are seventeen counties in the southern portion of the state that experience a frost-free period of more than 300 days. Of these, Cameron, Hidalgo, and Willacy counties have more than 325 days (Figure 2.16).

Severe weather conditions that periodically develop across Texas include droughts, tornadoes, hurricanes and other tropical storms, "blue northers" and blizzards, and floods. The very natures of these weather-related phenomena once again indicate the versatility and inconsistency of Texas weather. Of the severe weather conditions, drought has greatest impact over large areas for long periods (Figure 2.17). Defined as periods in which precipitation is less than 75 percent of what should normally occur, drought creeps into an area and inconspicuously dehydrates it almost before people are aware there is a drought. It may remain localized or may become so widespread that the entire state is involved. Prolonged periods of dryness usually occur when anticyclones become thoroughly entrenched, bringing about conditions that make the occurrence of precipitation virtually impossible. Such periods are more apparent during the summer half of the year, because most precipitation falls during the warm six months of the year. During the early days of settlement in Texas, dry periods were accompanied by an abnormal amount of dust in the air, but improved farm management and soil culture techniques have made the air cleaner during droughts.

Historically, the great drought periods in Texas have developed during odd-numbered decades, the first of consequence taking place in 1893–1894, a period in which dust storms spread over Northwest Texas. A state-wide drought occurred in 1916–1917, and the Great Plains dust bowl period developed during the early part of the 1930s. Although considerable amounts of airborne dust and sand were part of the major drought of the 1950s, the amounts were small when compared to the dust bowl period. The major dry period of the 1970s came at the end of the decade and was full-fledged by 1980, causing major crop reduction. Dry periods also bring more problems to urban areas as water supplies are reduced and reservoirs become depleted. Increased population places more stress on water systems, and water availability represents a growing problem Texans must learn to cope with.

Because of the state's large size, the availability of large amounts of water vapor from the Gulf of Mexico, and rapidly moving cold fronts, Texas is situated at the

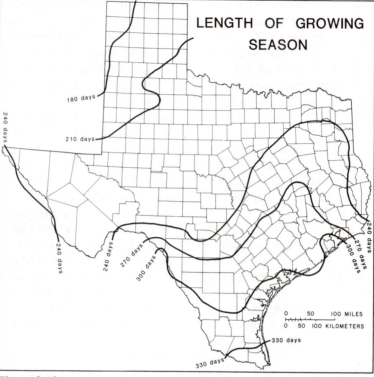

Figure 2.16.

Figure 2.17. Blown sand being removed from a West Texas highway. (Photo: Texas Highway Department.)

southern extremity of the most tornado-prone region in the world. Often referred to as Tornado Alley, this region stretches from South Central Texas to Iowa in a zone some 200 mi (322 km) wide. The spring months of April, May, and June are the tornado season in Texas, with May accounting for more than one-fourth of all tornadoes reported in the state for the period 1951–1976. That spring is tornado season in Texas is not surprising when one considers the atmospheric activity during that season. First, by April and May there has been ample time for the maritime tropical air mass of the Gulf to penetrate the southern United States, bringing with it a large quantity of water vapor. Second, even though considerable warming has taken place by then, it is not too late for an occasional outburst of cold air that may go as far south as the Gulf of Mexico, moving rapidly across Texas or becoming stationary. Finally, by April and May, the jet stream has usually assumed its southerly position, circulating from southwest to northeast across Texas.

Studies in recent years suggest that tremendous turbulence occurs within the zone where the jet stream intersects a cold front. Although this idealized condition is not mandatory for tornado and high-wind production, the most violent of tornadoes do seem to occur when this juxtaposition takes place. For example, the jet-stream–cold-front intersection was noted in the tornadoes of April and May 1970 at Clarendon (Donley County) and Lubbock, and at Wichita Falls in April 1979. Tornadoes customarily occur during the late afternoon on humid days, when the water vapor has been warmed just prior to the advance of a cold front. The highly charged warm, humid air is forced to rise, and the potential for severe weather increases. Often hailstorms accompanied by torrential rains precede the high winds. Even in those instances when tornadoes fail to materialize, the hail and rain may inflict considerable damage. Many a Texas wheat field, ripe with grain, has been destroyed by hail

Figure 2.18. Railroad damaged by Hurricane Celia, August 1970. (Photo: Texas Highway Department.)

only a week or two before harvest. Most of the great floods in Texas have occurred during the months of April, May, and June, resulting from the same atmospheric conditions that are capable of generating tornadoes. The drought of the mid-1950s was broken by torrential rains in April and May of 1957; and in most years through the 1960s and 1970s, there was some flooding activity in Texas during April, May, and June.

While spring is tornado season in Texas, late summer and early fall bring the hurricane and tropical storm season. These large cyclones develop over the superheated waters of the tropical Atlantic Ocean, Caribbean Sea, and Gulf of Mexico and move erratically, becoming progressively more energetic until they strike land, lose their punch, and dissipate. Characterized by high wind and torrential rain, these depressions frequently enter the Gulf of Mexico and wreak havoc along the Texas coast (Figure 2.18). The most notorious hurricane to hit

Texas was the great Galveston storm of September 1900. Some 6,000 lives were lost, and most of the structures on Galveston Island were destroyed or damaged. Most hurricanes develop during the months of July, August, September, and October, but of the thirty-one major hurricanes to hit the Texas coast, twenty-one have occurred during August and September. The term *hurricane* implies sustained winds in excess of 75 mi per hour (120 kph), often accompanied by torrential downpours of rain and flooding. The greatest rainstorm in U.S. history resulted from a hurricane that hit northern Mexico in September 1921 and moved across Texas. The town of Taylor northeast of Austin received 23.98 inches (60.9 cm) in thirty-five hours.

Blizzards are usually restricted to the High Plains and Rolling Plains. Characterized by winds exceeding 40 mi per hour (64 kph), freezing temperatures, and heavy snowfall, these most dreaded of Great Plains storms blast into Texas as they move south from Canada along the eastern edge of the Rocky Mountains. They have occurred as early as December, but, surprisingly, some of the most disastrous blizzards have developed in February and March. Regardless of when they occur, their characteristics are the same. They are usually preceded by abnormally warm weather. Then the norther, or blue norther, approaches as a wall of dark blue clouds that may be seen for several hours before the storm actually hits. Suddenly the wind shifts to the north, the temperature plunges, and snow begins to fall. As the storm intensifies, snow is blown horizontally and accumulates only on the lee side of obstacles in great drifts that may be several feet deep. Such storms may last for two or three days before they subside enough for people to begin assessing the damage. Livestock losses are often immense. The great blizzards during the winter of 1886/87 are alleged to have brought to a close the cattle boom period of the 1880s, and the blizzard of 1956 resulted in the previously mentioned record snowfall for Texas.

Ice storms occur when temperatures that are only slightly below freezing are accompanied by supercooled drizzle that freezes to objects at ground level. Tree limbs, power lines, and thoroughfares are especially vulnerable to this form of weather, and much urban activity ceases for the duration of such a storm. The ice storm that occurred in northern Texas on New Year's Day, 1979, is noteworthy since much of northern Texas was glazed over for ten days. Unprepared urban centers were especially hard hit.

CLIMATIC REGIONS

The variety of weather activity, the inconsistent character of the atmosphere from one year to the next, and the capability of the atmosphere to change abruptly from one extreme to another are sufficient grounds for Texans to cast wary eyes toward the sky. So unreliable is Texas weather that every year brings about the breaking of all-time records for individual days at weather stations across the state. Television and radio weather forecasters emphasize temperature and precipitation records for individual days, weeks, and months, stressing daily or monthly departures from "normal" weather activity. One might suggest that the most normal thing about Texas weather is its lack of reliability. It is not surprising that scholars have had considerable difficulty in establishing consistent climatic boundaries for Texas. Some scholars depict broad, sweeping regions bearing such names as humid subtropical, subtropical steppe, and subtropical desert, and others distinguish coastal from continental climate. The western humid, subtropical boundary has been located in eastern New Mexico by some observers, but others designate the 100th meridian as the dividing line between wet and dry Texas.

In the early work by Russell, the consistency factor of climatic years was utilized as the basis for climatic boundaries in Texas (Figure 2.19). Cutting a broad swath across Central Texas from Louisiana to the Rio Grande is the zone that Russell ascertained

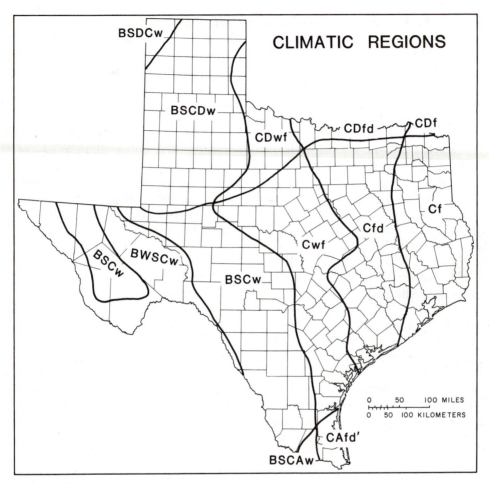

Figure 2.19.
Key: CDf = mesothermal in most years with occasional microthermal winter, good distribution of precipitation; Cf = mesothermal, good distribution of precipitation; CDfd = mesothermal in most years with occasional microthermal winter and occasional dry year; Cfd = mesothermal with occasional dry year; CDwf = mesothermal with occasional microthermal winter, normally dry winters with occasional wet year; Cwf = mesothermal, normally dry winters with occasional wet year; CAfd' = mesothermal in most years with occasional tropical winter, good precipitation in most years with occasional drought year; BSDCw = steppe, microthermal in most years with occasional mesothermal winter, winters are dry; BSCDw = steppe, mesothermal in most years with occasional microthermal winter, winters are dry; BSCw = steppe, mesothermal, winters are dry; BSCAw = steppe, mesothermal in most years with occasional tropical winter, winters are dry; BWSCw = desert with occasional steppetype precipitation, mesothermal, winters are dry.

has never experienced anything but mesothermal (mild), or type C, winters. Adjacent to this zone on the north, including most of the High Plains and a narrow strip along the Red River, is the portion of the state that is dominated by mesothermal winters but in a rare year is visited by a microthermal winter. The symbol CD designates the portion of Texas having winters of this type. In the northwest corner of the Panhandle is a small area in which more than one-half of the winters are microthermal (DC). To the south of the C zone a portion of the state is designated as region CA, which has C winters in most years but occasional tropical winters.

Although the temperature zones trend generally in east-west strips, the precipitation belts trend in north-south strips, intersecting the temperature zones and establishing Russell's climatic regions of Texas. His precipitation symbols are f, fd, w, wf, and fd′. The letter f represents regions with very reliable precipitation patterns, and fd suggests areas with normally reliable precipitation but with occasional dry years. The symbol w indicates dry winters, wf indictes dry winters with potential wet years, and fd′ denotes periodic major droughts in regions of usually reliable precipitation. BS and BWS indicate, respectively, semiarid steppes and arid desert areas with occasional steppetype precipitation years. Although Russell's work spanned only twenty years of weather data, a period of time seemingly not long enough to draw well-defined conclusions, geographer Lee G. Knox recently expanded Russell's data to sixty years. Knox determined that Russell's boundaries have remained unchanged except in the western part of the state, where weather stations were more scattered at the time Russell's data were collected.

Perception of Climate

Climate is not as easily observed as terrain, and the early settlers did not have the findings of years of weather observations on which to rely. Consequently, some decades of trial and error were necessary in order to learn how to live successfully in the area, and many mistakes were made.

Temperatures, for the most part, were correctly interpreted. If there was significant error, it lay in judging Texas to be more tropical than it actually is. For example, orange trees were planted before 1830 in the coastal area near present-day Houston, only, according to Mary Holley, to be destroyed or damaged by "colder than usual" winters in 1830–1831 and later. William Kennedy, a British resident, obviously applying his observations in Galveston to much of the rest of Texas, noted in 1840 that ice was seldom seen, except in northern parts of the Republic, and that "snow is a rare and transient visitor." The well-known "norther," a strong winter wind that brings rapid and pronounced drops in temperature, was known and described as early as 1820, and the word quickly became a part of Texas weather vocabulary. "These winds commonly burst forth so suddenly that the first notice of their advent is a violent gust that almost checks respiration, . . . and the temperature frequently falls fifteen or twenty degrees in as many minutes," wrote Francis Moore in 1840. Already by the mid-1830s, Texans knew that northers could change the temperature by 40 °F (23 °C) within twenty-four hours. Moore hastened to add, however, that a Texas winter in general "resembles a protracted Indian summer."

Summers presented no noticeable contrast to those of more-eastern portions of the South, from which the larger part of the Texas population was derived. July averages in the area between the lower Trinity and Colorado rivers were reckoned at around 85 °F (29 °C) as early as the 1830s, remarkably close to the actual temperature. Only European immigrants were bothered by summer temperatures. Ferdinand von Roemer wrote in 1849 that "the climate is so different from that of northern Europe, that initially it affects the German constitution rather severely. Of all the German immigrants who arrived in Texas while I was there, I can hardly name a single one whose health was not affected by the change of climate." A fellow German, Viktor Bracht, believed that two years were required for acclimatization.

German problems with acclimatization apparently did not distort the German immigrants' perception of the temperature characteristics of Texas. Immediately upon settlement, the German pioneer farmers abandoned the age-old European practices of winter housing for livestock and the accumulation of large amounts of winter feed for their animals, both of which were unnecessary in the mild climate of South Central Texas. Prince Carl von Solms-

Braunfels, founder of the German town of New Braunfels in Comal County, advised his colonists that it was not necessary to cut hay for winter feed. The Germans made no effort to combine house, barn, stables, and storage rooms under one roof, as had been the tradition in the cool, damp, northern German area from which many of the settlers came.

Correct perception of precipitation characteristics was more difficult, because the early immigrant Texans were on the western edge of the humid lands, a climate that was unfamiliar to Anglo-American and European alike. The possibility of drought became apparent almost at once, for the leader of the early Anglo settlers on the lower Brazos, Stephen F. Austin, complained of "an extraordinary drought" as early as 1822, long before he could have known what was ordinary or extraordinary. In July of 1824, the same settler lamented that "we are burnt up by the drought," and similar protests were registered in his journals in the summers of 1828 and 1830. Gradually, it became apparent that dry spells were part of the natural order of things, and in particular that summer was more prone to drought than the remainder of the year. In 1835 David B. Edward even designated the period from late April to early September as "the dry season." The decrease in annual precipitation from east to west was correctly observed quite early. Amos Parker noted in 1834 that the "portion of the country lying between the Colorado river and Louisiana is subject to powerful rains in the fall and spring, but as you go southward and westward . . . , the rains become less frequent, and not so abundant." Writing six years later, Francis Moore mentioned that "rains in eastern Texas fall more frequently and in greater abundance than in the counties west of the Trinity." It was also recognized that some years or cycles of years were much drier than others, and as early as 1861 the *Texas Almanac* ambitiously included a list of drought cycles for the period 1725–1860.

Perception of the seasonality of rainfall led to recognition of a flood season in spring and early summer, when the rivers were likely to spill out across their floodplains. Major inundations along the lower Brazos and Colorado rivers occurred in 1823, 1828, 1833, 1843, and 1852. The overflow of 1833 occurred in June, and one resident, Dilue Harris, described waters that reached from the Brazos to Buffalo Bayou, destroying crops in the entire area. As early as 1828, J. C. Clopper pessimistically calculated that the Brazos bottoms flooded about one of every three years, and in the same year, Stephen F. Austin accused the river of trying to emulate the Mississippi.

The rather astute observations of drought and diminishing rainfall to the west made by early residents along the lower Brazos apparently were not passed on to later pioneer farmers who pushed ever further into zones of increasing climatic hazard. These later settlers either did not realize or refused to admit that they were occupying semiarid lands, and they paid dearly for it. Many German colonists in counties such as Gillespie and Medina finally had to abandon their traditional crop-oriented economies and adopt livestock ranching, but to this very day many of them feel that drought is abnormal, which is by no means the case. Visitors often were more perceptive of the true nature of things, because they viewed the countryside free of the subjectivity of landowners. A German traveler, Benno Matthes, described the severe drought of 1856–1857, noting crop failures, dried-up creeks, stunted vegetation, and dead trees. He wrote that the Brazos and the Colorado were so low that one could ride through them on horseback; that cattle clung to the edges of the bottom forests even in winter, rather than grazing the adjacent prairies; and that huge cracks appeared in the earth, up to 3 ft (1 m) wide, 50 ft (15 m) long, and 12 ft (4 m) deep. Matthes watched horses and mules kick off thorns before devouring cacti, and he saw dead trees along the streambeds. But even the articulate Matthes could not have convinced his fellow Germans in New Braunfels or Fredericksburg, in nearby Gillespie County, that they had settled in semiarid country.

Greater disasters were experienced in West Texas after the Civil War, when farmers rushed in to displace ranchers in wet years, only to be wiped out by great droughts, such as those that occurred in the late 1880s. Some settlers approached the High Plains armed with such fancies as the belief that the windmill was an effective irrigator, and some people apparently still feel today that the supply of water pumped from the ground by electric pumps for cotton and sorghum fields is inexhaustible. West Texas was settled largely by East Texans, and it required decades of trial and frequent error for them to become aware of climatic realities. Even today, if the rains do not come, the residents petition heaven for relief from what is, for West Texas, the natural climatic condition.

In this respect, the Spaniards and Mexicans made a much better evaluation of semiarid Texas than did the Anglo-Americans and Europeans. The former were accustomed to drought in Spain and Mexico, and they adapted very well to it in Texas. Indeed, their difficulties were encountered in humid eastern Texas, where they never established a really successful colony or, for that matter, ever seriously attempted to do so. Their reliance on such items as dried beef, or jerky, helped them settle mainly in areas where evaporation exceeded precipitation.

Early Texans learned very little from their experiences with hurricanes on the Gulf Coast. Even the earliest settlers had heard of the storm of 1818, which sent ocean waters surging completely over Galveston Island, and the force of hurricanes was obvious from wrecks of old vessels that were found in timbered country 5 mi (8 km) from the seashore in the 1820s. In spite of the evidence, the town of Galveston was founded in 1837, only to be welcomed by a severe hurricane in October of the same year. Another storm struck on September 19, 1842, doing much damage, and the even more disastrous hurricane of 1900 virtually destroyed the city. William Bollaert, an observer of the Galveston hurricane of 1842, noted that the wind direction shifted from north-northeast to northwest during the storm, indicating that the center of the hurricane crossed the coast some distance to the east of the city. Indianola, a busy port town on Matagorda Bay, was wiped out in 1875 and again in 1886, and the surviving inhabitants decided not to rebuild it the second time.

ORIGINAL VEGETATION

The vegetational pattern of Texas, with only occasional exceptions, conforms largely to the precipitation pattern. Exceptions occur mainly in regions where earth materials are sufficiently high in calcareous materials that tree growth is minimal even though precipitation is sufficient to support forest growth. In all parts of Texas the growing season is of adequate length to encourage most forms of subtropical vegetation; the major limiting factor is precipitation reliability (compare Figure 2.20 with Figure 2.16).

The Piney Woods are located in the wetter portions of East Texas where the soils have been rendered extremely acidic through excessive leaching. This region of Texas represents the western margin of the southern coniferous forest belt that stretches to this point virtually uninterrupted from the Atlantic Ocean. The Texas Piney Woods are on the dry end of this belt, with precipitation ranging from about 45 to 60 inches (114 to 152 cm) per year, and include about 25,000 sq mi (65,000 sq km). Numerous species of pine, the most common of which are shortleaf, longleaf, slash, and loblolly, are found throughout the region, as well as cypress and hardwoods such as hickory, elm, tupelo, gum, and oak (Figure 2.21). Within the region are four national forests—Angelina, Sabine, Sam Houston, and Davy Crockett—and their aggregate area is more than 662,000 acres (269,000

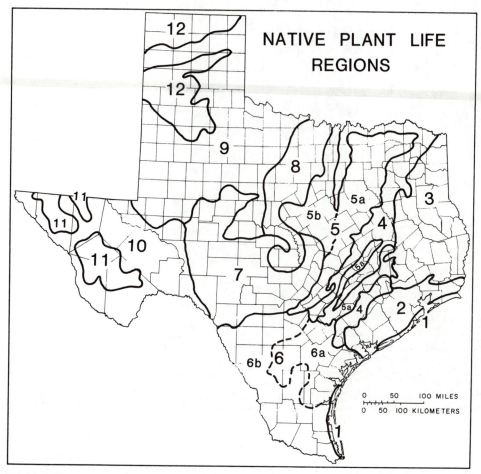

Figure 2.20.

Key: 1 = marsh and salt grasses of the Coastal Prairie adjacent to the Gulf; 2 = Coastal Prairie andropogons with panicum and grama grasses; 3 = Piney Woods with scattered hardwoods; 4 = Post Oak Belt and Eastern Cross Timbers consisting mainly of post oak, hickory, and other oaks with numerous scattered prairies; 5 = grasslands of the Blackland (5a) and Grand (5b) prairies consisting of andropogons, grama, buffalo, and bluestem grasses and scattered live oaks in the northwest and mesquite in the south; 6 = Brush Country of South Texas consisting of short buffalo and curly mesquite grasses with coarse bunch grass interspersed with prickly pear and thorny shrubs in 6b and scattered post oak and live oak in 6a; 7 = short grass, scattered timber of the eastern Edwards Plateau and Hill Country including live oak, shinnery oak, red oak, and juniper with a thin cover of buffalo and mesquite grasses; 8 = Western Cross Timbers with post oak and blackjack oak and numerous prairies of grama and bluestem grasses; 9 = short-grass steppeland of Lower and High Plains, including buffalograss, wheatgrass, and Indiangrass, with scattered mesquite and other xerophytes; 10 = desert vegetation with thin bunch grass and numerous xerophytes, including yucca, sotol, catclaw, cenizo, and huisache with tussock, burro, and salt grasses; 11 = mountain vegetation with grasses and small shrubs on lower slopes and oak, juniper, piñon pine, and ponderosa pine; 12 = steppeland of the High Plains with mesquite, yucca, and other xerophytes.

Figure 2.21. Longleaf pine and fern in the Piney Woods. (Photo: Texas Highway Department.)

ha). Another area of special interest within the Piney Woods is the Big Thicket National Preserve, a unique middle-latitude rain forest whose surviving remnant includes over 84,000 acres (34,000 ha). Throughout most of Texas vegetational outliers occur, evidence of the status of the state as an environmental transition zone. A notable outlier of the Piney Woods occurs in the vicinity of Bastrop, near Austin, and is known as the Lost Pines (Figure 2.22). Still further west, in the Hill Country, magnificent galeria stands of cypress appear, several hundred miles from their nearest kindred species in the Piney Woods.

The Central Hardwoods region of the United States, in its western margins, bends southwest across Missouri, eastern Kansas, and Oklahoma and crosses the Red River into Texas as three major southward-projecting prongs. In Texas, from east to west, these are identified as the Post Oak Belt, the Eastern (or Lower) Cross Timbers, and the Western (or Upper) Cross Timbers. The natural vegetation of all three regions is similar, consisting of hardwoods—such as post oak, blackjack oak, hickory, pecan, and assorted elms—interspersed with a wide variety of grassland species, suggesting in places a savannalike appearance.

The three hardwood belts are separated by two formidable prairies, which have developed on alkaline materials unsuitable for extensive tree growth. The Blackland Prairie lies between the Post Oak Belt and Eastern Cross Timbers, occupying the west-

Figure 2.22. A scene in Lost Pines State Park, Bastrop County. (Photo: Texas Highway Department.)

ern portion of the Upper Cretaceous calcareous limestone and shale region. Although some trees may be found along water courses, the uplands were originally dominated by tall, lush grasslands, which made this region the outstanding prairie in Texas. Consisting of 17,000 sq mi (44,500 sq km), the Blackland Prairie extends from the Red River to San Antonio in one long narrow strip, with several smaller eastern outliers. Its border with the adjacent woodland was originally highly intricate, as was typical of most vegetational boundaries in Texas (Figure 2.23).

The Grand Prairie separates Eastern and Western Cross Timbers. Like the Blackland, the Grand Prairie's rock materials are predominantly limestone, but much harder and more resistant to weathering. The native vegetation, nevertheless, originally resembled that of the Blackland Prairie, consisting of tall grasses in the uplands and hardwoods along water courses, where much

of the calcareous material had been removed. In recent times, however, the region has been encroached upon by mesquite and other noxious forms of vegetation.

The third major prairie in Texas extends along the Gulf shore. Known as the Coastal Prairie, this grassland is also underlain by calcareous clays derived from recently emerged limestones and shales. The region consists of two major subdivisions. Coastal marshes parallel the Texas Gulf Coast for its entire length, at no point extending very far inland. The marsh terrain is flat and poorly drained, capable of supporting only halophytic wetland grasses of little value for livestock (Figure 2.24). Toward the interior, an upland prairie emerges, with a lush bunch-grass and bluestem cover that is excellent for livestock. Hardwoods also are found along the water courses.

The eastern portion of Texas, then, is well endowed with vegetational variety in its seven major plant regions, including

32

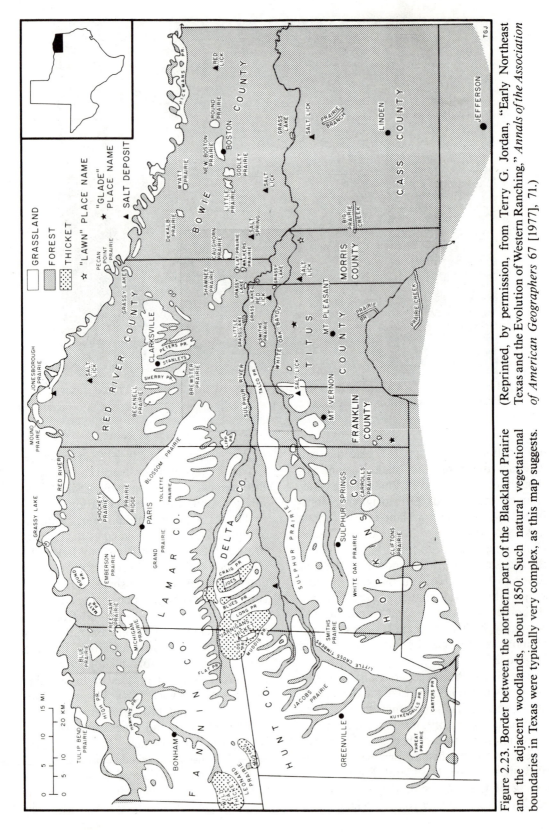

Figure 2.23. Border between the northern part of the Blackland Prairie and the adjacent woodlands, about 1850. Such natural vegetational boundaries in Texas were typically very complex, as this map suggests. (Reprinted, by permission, from Terry G. Jordan, "Early Northeast Texas and the Evolution of Western Ranching," *Annals of the Association of American Geographers* 67 [1977], 71.)

Figure 2.24. Deer in marsh grass near the Gulf Coast. (Photo: William M. Holmes, 1981.)

three prairies and four forests. To the west, however, conditions become more arid, trees and taller grasses are widely scattered or absent, and the demarcation of vegetative boundaries is increasingly more difficult. Close scrutiny of the vegetation distribution in western Texas reveals that although several subdivisions of the Great Plains are represented, they all are covered by essentially the same grassland species. West of the 28-inch (71-cm) isohyet, the subtropical steppes prevail, extending across western Texas to the mountains. From the southern tip of the state to the northwestern corner, the predominant native species are various bluestems, side oats and hairy grama, Indiangrass, buffalograss, switchgrass, and western wheatgrass. They become shorter and more widely scattered to the west and in many instances are interrupted by yucca, mesquite, shinnery oak, sagebrush, and various other xerophytic shrubs. Considerable live oak and juniper are found along the eastern margins and as shinnery enclaves, while cottonwood, willow, and hardier elms are found in galeria stands along the water courses.

Semiarid South Texas is dominantly the Brush Country, a chaparral zone dominated by mesquite, scrub oaks, a host of thorny bushes, cacti, and short grasses (Figure 2.25). Visibility is generally restricted by this tangle of xerophytic vegetation, and much of the area remains very thinly settled to the present day. Further west, particularly in the Trans-Pecos country, vegetation in the desert lands of Texas is highly sensitive to elevation differences (Figure 2.26). In the high altitudes, generally above about 6,000 ft (1,830 m), precipitation is more abundant, evaporation is reduced, and the resultant vegetation cover is a mixture of western mountain and eastern hardwood trees interspersed with numerous shrubs and grassland species not common to other parts of Texas (Figure 2.27). Piñon and ponderosa pines, western red cedar, and substantial stands of oak and hickory are common. On the lower slopes, steppe grasslands mingled with yucca, creosote bush, and other thorny shrubs occur before the surrounding basin deserts intrude and the hardier xerophytes become dominant.

Figure 2.25. Brush Country of South Texas. (Photo: William M. Holmes, 1981.)

Figure 2.26. Desert vegetation of the Black Gap Wildlife Refuge. (Photo: Texas Highway Department.)

Figure 2.27. Mountain vegetation in McKittrick Canyon. (Photo: Texas Highway Department.)

Perception of Vegetation

To the southern pioneer, the vegetational cover in East Texas offered little that was unfamiliar, and early travelers rarely felt any compulsion to describe the Piney Woods. Joshua James and Alexander McCrea, visiting Shelby County in 1835, did describe a well-timbered county, "literally covered with oak of various kinds, black hickory, ash, dogwood, etc., and occasionally mixed with short-leaf pine," but only the Big Thicket, which occupies the southeasternmost part of the Piney Woods, was deemed worthy of lengthy description. "The thickest woods I ever saw," wrote

Gideon Lincecum of the thicket in 1835, "it perhaps surpasses any Country in the world for brush; there is 8 or 10 kinds of ever green undergrowth, privy, holly, 3 or 4 Sorts of bay, wild peach tree [laurel], bay berry, &c., and so thick that you could not see a man 20 yards [away]."

Few travelers who encountered the Cross Timbers failed to be impressed. It is "a belt of thick and almost impenetrable forests," wrote Frederick Marryat about 1840, our "every attempt to penetrate into the interior proving quite useless, so thick were the bushes and thorny briers." George Wilkins Kendall, at about the same time, noted that "the growth of timber is principally small, gnarled post oaks and black jacks," and he further described the Cross Timbers as "an immense natural hedge."

Scattered through the forests of the Piney Woods and Post Oak Belt were hundreds of small prairies, islandlike in a woodland sea and probably the result of forest clearance by the farming Indians of East Texas. These small grasslands grew more numerous and larger as one progressed westward through the forested regions of Texas, producing an intricate vegetational mosaic across much of the state. The Anglo-Americans who settled most of East Texas preferred to settle on the fringes of one of the small prairies, locating their houses just within the woods. Fields and pastures were situated in the prairie, where no laborious clearing was necessary, and the forest served as a hunting ground for the settler; provided wood for housing, fencing, and fuel; and offered abundant roughage for the settler's scavenging hogs. In choosing such mixed vegetational sites, the Anglo-American pioneers of eastern Texas were following the example of their ancestors, who had exhibited a preference for the fringes of small grasslands since they settled on the Atlantic seaboard in colonial times. Until the vanguard of settlement reached the treeless High Plains, settlers across much of Texas were able to combine forest and prairie in their landholdings.

The Coastal Prairie, driven like a wedge between the forests of East Texas and the Gulf shore, figured prominently in the early settlement of Texas. This belt of tall, coarse grasses served as range for tens and hundreds of thousands of cattle beginning in the 1820s. Indeed, the Coastal Prairie seems to have served as a route in the expansion of an Anglo-American cattle ranching tradition westward from the Carolinas and Gulf Coast pine barrens of the Lower South to meet the Spanish-Mexican ranching complex in South Texas. The most preferred sites for settlement in the colony of Stephen F. Austin lay on the border between the Coastal Prairie and bottom forests along the streams. Crops were planted in "peach and cane lands," which lined the stream courses and consisted of huge cane breaks interspersed with laurel, or "wild peach." The adjacent prairie served as a natural pasture. The portion of the Coastal Prairie known as Bay Prairie, around Bay City in present Matagorda County, was one of the earliest and most desired areas of settlement. One of the first pioneers there, E. Flowers, reported in 1826 that he was "plowing the praira," indicating that crops were to be raised there.

Travelers were generally impressed by the Coastal Prairie, which, according to Lincecum, "spread out before the wondering eye, as large as infinity," with the view "only here and there obstructed by the islands of timber which are thinly interspersed over the wide expanse." In springtime, "the wild flowers . . . were often spread around . . . in the utmost profusion, and in wonderful variety," wrote the anonymous author of *A Visit to Texas* in describing the Coastal Prairie in 1831. It was the practice of pioneer American cattle raisers, and of Indian bison hunters before them, to fire the prairies in winter to destroy the brush and ensure a lush growth of grass in the following spring and summer.

The other great grassland zone in eastern Texas, the Blackland Prairie, also attracted early attention and admiration. In the Blackland north of Austin in 1841, Kendall wrote of "rolling and beautiful prairies, occasionally relieved by the slight skirting of timber which fringes the margins of the small streams, or by a grove of timber so regularly planted by nature that it would almost seem the hand of man had assisted in its production." In 1833 Benjamin Lundy described an eastern outlier of the Blackland, near La Grange and south of the Colorado River, as "a country magnificently checquered with alternate prairie and woodland." Pioneers from the forests of the South readily chose settlement sites on the fringes of the Blackland, where timber was at hand, just as they had done earlier in the small grasslands of East Texas and in the Coastal Prairie, but they left the open expanses of

grassland, distant from timber, empty for
Europeans and Midwesterners to settle at
a later time. In this way, latecomers from
Germany, Czechoslovakia, or Illinois were
able to obtain some of the best land in
Texas—the fertile, black prairie soils.

One of the most unusual outliers of the
Blackland is the famous San Antonio or
String Prairie, not over 5 mi (8 km) wide
and reaching some 100 mi (160 km) from
near Bastrop northeast beyond the Brazos
River almost to the Trinity. As a corridor
leading through the Post Oak Belt, it formed
a magnificent natural route. The early Spanish explorers found this prairie strip and
used it as their major route between Bexar
(San Antonio) and East Texas, in which
capacity it became known as the Old San
Antonio Road. Part of this ancient road is
now duplicated by Texas state highway 21,
and the motorist traveling from the town
of Caldwell in Burleson County can observe
that the highway passes through largely
treeless country, with a dense growth of
oak timber visible 2 or 3 mi (3.2 or 4.8
km) distant on either side. Similarly, one
of the main overland routes in South Central Texas in the 1820s and 1830s branched
off from the Old San Antonio Road just
west of the Trinity River and followed
another narrow corridor of the Blackland
Prairie south and southwest to the Brazos
River in the vicinity of Navasota. In addition, the Spaniards laid out the Atas-
cosito-Opelousas Road, which ran from
Refugio and Goliad eastward to Liberty
and on beyond into southwestern Louisiana
by following the Coastal Prairie to avoid
the dense Big Thicket to the north. The
main roads of early Texas, then, typically
followed the lines of least vegetational resistance.

Few early observers were charmed by
the Brush Country of South Texas. William
A. McClintock, obviously speaking with
the voice of experience, protested in 1846
that "there is nothing of the vegitible world
on the rio grand but what is armed with
weapons of defence and offence," including
a variety of "pricks, thorns, or burs." Wil-

liam B. DeWees, riding between San Antonio and the Rio Grande in 1827, found
the countryside "covered with shrubs, mis-
quit trees, and prickly pear," adding that
the cacti reached as high as 15 ft (5 m).
"The road is oftimes completely hedged in
for miles by long rows of prickly pear," he
continued, and "all the shrubbery throughout this country is covered with thorns."

SOIL REGIONS

As a rule the distribution of soils in
Texas corresponds to climate and vegetation. Early soil maps of Texas simply partitioned the state into two groups, the pe-
dalfers of humid East Texas and the pedocals
of semiarid West Texas. More recently,
extensive county soil surveys have been
completed, and more than 800 soil series
have been recognized. A convenient compromise between these extremes is the
grouping of soils into broad classes or
orders.

Of the ten great soil orders recognized
around the world, seven are found in abundance in Texas (Figure 2.28). Some orders,
such as Aridisols and Ultisols, represent
the extremes of Texas soils. Aridisols occur
in the desert areas of West Texas and are
generally light-colored calcareous soils possessing distinctive horizons of calcium car-
bonate and brines. Ultisols, on the other
extreme, are severely leached, acidic, sandy
or sandy-loam soils found in the Piney
Woods of eastern Texas. Between these two
extremes lie the three most prominent Texas
orders: Vertisols, Alfisols, and Mollisols.
Alfisols characteristically consist of thin,
light-colored A-horizon materials overlying
B-horizons consisting of heavy, almost im-
permeable clays. Regional distribution in
Texas suggests that Alfisols are found in
such diverse areas as the Blackland Prairie,
Post Oak Belt, Cross Timbers, and southern
High Plains. Mollisols are dark loamy soils
consisting of soft granular surface materials
of alluvial origin overlying calcareous sed-
iments. Normally, Mollisols are more prominent in the semiarid portion of the north-

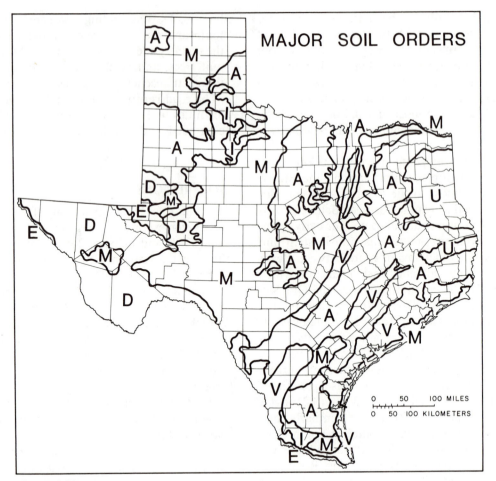

Figure 2.28.
Key: A = Alfisols; D = Aridisols; E = Entisols; I = Inceptisols; M = Mollisols; U = Ultisols;
V = Vertisols.

ern High Plains and Rolling Plains, but they are also found in the Grand Prairie and along the Gulf Coast. Vertisols are the black, waxy clays of calcareous origin found in the Blackland and Coastal prairies.

Inceptisols and Entisols occur only in small areas of Texas. The latter have poorly developed horizons, consisting largely of uniform sands, and are confined to river valleys and barrier beaches. Inceptisols are reddish brown loams formed over the loosely cemented calcareous sands found in isolated portions of the Rolling Plains. Generally the soils of Texas are sufficiently fertile to support a great variety of agri-

cultural products, as long as water availability is reasonably constant. The nature of soils is also important to urban dwellers as they attempt to maintain yards, grow household garden products, and keep proper moisture levels around the foundations of houses in an effort to minimize shifting.

Perception of Soils

Soil, perhaps more than any other feature of the environment, attracted the attention of pioneers, for they were interested in obtaining good farmland. Alluvial soils were universally recognized as being among the best, though a heavy growth of timber and the frequency of flooding in the bottomlands decreased the attractiveness of these areas. River-bottom prairies, many of which were found in the valleys of the Red, Brazos, and Colorado rivers, were much sought after because in them the laborious task of forest clearance was unnecessary. Thomas Nuttall observed as early as 1819 that Anglo-American settlers in the valley of the Red River in far northeastern Texas were raising corn and cotton on a bottom prairie. Especially prized were the numerous fertile "weed prairies" in the Brazos bottoms of Falls, Robertson, and Milam counties, where even the troublesome, tough prairie sod was absent, replaced by a growth of weeds up to 25 ft (7.6 m) tall. The fertile soil was ready for use with only a minimum of effort. Similarly, the canebreaks of alluvial valleys near the coast in the Austin Colony covered extremely fertile soils, which could be had by the simple expedient of burning off the cane. In general, alluvial soils became the domain of wealthy slaveowners, and most of the large cotton and sugar plantations were lined up in succession along the river courses of eastern Texas. By 1840, O. Fisher noted that "the bottom lands on Brazos and San Bernard rivers and Old Caney creek are thought to be the richest lands in Texas." In northwestern Texas, the Canadian River bottomlands in Oldham County were the soils first cultivated by Mexican-American farmers in the early 1870s. The uplands were pastures for sheep.

Next to the cane lands, Brazos weed prairies, and other alluvial soils, perhaps the most highly valued soils were those of the famous East Texas Redlands. This zone begins near the Sabine River and extends west and north through San Augustine, Nacogdoches, Cherokee, and Smith counties. The Redlands were more thinly timbered than the surrounding regions, with a luxuriant growth of grass among the trees, and this area of loamy, reddish soils was described by D. Edward as early as 1835 as "one of the richest landed districts in the whole province" of Texas. Here, as in the alluvial areas, large plantations came to dominate the rural economy. Even before the coming of the Anglo-Americans, Spanish settlers had occupied parts of the Redlands around Nacogdoches in the 1700s, farming the rich soil and grazing herds of cattle on the abundance of grass among the trees.

The fertility of the upland prairies, such as the Blackland, was recognized quite early, though the astute pioneers learned quickly that not all prairie soils were of equal quality. Many rules of thumb were followed. James W. Parker, in 1844, declared that "it is almost an invariable rule that where you find prairies bordered by pine timber, the land is generally poor, but where it is bordered by post-oak, the land is generally good." Another observer, Benno Matthes, noted that prospective Texas prairie farmers sought out milky-juiced spurge plants and certain snails as reliable indicators of fertile soils. Fisher, in 1840, warned that the black waxy soil of the Blackland Prairie became hard when dry, though admitting that "some think it pays them well for cultivation." There were few hints of an old misconception that treelessness was an indicator of soil infertility. By 1849, Edward Smith could report that the Blackland "is universally admitted to be the finest soil in the country," and apparently the interiors of the larger prairies were avoided only because the absence of timber imposed hardships in regard to fencing, acquisition of fuel, and construction of houses and other buildings.

Generally recognized as less desirable were the sandy soils of the post-oak areas. They attracted small populations of lower-class "poor whites," the so-called sandhillers and mountaineers from similarly poor areas farther east in the South, who preserved a frontier life well into the present century in the post oaks of the Cross Timbers regions and elsewhere. Their only major competition for these infertile soils were Slavic Wendish settlers from the sandy

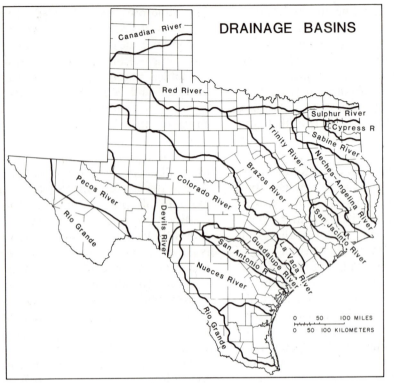

Figure 2.29.

HYDROGEOGRAPHY

Spree Forest of East Germany, who settled in the similarly sandy post-oak woods of Lee County in the 1850s.

Texas is large enough that eight independent river systems rise and remain within the state, in addition to five others that rise beyond its limits and either flow across the state or form boundaries (Figure 2.29). The largest drainage basin totally within Texas is that of the Colorado River, and the Trinity, Neches-Angelina, and Sabine rivers are the other major rivers of eastern Texas. Although none of those three equal the Colorado in area drained, each has a greater annual water discharge than the Colorado. The Sabine has the largest annual water discharge of any river in Texas, with more than 6,800,000 acre-ft (840,000 ha-m), but in 1941, which was a maximum rainfall year, the Sabine discharged more than 13,000,000 acre-ft (1,600,000 ha-m) of water.

The San Jacinto and Lavaca rivers have small drainage basins confined to the coastal plain. The San Jacinto flows into Galveston Bay and is important in constituting part of the port facility at Houston. The Guadalupe, San Antonio, and Nueces are also mainly coastal plain rivers, but much of their discharge is contributed by springs emerging from the Balcones fault zone. The huge Brazos River Basin is the largest in Texas and has its headwaters in New Mexico.

The Rio Grande not only forms the southwestern boundary of Texas, but serves also as the international boundary between the United States and Mexico. With its headwaters in southern Colorado, it is one of the longest rivers in North America. The Pecos River, which enters from New Mexico, is the major Texas tributary of the Rio Grande. The Canadian River also enters Texas from New Mexico, flowing across the northern portion of the High Plains before crossing into Oklahoma. Its bed is usually dry, and only in those brief periods following rare downpours of rain in its watershed area does the Canadian have a discharge worth mentioning. In spite of this, however, the Canadian has the capability of supporting the tenth-largest lake in Texas in terms of storage capacity, suggesting that every river in the state can support formidable reservoirs (Figure 2.30).

In 1920 Texas had 11 major reservoirs possessing an aggregate storage capacity of only 450,000 acre-ft (55,000 ha-m), more than half of which was contained in Medina Lake, completed in 1913. By 1980 there were more than 160 major reservoirs in Texas whose total capacity exceeded 29,000,000 acre-ft (3,6000,000 ha-m) (Table 2.1). Two-thirds of this storage capacity is contained in the 9 largest reservoirs of the state, but in 4 of those the water must be shared. Mexico receives almost half of the water from Amistad and Falcon reservoirs, Oklahoma gets most of the water from Texoma, and half of the Toledo Bend allotment goes to Louisiana. Twenty-one of the state's reservoirs have a storage capacity of more than 400,000 acre-ft (49,000 ha-m) of water and account for more than 27,000,000 acre-ft (3,320,000 ha-m) of the storage capacity in Texas.

The freshwater aquifers of Texas, until recent times, constituted the major source of water for irrigation, municipal water supplies, and industrial uses. With the development of reservoirs on a large scale, however, virtually all municipal and industrial water needs are now supplied by surface sources. Some irrigation water is extracted from the reservoirs in the west, but groundwater sources continue to be important.

The Texas Department of Water Resources recognizes six major freshwater aquifers in Texas, in addition to scattered alluvial deposits along river valleys and in bolson (box canyon) deposits of the desert west (Figure 2.31). The aquifers are the Ogallala formation of the High Plains, the Trinity Sands of North Central Texas, the Edwards Limestone–Trinity Sands group of the Edwards Plateau, the smaller Edwards Limestone of the Balcones fault zone, the Carrizo-Wilcox Sands of the inner coastal plain, and the Gulf Coastal Sands. Generally, all are reliable sources of water, but localized problems do occur. Saline conditions are often found in the Coastal Sands and within the coastal border of the Carrizo-Wilcox Sands. Otherwise the Carrizo Sands are the principal aquifers in the South Texas fruit and vegetable districts, and the Wilcox Sands are more important in the eastern part of the region. The Trinity Sands aquifer is the most reliable in North Central Texas, but the Paluxy and Woodbine Sands are significant members of this group. The Ogallala Formation is the only major aquifer in Texas whose immediate future is questionable. Although it is an excellent aquifer, the Ogallala has been the lone source of irrigation water on the High Plains for many years. The annual depletion rate so greatly exceeds its recharge rate that the demise of the Ogallala as a source of irrigation water may occur before the end of the century.

FAUNA

When the first Anglo-Americans colonized Texas, they found a land very rich in wildlife. The prairies and forests abounded with bison, wolves, bears, deer, wild turkeys, javelinas, prairie hens, wildcats, and many other animals, and the waters were home to alligators, redfish, oysters, catfish, and the like. The Spanish-Mexican occupation had not adversely affected the fauna. Indeed, huge herds of wild horses, or mustangs, and wild longhorn cattle had been added to the fauna of Texas as a result of the Spanish activity. In contrast, the Anglo-American colonization proved disastrous for several species of land animal.

The destruction of bison began very early. These animals ranged throughout the

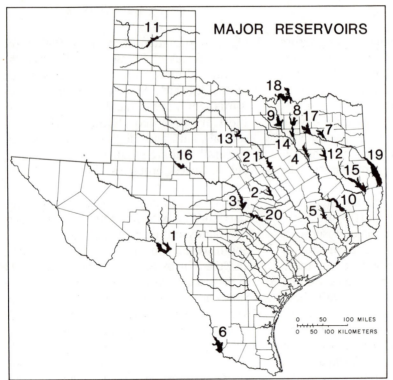

MAJOR RESERVOIRS

Figure 2.30. For key to numbers, see Table 2.1.

Table 2.1. Texas Reservoirs with Conservation Storage Capacity of More Than 400,000 Acre-feet

Reservoir	River	Surface Area		Storage Capacity (acre-feet)
		Acres	Hectares	
1. Amistad	Rio Grande	64,900	26,382	3,505,400
2. Belton	Brazos	12,300	5,000	457,600
3. Buchanan	Colorado	23,060	9,374	992,000
4. Cedar Creek	Trinity	33,750	13,720	679,200
5. Conroe	San Jacinto	20,985	8,532	430,260
6. Falcon	Rio Grande	87,210	35,450	2,667,400
7. Lake Fork	Sabine	27,690	11,256	675,819
8. Lavon	Trinity	21,400	8,700	456,500
9. Lewisville	Trinity	23,280	9,463	464,500
10. Livingston	Trinity	82,600	33,577	1,750,000
11. Meredith	Canadian	16,504	6,709	864,400
12. Palestine	Neches	25,560	10,390	411,840
13. Possum Kingdom	Brazos	17,700	7,195	570,243
14. Ray Hubbard	Trinity	22,745	9,246	490,000
15. Sam Rayburn	Angelina	114,500	46,545	2,898,200
16. Spence	Colorado	14,950	6,077	488,760
17. Tawakoni	Sabine	36,700	14,919	936,200
18. Texoma	Red	89,000	36,179	2,722,000
19. Toledo Bend	Sabine	181,600	73,821	4,477,000
20. Travis	Colorado	18,930	7,695	1,172,600
21. Whitney	Brazos	23,560	9,577	627,100
TOTAL		958,924	389,807	27,737,022

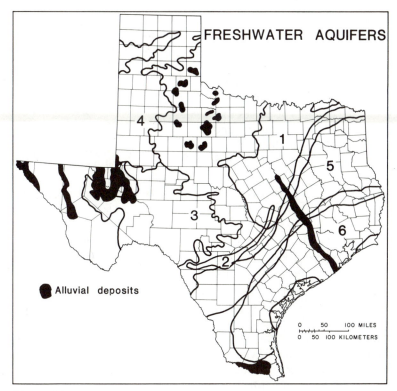

FRESHWATER AQUIFERS

Figure 2.31.
Key: 1 = Trinity Sands; 2 = Edwards Limestone; 3 = Edwards Limestone–Trinity Sands; 4 = Ogallala formation; 5 = Carrizo-Wilcox Sands; 6 = Gulf Coastal Sands.

state, thriving on the prairies and also the grassy Indian old fields in wooded eastern Texas. William DeWees, one of the earliest Anglo pioneers, claimed that he had "frequently seen a thousand in a day" near the confluence of the Brazos and Little rivers in present Milam County, and they also abounded on the Coastal Prairie. The name of Buffalo Bayou, in Houston, suggests the former presence of bison there. As early as 1835, however, bison were seldom seen east of the Balcones Escarpment. In the same area where DeWees had seen 1,000 bison in one day in the 1820s, A. W. Moore saw only a herd of 40 in 1846. A large number of bison were observed on the east bank of the lower Brazos near present Richmond in 1836, but that was one of the last times the animals were seen on the Coastal Prairie. Thirty bison were sighted in the mainland section of Gal-

veston County in 1838, but they were by that time a curiosity, as were the few head observed running with domestic cattle on a Grimes County ranch in the early 1840s. Further north, a herd of 125 bison was reported in the Blackland Prairie, perhaps in Limestone County, in 1846, and they were still numerous in the Austin area in 1840. By the late 1850s bison were so rare in the Hill Country of Mason County, considerably west of the Balcones Escarpment, that the appearance of one isolated beast caused several local German farm children to run home screaming that the devil was among the cattle. The systematic slaughter of bison on the plains of West Texas after the Civil War completed the removal of this animal from the state.

Daniel Shipman, who went to Texas in the 1820s, recalled in later years that "in the first settling of Austin's Colony the bears were very bad on the corn in the fields," but by 1836 they had withdrawn to the refuge of the canebreaks and bottom forests. At mid-century, Edward Smith wrote that bears were rapidly disappearing. Wild-cats were also in retreat by the mid-1830s.

Mustangs, the descendants of horses that had escaped from Spanish settlements and exploration parties, were found on all the prairies of Texas, as well as in the Brush Country. They were sought by Indian, Mexican, and Anglo-American alike for a variety of reasons. Stephen F. Austin, as early as 1824, considered a law "to prevent the killing of Deer and Wild horses for the Skins alone," an indication that mustangs were being subjected to the same indiscriminate slaughter as bison. Generally, however, mustangs were sought as animals to be domesticated and sold. Anglo-American "mustangers" were among the earliest of that cultural group to enter Texas, engaging in the horse trade there as early as the 1790s. By the 1830s many Mexicans in the San Antonio area were engaged in rounding up wild mustang mares, which were then lamed and used as broodmares. Others simply sold the wild horses. In June 1834, for example, Mexican traders arrived in the Brazoria area with droves of mustangs for sale, continuing on to Anahuac on Galveston Bay and Nacogdoches. Some traders drove horses into Louisiana, as far as New Orleans.

* * *

The Texas environment, then, is both diverse in reality and variously perceived by different groups of settlers. In the following chapters, the confluence of peoples and cultures in this varied land are outlined, adding human variety atop the physical environment mosaic.

SOURCES AND SUGGESTED READINGS

Arbingast, Stanley A., et al. "Location and Physical Setting." In *Atlas of Texas*, pp. 1–26. 5th ed. Austin: University of Texas, Bureau of Business Research, 1976.

Climatological Data, Texas. Asheville, N.C.: National Oceanic and Atmospheric Administration, Environmental Data Service, National Climatic Center, published monthly.

Godfrey, Curtis L., McKee, G. S., and Oakes, Harvey. *General Soil Map of Texas*. College Station: Texas Agricultural Experiment Station, 1973.

Gould, F. W. *Texas Plants: A Checklist and Ecological Summary*. College Station: Texas Agricultural Experiment Bulletin MP-585, June 1962.

Hammond, Edwin H. "Classes of Land-Surface Form in the Forty-Eight States, U.S.A." *Annals of the Association of American Geographers* 54 (1964), Map Supplement no. 4.

Jordan, Terry G. *Environment and Environmental Perceptions in Texas*. Boston: American Press, 1980.

————. "Pioneer Evaluation of Vegetation in Frontier Texas." *Southwestern Historical Quarterly* 76 (1973), 233–254.

Land Use/Land Cover Maps of Texas. Bulletin LP-62. Austin: Texas Department of Water Resources, February 1977; reprinted 1978, pp. 233–254.

Marriott, Alice L. "The Cross Timbers as a Cultural Barrier." *Texas Geographic Magazine* 7:1 (1943), 14–20.

Mattoon, W. R., and Webster, C. B. *Forest Trees of Texas*. Bulletin no. 20. College Station: Texas Forest Service, 1928.

Parks, H. B., and Cory, V. L. *Biological Survey of the East Texas Big Thicket Area*. College Station: Texas Agricultural Experiment Station, 1936.

Renfro, H. B., et al. *Geological Highway Map of Texas*. Tulsa, Okla.: American Association of Petroleum Geologists and the U.S. Geological Survey.

Russell, Richard J. "Climates of Texas." *Annals of the Association of American Geographers* 35 (1945), 37–52.

Sellards, E. H., and Baker, C. L. *The Geology of Texas, Volume II*. Bulletin no. 3401. Austin: University of Texas, January 1934.

Water Resources Development. Dallas: U.S. Army, Corps of Engineers, Southwestern Division, January 1977.

SOURCES OF QUOTATIONS

Austin, Stephen F., as quoted in *The Austin Papers*, ed. Eugene C. Barker (Washington,

D.C.: American Historical Association, vol. 1, 1924, vol. 2, 1928; Austin: University of Texas Press, vol. 3, 1926).

Bollaert, William, *William Bollaert's Texas*, ed. W. Eugene Hollon and Ruth L. Butler (Norman: University of Oklahoma Press, 1956).

Bracht, Viktor, *Texas im Jahre 1848* (Elberfeld and Iserlohn: Baedeker, 1849).

Clopper, J. C., "J. C. Clopper's Journal and Book of Memoranda for 1828," *Quarterly of the Texas State Historical Association* 13 (1909–1910), 44–80.

DeCordova, Jacob, *Texas: Her Resources and Her Public Men* (Philadelphia: E. Crozet, 1858).

DeWees, William B., *Letters from an Early Settler of Texas* (Louisville, Ky.: Morton & Griswold, 1852).

Edward, David B., *The History of Texas; or, The Emigrant's, Farmer's, and Politician's Guide to the Character, Climate, Soil, and Productions of That Country* (Cincinnati: J. A. James, 1836).

Fisher, Orceneth, *Sketches of Texas* (Springfield, Ill.: Walters & Weber, 1841).

Flowers, Elisha, as quoted in *The Austin Papers* vol. 2, ed. Eugene C. Barker (Washington, D.C.: American Historical Association, 1928).

Harris, Dilue, "Reminiscences of Mrs. Dilue Harris," *Quarterly of the Texas State Historical Association* 4 (1900–1901), 85–127, 155–189; 7 (1903–1904), 214–222.

Holley, Mary A., *Texas* (Lexington, Ky.: J. Clarke & Co., 1836).

James, Joshua, and McCrea, Alexander, *A Journal of a Tour in Texas* (Wilmington, N.C.: T. Loring, 1835).

Kendall, George Wilkins, *Narrative of the Texan Santa Fé Expedition* (London: Wiley & Putnam, 1844).

Kennedy, William, *Texas: The Rise, Progress, and Prospects of the Republic of Texas* (London: R. Hastings, 1841).

Lincecum, Gideon, "Journal of Lincecum's Travels in Texas, 1835," *Southwestern Historical Quarterly* 53 (1949–1950), 180–201.

Lundy, Benjamin, *The Life, Travels, and Opinions of Benjamin Lundy, Including His Journeys to Texas and Mexico* (Philadelphia: William D. Parrish, 1847).

McClintock, William A., "Journal of the Trip Through Texas and Northern Mexico in 1846–1847," *Southwestern Historical Quarterly* 34 (1930–1931), 20–37, 141–158, 231–256.

Marryat, Frederick, *Narrative of the Travels and Adventures of Monsieur Violet in California, Sonora, and Western Texas* (London: Longman, Brown, Green & Longmans, 1843).

Matthes, Benno, *Reise-Bilder von Dr. Benno Matthes: Bilder aus Texas* (Dresden: H. J. Zeh, 1861).

Moore, A. W., "A Reconnaissance in Texas in 1846," *Southwestern Historical Quarterly* 30 (1926–1927), 252–271.

Moore, Francis, Jr., *Map and Description of Texas, Containing Sketches of Its History, Geology, Geography, and Statistics* (Philadelphia: H. Tanner, Jr.; New York: Tanner & Disturnell, 1840).

Nuttall, Thomas, *A Journal of Travels into the Arkansa Territory During the Year 1819* (Philadelphia: Thomas Palmer, 1821).

Parker, Amos A., *Trip to the West and Texas* (Concord, N.H.: White & Fisher, 1835).

Parker, James W., *Narrative of the Perilous Adventures, Miraculous Escapes, and Sufferings of Rev. James W. Parker, With an Impartial Geographical Description of Texas* (Louisville, Ky.: n.p., 1844).

Roemer, Ferdinand von, *Texas, mit besonderer Rücksicht auf deutsche Auswanderung und die physischen Verhältnisse des Landes* (Bonn: Adolph Marcus, 1849).

Shipman, Daniel, *Frontier Life: 58 Years in Texas* (n.p., 1879).

Smith, Edward, *Account of a Journey Through North-Eastern Texas Undertaken in 1849* (London: Hamilton, Adams & Co., 1849).

Solms-Braunfels, Carl von, *Texas: Geschildert in Beziehung auf seine geographischen, socialen, und übrigen Verhältnisse* (Frankfurt am Main: Johann David Sauerländer, 1846).

A Visit to Texas: Being the Journal of a Traveller Through Those Parts Most Interesting to American Settlers (New York: Goodrich & Wiley, 1834).

CHAPTER 3

POPULATION GEOGRAPHY

Most of this book is concerned with people and their characteristics. Subsequent chapters focus on topics such as ethnicity, language, religion, political patterns, settlement patterns, economic activity, etc.; this chapter sets the stage by presenting an overview of past and present patterns of Texas demographics. Major topics include trends in population growth, urban-rural patterns, distribution of population, age structure, the ratio of men to women, income patterns, and health patterns. The focus is on both temporal and spatial variations.

A land without people would seem empty to most of us—it might be cleaner, more structured, less polluted, and less changing, but it certainly would be devoid of an essential ingredient. Similarly, a land in which the people were all alike might strike us as being somewhat sterile. Fortunately, Texas fits neither of these patterns as its people are even more varied than its physical environment. Some regions are growing rapidly, and others are static or are experiencing depopulation. The ethnic pattern is complex both statewide and within individual regions, and variations exist between and within the state's regions in such diverse elements as religion, language, and means of earning a livelihood.

The visual and print media have long presented an overly simplistic image of Texas as a vast, subhumid region sparsely populated by a few hardy individuals amassing wealth and power from cattle ranching and petroleum production. This image was never accurate, and it is grossly deficient today when Texas ranks as the third most populous state in the United States and is home to more than 14 million people of widely varying characteristics and cultural backgrounds.

Texas is, and has been for more than a century, a land of rapid demographic changes. These changes have accompanied the transformation of Texas from a rural, agrarian backwater into a modern urban and industrial state.

POPULATION GROWTH

The first humans to live in what is now Texas were American Indians. These peoples were never very numerous and were concentrated largely in the more-humid eastern woodlands until they were dispossessed by people of European heritage in the first half of the nineteenth century.

The beginnings of European settlement in Texas commenced about two centuries ago during the period of Spanish rule of the American Southwest. The number of settlers grew very slowly, however—even with a small continuing influx of people during the period of Mexican rule and the subsequent brief existence of the Republic of Texas (1836–1845), the population remained small. It was not until after the middle of the nineteenth century that the population of Texas approached one-quarter of a million people.

The annexation of Texas into the United States in 1845 was accompanied by the beginnings of rapid population growth, and the state's population doubled on the average of once every seven years during the 1840s and 1850s. Several factors contributed to this rapid growth, including the apparent "elimination" of the Indians, the perception of increased political stability with statehood, the availability of free or very cheap agricultural land, and the promotion of Texas—both in the rest of the United States and in parts of Europe—as a land of economic opportunity for anyone who could migrate there. Reality was not as pretty as the image, however, as transportation facilities were poor, the land varied enormously in quality, and many of the materials needed to support rapid economic development were lacking. Nevertheless, few of the early immigrants gave up.

The population of Texas has continued to increase at a relatively high rate (Table 3.1 and Figure 3.1). The only two significant interruptions of this pattern occurred during the period of the Civil War (1861–1865) and its immediate aftermath and during the period of the Great Depression of the 1930s. The state's growth rate has consistently exceeded the national growth rate by a very large margin—always by at least one-third and frequently by much more. Because Texas has consistently grown much faster than most other states, its population rank has gradually increased until it now ranks third, following only California and New York.

All of the state's regions experienced significant population growth during the latter part of the nineteenth century and the first few decades of the twentieth century, but during the last few decades this pattern of universal growth has altered, and the population increase has become more spatially concentrated. As a result of this change, a few regions are growing very rapidly, others are remaining stable, and a few are losing population. Some of the results of this change are illustrated in Figure 3.2. For example, more than one-third of the state's 254 counties had achieved

Table 3.1. Population Growth in Texas, 1850–1980

Year	Total	Urban	Rural	Percent Growth in Previous Decade	Rank Among U.S. States
1850	212,592	7,665	204,927	173	25
1860	604,215	26,615	577,600	184	23
1870	818,579	54,521	764,058	36	19
1880	1,591,749	146,795	1,444,954	95	11
1890	2,235,527	349,511	1,886,016	40	7
1900	3,048,710	520,759	2,527,951	36	6
1910	3,896,542	938,104	2,958,438	28	5
1920	4,663,228	1,512,689	3,150,539	20	5
1930	5,824,715	2,389,348	3,435,367	25	5
1940	6,414,824	2,911,389	3,503,435	10	6
1950	7,711,194	4,838,060	2,873,134	20	6
1960	9,579,677	7,186,011	2,393,666	24	6
1970	11,196,730	8,920,946	2,275,784	17	4
1980	14,229,191	11,333,017	2,896,174	27	3

Source: U.S. Census.

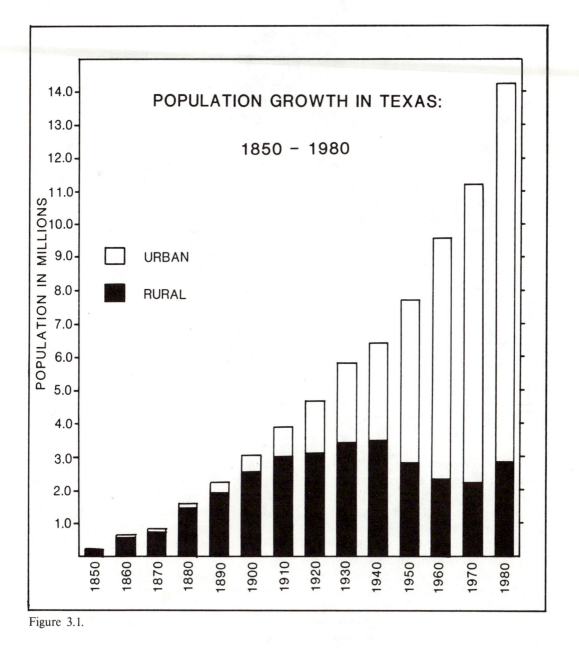

Figure 3.1.

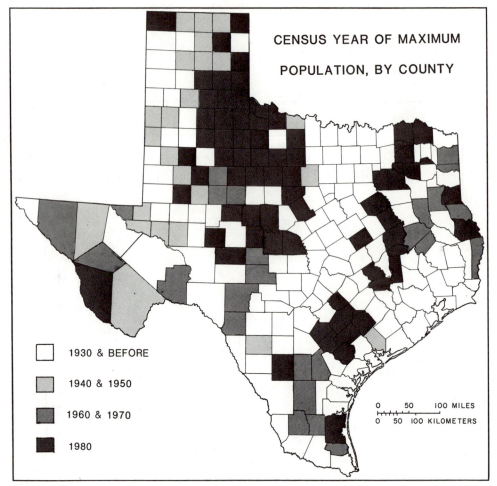

Figure 3.2.

their maximum population by 1930; these counties are largely concentrated in the southeastern Panhandle, the Blackland Prairie, and the northeastern part of the state. The reduced population of these regions is at least partially attributable to the fact that many farm laborers and small-farm families have been replaced by modern agricultural machinery. Another one-quarter of the state's counties registered their largest number of residents between 1930 and 1960; most of these are located in the western Panhandle and in the far west. Further, the 1980 population of nearly all of the counties that have been characterized by population loss is significantly below each

county's maximum population (Figure 3.3) as only a few have once again grown after there has been significant depopulation. Most of the state's recent population growth has been concentrated within and adjacent to the major urban counties (see Chapter 10).

The population of Texas increased by more than 3 million people between 1970 and 1980, which represents an increase of more than 27 percent over 1970 and accounts for more than one-fifth of the state's 1980 populaiton. Most parts of the state gained population during this period, and only the southeastern Panhandle, the southern High Plains, and the far west contain

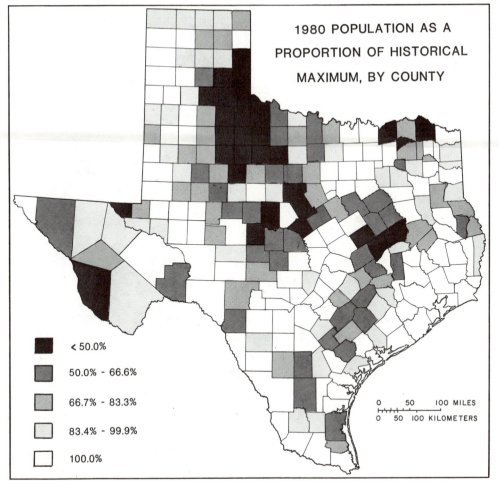

Figure 3.3.

significant clusters of counties that lost population during the period (Figure 3.4). Nevertheless, most of the population growth remained concentrated in a relatively few regions. Nearly one-half (46.6 percent) of the growth occurred in the six large urban counties that contain the cities of Houston, Dallas, San Antonio, Fort Worth, Austin, and El Paso. Most of the remainder was concentrated in the suburban counties in various parts of the state. Numerically and spatially, this recent growth is largely attributable to the continuing rapid development of secondary and tertiary economic activities in Texas and the concomitant increase in the demand for labor. The re-

gions that have lost population are largely those that continue to be highly dependent upon either agriculture or mineral exploitation for an economic base.

URBAN-RURAL PATTERNS

Many changes in the character of Texas's population have resulted from more than a century of rapid population increase and major economic transformations. One of the most pronounced, and culturally significant, changes has been the transition from a dominantly rural, agrarian population to a dominantly urban population.

The population of Texas was overwhelm-

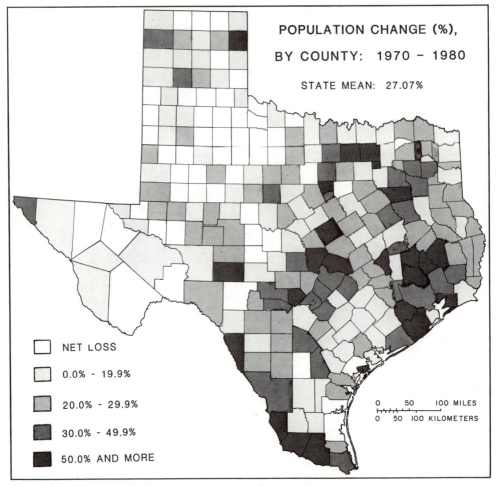

Figure 3.4.

ingly rural as late as 1900 (see Table 3.1), and this rural population consisted of people who lived and worked on individual farmsteads and ranches as well as people who lived in small towns and villages. The numerical dominance of the rural population continued as long as it did because the rural population grew faster numerically than the urban population did until shortly after the beginning of the twentieth century, but the pattern of rural dominance began to wane following 1910. Although the rural population continued to grow for the next three decades (1910–1940), its growth was considerably slower than that of the urban population. The result was a near balance between rural and urban populations in 1940—about 55 percent rural and 45 percent urban.

The urban-rural pattern has been transformed during the last four decades (1940–1980). At the beginning of the period, a large number of people left their farms and small towns for wartime jobs in the larger cities, and relatively few returned to their former rural homes after World War II. The first two decades of the period also witnessed the displacement of many tens of thousands of sharecroppers and farm laborers by modern farm machinery. At the same time, large numbers of small family-owned-and-operated farms and ranches were being absorbed into modern corporate farms. These factors, combined

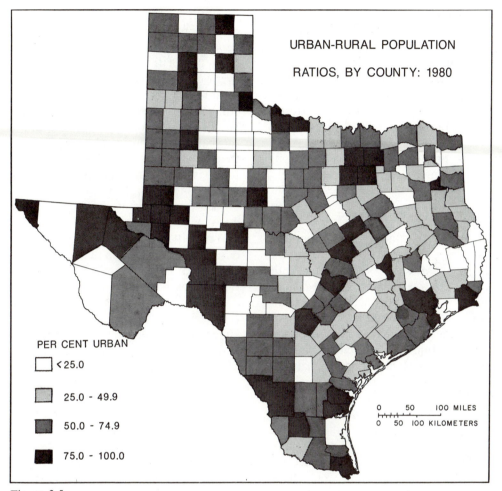

Figure 3.5.

with the large-scale in-migration of several million people from other parts of the United States and foreign lands into the metropolitan centers of Texas, resulted in the fact that approximately four-fifths of the state's 1980 population was concentrated in urban centers.

The growth in the total number of people living in rural areas during the 1970–1980 decade does not appear to reflect a reversal of the trend toward increasing the concentration of Texans in urban regions. Most, if not all, of this net increase in the rural population can be attributed to growth in the rural parts of counties that are located adjacent to or in close proximity to metropolitan centers. This situation appears to

be part of a nationwide pattern, according to which large numbers of families move to the "country" but commute to jobs in the metropolitan centers.

The spatial distribution pattern of counties according to their rural or urban status is relatively complex, although a number of generalizations are possible. Nearly one-quarter of the state's counties contained no urban settlement in 1970, and these counties are concentrated in the western half of Texas (Figure 3.5). Another one-quarter had a majority of their population in rural areas; most of these counties are in the eastern and central areas. Most, but not all, of the counties that exceeded the state's urban percentage contain one or more SMSA

(Standard Metropolitan Statistical Area) central cities, with the notable exceptions of several western counties that have relatively small total populations but nearly all of their residents are concentrated in a small city. Counties that are marginally urban (50.0–74.9 percent) are scattered throughout the state and tend to be either suburban in nature or else have a small population that is largely concentrated in one or two small cities.

POPULATION DISTRIBUTION

The spatial distribution of the population could have been described relatively simply in the middle of the nineteenth century. Texas was a sparsely settled land, and there was a pronounced decrease in the number of residents from east to west. The subsequent very rapid growth of the state's population contributed to the development of a much more complex pattern; a second contributor was the partial depopulation of several rural areas.

At the time of the 1980 national census, a total of 14,229,191 people inhabited the 267,338 sq mi (692,405 sq km) of land and surface water that compose Texas. An evenly distributed population would have resulted in approximately 53 people residing within each square mile (20 per sq km) or one person for each 12 acres (5 ha), but the population is not at all evenly distributed. Texas, like all large regions, is characterized by marked variations in the spatial distributional pattern of its population. For example, Loving County in the west contains only 91 residents within its 647 sq mi (1,676 sq km), but Dallas County, which covers an area of 893 sq mi (2,313 sq km), has 1,551,032 residents. Thus, Dallas County is more than 12,000 times as densely populated as Loving County.

Although Texas has a few areas that have relatively dense concentrations of population, most of the state remains quite sparsely populated even after the rapid population growth of the last few decades. More than

four-fifths of the state's counties have a mean population density of fewer than 50 people per sq mi (19 per sq km), and nearly one-tenth of the total surface area has an average density of less than 1 person per sq mi (0.4 per sq km). Overall, there is still a marked general decrease in population density from east to west, although the pattern is considerably more complex than in earlier times. Today this general trend is frequently disrupted by areas of sparse concentrations in the east and nodes of denser settlement in the west (Figure 3.6).

Very little of Texas can accurately be described as being even moderately densely populated. Less than one-fifth of the counties approach or exceed the national mean population density of 61 people per sq mi (24 per km), and these few counties are largely concentrated in three clusters: around Dallas–Fort Worth in the north-central part of the state, along a north-south belt extending from Waco through Austin to San Antonio in the central part, and north and south of Houston. Each of the ten counties that have a density of more than 1 person per acre (0.4 per ha) is the location of an important urban complex. Ranked according to decreasing order of county population, the cities involved are Dallas, Houston, Fort Worth, San Antonio, El Paso, Galveston–Texas City, Austin, Longview, Corpus Christi, and Beaumont–Port Arthur. Even in the counties that contain these cities, however, there are still substantial areas that are sparsely populated.

Using only density patterns to examine the distribution of population frequently leads to distorted images. For example, it is quite possible for a relatively large, highly concentrated group of people located within a geographically large and otherwise sparsely settled area to be masked. Webb County, which is located along the lower Rio Grande and contains the city of Laredo, is one example. More than 90 percent of the county's population of nearly 100,000 people is concentrated in Laredo, but the city ac-

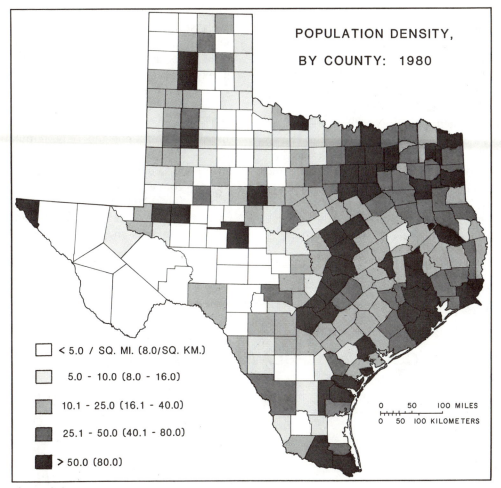

POPULATION DENSITY,
BY COUNTY: 1980

< 5.0 / SQ. MI. (8.0/SQ. KM.)

5.0 - 10.0 (8.0 - 16.0)

10.1 - 25.0 (16.1 - 40.0)

25.1 - 50.0 (40.1 - 80.0)

> 50.0 (80.0)

0   50   100 MILES
0   50   100 KILOMETERS

Figure 3.6.

counts for less than 5 percent of the county's area of 3,295 sq mi (8,534 sq km). Thus, Webb County has a population density of only about 30 people per sq mi (12 per sq km) even though it has nearly 100,000 residents. Similarly, a much less numerous group of people located within a geographically smaller area can be made to appear quite significant. Rockwall County, a suburban area adjacent to Dallas County, is an example. This county, with a population of only 14,433 people in an area of 147 sq mi (381 sq km), has a population density that is more than three times greater than that of Webb County. Such distortions can be avoided by examining the distribution of population according to numerical patterns and comparing the results with those obtained from examining the density patterns.

Most Texas residents are spatially concentrated in a few parts of the state (Figure 3.7). For example, more than one-quarter of the total population is concentrated in just two counties—Harris County (Houston) and Dallas County (Dallas)—and more than one-half of the people of Texas are located in the state's eight most populous counties. By contrast, the twenty-five least populous counties combined contain less than 0.33 percent of the total state population.

The more heavily populated counties generally are located in the eastern and central regions of Texas (Figure 3.8). There are only two notable clusters: one centered on Harris County in the southeast and the other centered on Dallas and Tarrant counties in the north-central area. Combined, these clusters contain nearly 6,000,000 of the state's 14,229,191 residents. The Harris County cluster alone accounts for more than 21 percent of the state's population, and the Dallas–Fort Worth area contains very nearly as large a share. No other part of the state comes close to assuming such importance in the overall distribution of population. With the exception of a relatively small concentration in the corridor between Dallas–Fort Worth and San Antonio, other notable agglomerations are relatively small and reflect the presence of secondary urban centers scattered in various parts of the state.

The number of people and their spatial distribution are not the only population aspects that are subject to change; many others may change as well, often greatly. And, of course, there is considerable variation in the spatial patterns of most of the characteristics of a region's population. The remainder of this chapter is devoted to an

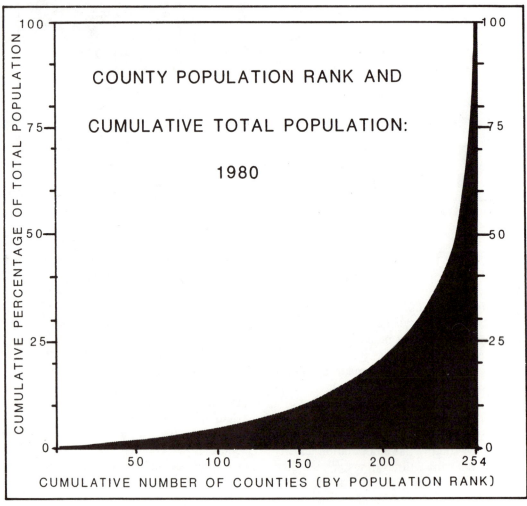

Figure 3.7.

examination of several of these population attributes.

AGE STRUCTURE

The rapid growth and marked changes in the spatial distribution of the population of Texas during the past century have been accompanied by significant changes in the age structure of the overall population. This section does not attempt to examine the changing age structure of the state in great detail; rather, it seeks to present an overall description that will be sufficient to provide a base for understanding the general trends in median age, proportion of children in the total population, proportion of the aged in the population, and the overall spatial distribution patterns of various age groups.

Several factors have a strong direct influence on the evolving age structure of a complex region, including natural fertility, life expectancy, and the relative age of migrants both to and from the region. These factors are affected, in turn, by secondary influences such as the society's attitudes toward children and family size, ethnicity, perceived economic opportunity both within and outside the region, and the quality and availability of health care. It is beyond the scope of this book or this chapter to assess the contribution of each of these factors to

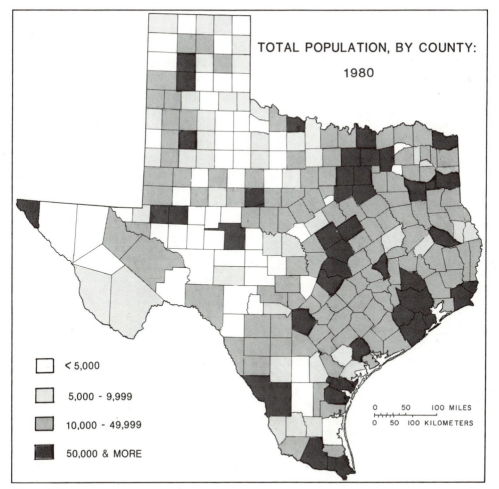

TOTAL POPULATION, BY COUNTY: 1980

☐ < 5,000
▨ 5,000 - 9,999
▨ 10,000 - 49,999
■ 50,000 & MORE

0   50   100 MILES
0 50 100 KILOMETERS

Figure 3.8.

the changing demographic patterns in Texas. What is of concern is to examine the overall types of change that have occurred and to describe the current structural and spatial patterns.

Compared with the rest of the United States as a whole, Texas has consistently had a very young population. The disparity between the pattern in Texas and the national pattern has frequently been quite pronounced. However, since the early 1950s, the differential between the national and the Texas median ages has narrowed considerably.

During the past century, the median age of the state's population has increased by more than 50 percent, from 17.6 years in 1880 to 28.0 years in 1980 (Table 3.2). With the exception of what appears to have been a temporary decline in 1960 and 1970, the trend toward an increase in the population's median age has been very consistent, and it has been accompanied by significant changes in the proportions of the very young and the older age groups. The percentage of the state's population that was younger than fifteen years of age decreased by more than 45 percent between 1880 and 1980, and the rate of that decrease seems to be accelerating. Further, the pro-

portion of people aged sixty and older more than tripled during the 1880–1980 period, but there is some evidence that this group's proportion may be stabilizing. These trends generally parallel the national trends for the same period, but they have been much more intense in Texas than in the United States as a whole.

A frequent pattern in areas of "pioneer" agrarian settlement is that rural areas are characterized by somewhat younger populations than are the scattered towns and small cities in such areas. This pattern reflects, at least partially, the largely one-way movement of adults—but few children—from farm to city as such areas begin to mature. This pioneer age-structure pattern was characteristic in much of Texas through the first few decades of the twentieth century, but as the state's economy matured and became more industrial in orientation, increasing numbers of young adults left their rural homes for better economic opportunities in the cities of Texas— many thousands more left the state for other parts of the nation. This movement has been strong since the early 1940s and has resulted in a reversal of the earlier urban-rural dichotomy with respect to age structure. Today the cities are characterized

Table 3.2   Male and Female Population, Sex Ratio, and Age Structure, 1880–1980

Year	Males	Females	Sex Ratio[a]	Median Age	Percent Under 15 Years	Percent Over 60 Years
1880	837,840	753,909	111.1	17.6	45.2%	3.2%
1890	1,172,556	1,062,971	110.3	17.9	43.6	4.2
1900	1,578,900	1,469,810	107.4	18.7	41.6	4.5
1910	2,017,626	1,878,916	107.4	20.2	38.6	5.1
1920	2,409,222	2,254,006	106.9	22.0	35.4	5.9
1930	2,965,994	2,858,721	103.8	23.7	32.2	6.4
1940	3,221,103	3,193,721	100.9	26.8	28.1	8.3
1950	3,863,142	3,848,052	100.4	27.9	29.1	9.9
1960	4,744,981	4,834,696	98.1	27.0	33.1	10.8
1970	5,481,169	5,715,561	95.9	26.4	29.7	12.2
1980	6,998,723	7,230,468	96.8	28.0	24.7	11.5

[a]Index of males to females (females = 100)
Source: U.S. Census.

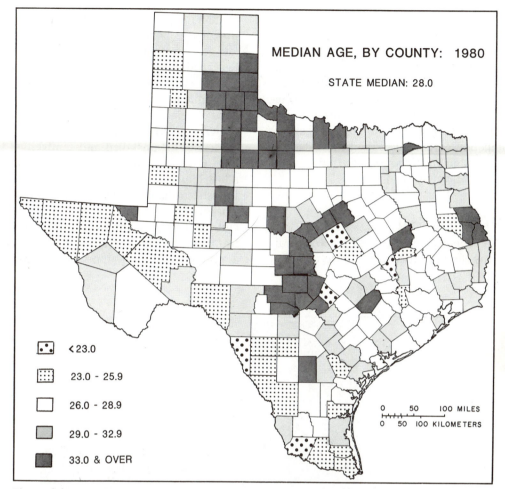

Figure 3.9.

by younger populations, and the rural areas have a disproportionately high percentage of the state's older residents.

The intensity of the disparity in relative ages between rural counties and urban counties in Texas is clearly reflected in Figure 3.9, and a comparison with Figure 3.5 shows the relationship between counties with high median ages and dominant rural populations. Very nearly 40 percent of the state's counties have a population with a median age of thirty-three years or more, and none of these counties reach the state mean in the proportion of urbanized population. Generally, these are the same counties that have been losing population in recent decades. The most notable exception occurs northwest of San Antonio in a part of the Hill Country that has attracted many thousands of retirees in recent decades. The populations of rapidly growing urban counties are generally at or below the state median age. Other types of areas that are characterized by relatively low median ages are counties in which a relatively large proportion of the population consists of college students or military personnel and counties along the Rio Grande that have relatively large numbers of families with several children that have recently arrived from Mexico.

There are approximately three times as

many people in Texas under eighteen years of age as there are people sixty-five or older. In several areas the ratio is greater than four to one—especially the Houston area, the southern and central Rio Grande area, and much of the Trans-Pecos section (Figure 3.10). In many counties, however, the ratio of young to old among the general population is considerably below the average, and in a few counties, the old actually exceed the young in numbers.

MALE/FEMALE RATIO

Another significant demographic indicator is the sex ratio, or the ratio of males to females in the general population, as this figure is informative both culturally and economically. For example, regions with fewer adult males often encounter labor shortages, which serve to restrict or limit economic growth. In contrast, regions with a large relative surplus of males may experience a downward pressure on wages, especially for unskilled and semiskilled labor. Regions with a high proportion of adult females are frequently attractive to industries that require low skill–low wage workers for assembly lines in textile mills, clothing factories, and the assembly of electronic components. And, historically at least, a preponderance of males in the general

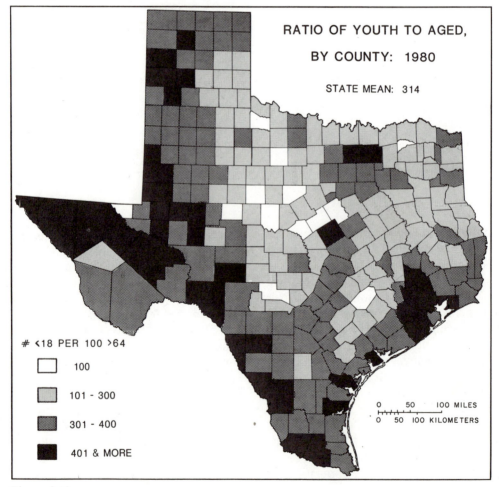

RATIO OF YOUTH TO AGED,
BY COUNTY: 1980

STATE MEAN: 314

<18 PER 100 >64

100
101 - 300
301 - 400
401 & MORE

0   50   100 MILES
0   50   100 KILOMETERS

Figure 3.10.

population was often perceived as a potential source of political and military strength.

In the early decades of the twentieth century, Texas fit the general pattern of a region with a major imbalance between males and females very well. Much of Texas was a sparsely settled, pseudopioneer region, dependent upon immigration from outside the state for a significant part of its population growth, and the dominant economic activities were those that required large amounts of male labor. Most men were employed in farming, ranching, and mineral exploitation—activities that even today are male dominated. As a consequence, the ratio of males to females in the state's population remained high, generally on the order of about 110 males for each 100 females (see Table 3.2). However, it is important to recognize that although a sex ratio of 110 is considered quite high today, it was not so unusual in the United States at the beginning of the twentieth century—the national ratio was 106 as late as 1910, and parity between males and females was not achieved nationally until about 1940.

Jefferson County, located on the Texas coast adjacent to Louisiana, provides a very good example of why the high sex ratio continued in Texas for so long. The county's economy was dominated by the processing and shipping of forest products in 1900. Its total population was slightly less than 15,000, and there was a marked, but not unusually excessive, preponderance of males. Then, in January 1901, the Spindletop oil field was discovered, and it became the scene of the first large-scale production in Texas. The oil boom resulted in a massive influx of common laborers, skilled workers, businessmen, promoters, etc.—some estimates indicate that perhaps 30,000 newcomers arrived during the first six months of 1901 alone—and by 1910 the permanent population of Jefferson County had increased to nearly 40,000. The county's sex ratio was extremely high through 1920 because many of the recently arrived workers either had no families or refused to bring them to a boom area where living conditions were notoriously difficult.

As is true for age structure, growing industrial development and the increasing concentration of the population in urban centers have resulted in significant changes in the state's sex ratio since about 1940. Although the overall ratio remains slightly above the national mean, females now outnumber males in Texas—the ratio in 1980 was 96.8 males for every 100 females—and it seems likely that females will retain their numerical majority in Texas for the foreseeable future, even though slightly more males than females moved into Texas during the early years of the 1980s.

The sex ratios of the individual counties vary widely from the state average of 96.8. In 1980 the ratios for individual counties ranged from a low of 84 to a high of 144, but a majority of the counties had ratios that were relatively near the state mean (Figure 3.11). Slightly more than one-quarter of all the counties had sex ratios that were well below the state norm, and nearly all of these were rural counties and most had been losing population for the past several decades. The low sex ratio in these counties is largely attributable to a significantly higher out-migration rate for males than for females.

Ten counties in various parts of the state have very high sex ratios, but in nearly every case, relatively easily identifiable circumstances account for the very high ratio of males to females. The situations in these ten counties are so unusual, yet so instructive, that a brief description of the special conditions that prevail in each will be presented. Four of the five counties clustered in the east-central part of the state reflect the presence of multiple units of the state's prison system for men. Another county, located near the geographic center of Texas, is the site of one of the largest military bases in the United States. A county in the western Panhandle contains a large, privately financed "boys ranch," and two sparsely populated counties located in the

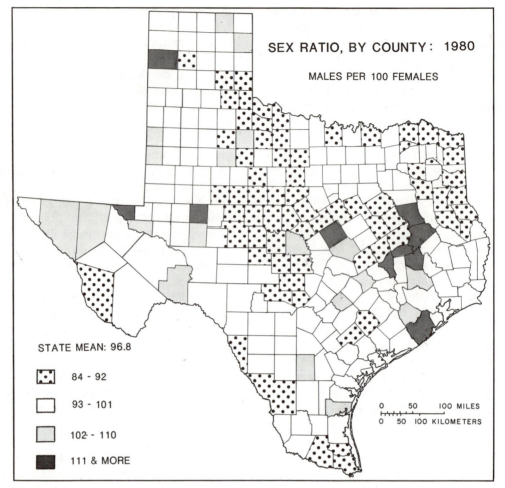

SEX RATIO, BY COUNTY: 1980

MALES PER 100 FEMALES

STATE MEAN: 96.8

84 - 92

93 - 101

102 - 110

111 & MORE

0   50   100 MILES

0   50   100 KILOMETERS

Figure 3.11.

southern High Plains and the west have economies that are strongly dominated by ranching, farming, and mineral production. Only two of the counties are dominantly urban and/or industrial. One—the fifth in the cluster in the east-central part of the state—is the location of a large state university (Texas A.&M.) that restricted enrollment to males until recently. The other is a suburban county adjacent to Harris County (Houston) that has been undergoing very rapid industrial growth and population growth for the past several decades.

PERSONAL INCOME

Texas has a relatively long-standing reputation of being a wealthy state, and the stereotype of the typical Texan is that of an individual with considerable wealth derived largely from cattle and oil wells. However, the truth is that the incomes of Texans are as varied as the incomes of people living in the rest of the United States. Texas is certainly relatively wealthier than many states in the nation, but it is not among the wealthiest on a per capita basis. Overall, the median household income in Texas slightly exceeds the national average, but some parts of the state are clearly among the poorest parts of the nation—a prime example is Starr County in the Rio Grande Valley. Other parts of the state are relatively wealthy—for example, Collin County, which is a very fast growing, largely upper-middle-class sub-

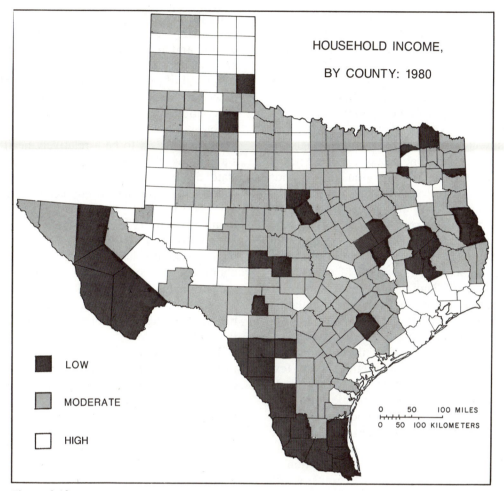

HOUSEHOLD INCOME,
BY COUNTY: 1980

LOW

MODERATE

HIGH

0   50   100 MILES

0   50   100 KILOMETERS

Figure 3.12.

urban county near Dallas.

The spatial distribution of the mean household income appears very complex at first view (Figure 3.12). In fact, however, the pattern has a considerable degree of internal consistency, and the variables that are particularly important in explaining the pattern are not numerous. These variables include the percentage of Hispanics within the population, the urban-rural status of a county, the importance of mineral production in a county's economic picture, and the size of the agricultural land holdings.

Perhaps the most apparent spatial pattern in the distribution of household income for Texas counties is the concentration of very low-income counties along the state's southern border with Mexico. This region has a very large Hispanic component in its population, and relatively low skill, low paying jobs dominate the employment picture even though several of these counties are relatively highly urbanized. A totally different distribution picture exists for the counties that can be classed as being significantly below the state mean but not really poor. Most of these counties are dominantly rural and rely on agriculture for most of their economic activity. In addition, the farms and ranches in these counties are relatively small and are owned, operated, and worked by individual families. This pattern is particularly evident in the Blackland Prairie, parts of the Edwards Plateau, and much of central and north East Texas.

Counties containing a large urban agglomeration generally have average household incomes that are considerably above the state average. The most notable exceptions are El Paso County and Bexar County (San Antonio), and each of these has a very large Hispanic component in its population. Two other types of counties are also generally characterized by relatively high average incomes. One group is located in the southern High Plains region and extends west to the Pecos River. Much of the economic activity in this region focuses on mineral production, with a secondary contribution from ranching. A very different economic base accounts for the relatively high incomes of the group of counties in the northern Panhandle. These counties are characterized by relatively low population densities and very large agricultural operations; mineral production is a secondary contributor in several of these counties.

For much of the twentieth century, Texans believed that their state was largely immune to most of the economic downturns that periodically afflict modern industrial societies. This optimism was based on the assumption that since the state's economy is supported largely by the production of foodstuffs and petroleum, Texans would always be able to find a market for their goods at a price that was sufficient to maintain relatively satisfactory income levels. Recent world events that have severely disrupted the market for crude petroleum have made Texans recognize the fact that the state's economy is as subject to outside negative influences as are the economies of other parts of the nation.

MORTALITY PATTERNS

One of the more interesting and informative ways to study the characteristics of a population is to look at the spatial pattern of disease and mortality—an aspect that is frequently overlooked. The occurrence of diseases and the causes of death within a population are strongly influenced by a wide variety of factors, the more important being age, place of residence, occupation, quality and availability of health care, diet, and marital status. The geographic patterns of several of these factors have been briefly described already; others, such as that of occupation, are discussed in subsequent chapters.

Texas appears to be a relatively healthy state in which to reside if one compares state death rates across the nation. The death rate (expressed in number of deaths per 1,000 residents) for Texas was approximately 8.0 in 1978. This figure was relatively low on a national basis, and Texas has consistently had a death rate that is about one full point (0.1 percent) below the national average since 1970. As a result, Texas ranked among the top five states in regard to having a low mortality rate through the 1970s.

Four causes account for more than two-thirds of all deaths in Texas: in order, heart disease, cancer, stroke, and accident. The remaining one-third of the deaths occur as the result of a wide number of causes, no one of which approaches the importance of any of the four primary causes. The geographic patterns of cause of death in Texas vary in several respects, but there are also striking similarities in several instances. Generally, the major causes can be related to a significant degree to one or more of the demographic elements discussed earlier in this chapter.

The overall death rate (i.e., from all causes combined) varies considerably from one part of Texas to another. Some parts of the state are generally characterized by relatively low rates; others have quite high rates (Figure 3.13). However, variations in the death rate appear to correlate much more closely with characteristics of the population than with precise regional location. For example, the overall death rate for people residing in major urban counties is quite markedly below the state mean—the major exceptions being Potter County (Amarillo) and McLennan County (Waco), each of which has a population that is older

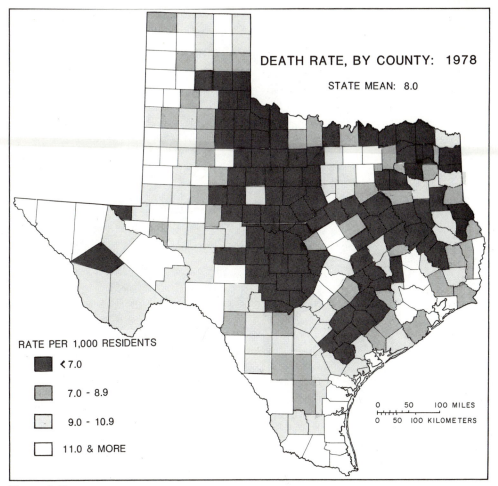

DEATH RATE, BY COUNTY: 1978

STATE MEAN: 8.0

RATE PER 1,000 RESIDENTS

< 7.0

7.0 - 8.9

9.0 - 10.9

11.0 & MORE

0   50   100 MILES

0   50   100 KILOMETERS

Figure 3.13.

than is normal for one of the state's major urban counties. Similarly, there is a strong relationship between the geographic distribution of recent death rates on a county basis and counties with a low median age. This latter pattern is particularly evident in such regions as the Rio Grande Valley, West Texas, and the western part of the Panhandle. Areas characterized by relatively high death rates have much the same spatial distribution pattern as counties with a high median age, and these counties also are generally characterized by a continuing rural depopulation and a low degree of urban development.

It is interesting to note an apparent relationship between death rates and ethnic patterns in Texas. For example, areas in which Hispanics are numerically dominant, or in which they constitute the largest ethnic minority, appear to be characterized by relatively low death rates, but this correlation is probably the result of a younger population rather than of an ethnic factor. Conversely, however, areas in which blacks are numerically important seem to have relatively high death rates, and the median ages of blacks are not too different from those of Hispanics in Texas. Finally, the parts of the state that retain a strong ethnic remnant of people of Slavic or Scandinavian origin are characterized by relatively high death rates. Probably this relationship largely reflects the "leaving behind" of older

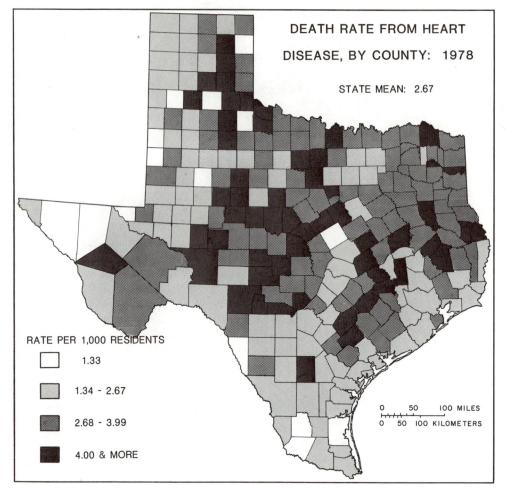

Figure 3.14.

family members as the youth of such families leave for better economic opportunities elsewhere.

The leading cause of death among Texans is heart disease, which alone accounts for more than one-third of all deaths, and cancer is the cause of nearly one-fifth of all deaths. Comparisons of the geographic pattern of death rates from heart disease (Figure 3.14) with patterns of urban-rural status, period of maximum county population, and median age indicate a considerable similarity, and much the same is true for the pattern of death rates resulting from cancer (Figure 3.15). For example, counties that have recently been experiencing rapid population growth, that are

highly urbanized, or that have a relatively young population tend to have very low death rates from both heart disease and cancer. Conversely, however, rural counties with a consistent pattern of recent depopulation tend to be characterized by quite high death rates from both diseases. These patterns are not unexpected, considering that both heart disease and cancer occur with greater frequency among the elderly than among the young.

At first glance, it might appear surprising that the more highly urbanized counties have both lower overall death rates and lower heart disease and cancer death rates than do the supposedly more healthy rural areas. However, this circumstance largely

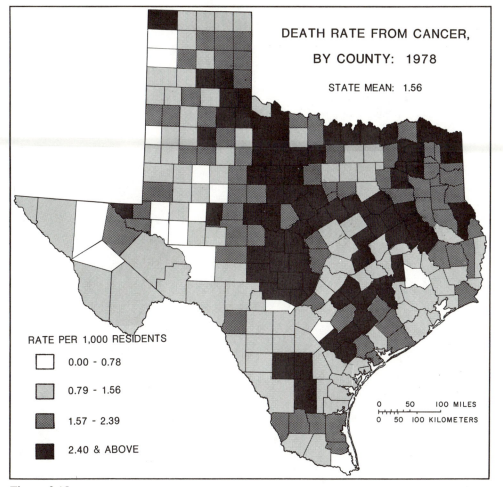

DEATH RATE FROM CANCER,
BY COUNTY: 1978

STATE MEAN: 1.56

RATE PER 1,000 RESIDENTS

☐ 0.00 - 0.78

▨ 0.79 - 1.56

▩ 1.57 - 2.39

■ 2.40 & ABOVE

Figure 3.15.

reflects the much lower age of the urban population as compared with the rural population of Texas. Only if mortality rates, both collectively and for individual causes, are adjusted for the age structure of the population does an accurate picture develop.

This chapter has very briefly described a few of the more important and more interesting demographic characteristics of the population of Texas. Subsequent chapters will explore several of these topics in additional detail. The next chapter focuses on settlement patterns, a topic that is closely related to several of the demographic elements covered in this chapter.

For more information, please see the Sources and Suggested Readings sections at the ends of Chapters 4 and 10.

CHAPTER 4

CONFLUENCE OF CULTURES

Implantation of the present cultural/ethnic diversity in Texas has been a lengthy process, which began in the late 1600s and continues still today. Four broadly defined groups account for the overwhelming majority of Texans: old-stock Anglo-American, Afro-Americans, Mexican-Americans, and persons of direct European ancestry. Of these the largest, forming the host culture, consists of the Anglos, primarily southern in origin, who make up about 60 percent of the Texas population.

THREE ANGLO-AMERICAN SUBCULTURES

By the time of the American Revolution, three major Anglo subcultures already had developed in the eastern half of the United States, and each was to play a role in westward migration and the shaping of Anglo-Texas. Along the northern fringe of the nation lay the domain of the New Englander, stretching in a narrow belt west from the rocky shores of Massachusetts and Maine across New York and into the northern part of the Old Northwest. The Yankee realm was the offspring of the Massachusetts Bay Colony, whose stern imprint was revealed in religion, dialect, education, architecture, and economy. It represented perhaps the purest transplantation of the people and culture of Old England, tempered by two centuries in a difficult environment that offered rocky soils and bitter winters. Those among the children of New England who sought wealth turned by necessity away from the soil and became merchants or artisans, in such numbers as to establish the "Yankee trader" permanently in American folklore. The dictates of distance provided little opportunity for Yankees to put their stamp on Texas, but those who did settle in Texas generally attained influence out of proportion to their numbers.

In the Atlantic and Gulf coastal plains of the southern states, another and quite different culture area had developed, perhaps most commonly referred to as the Lower South. It was a land of cotton and Negro slavery dominated economically by the plantation type of agriculture. It had arisen in the seventeenth and eighteenth centuries in the Tidewater coastal fringe of the Chesapeake Bay colonies and in the tidal swamps and sea islands of South Carolina. In these areas, the plantation first took root in Anglo-America, flourishing on the cultivation of tobacco, rice, and indigo. In neighboring areas of poorer soils, such as the pine barrens, slaveless "poor whites" earned a comfortable living from hunting and herding. Not until after the American Revolution did the economy of the lower-southern planters become linked to cotton, but under the impetus provided by that

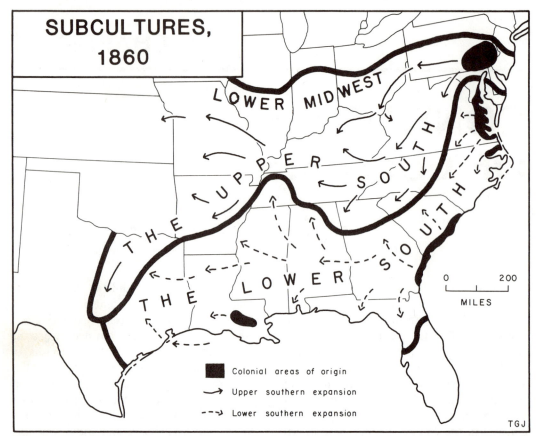

Figure 4.1. Anglo-Texans are derived primarily from the Upper and Lower South. Together, the Upper South and Lower Midwest constitute the Middle Atlantic subculture, which originated in the Delaware Valley.

single crop, the plantation domain rapidly expanded. The planters surged westward out of their colonial Tidewater base, crossed the Gulf Coastal Plain, and reached the Sabine River. Paralleling their advance, poor whites followed the pine barrens west. Only a little over half a century was required to complete the expansion from the Atlantic seaboard states to the pine forests of eastern Texas (Figure 4.1). The Lower South was to play a major role in the shaping of the Lone Star State.

Sandwiched between the Yankee and the lower-southern realms was the Middle Atlantic culture area, the largest and most important in the eastern United States. It formed a wedge-shaped zone that broadened to the west from an eastern apex in Pennsylvania and New Jersey. The center

of the Middle Atlantic culture lay in the valley of the Delaware River and its tributaries, particularly in southeastern Pennsylvania, the source of much that later came to be thought of as typically American—the log cabin, covered wagon, and long rifle; the independent family farm, livestock barn, and isolated farmstead; the Corn Belt and Wheat Belt; the "melting pot" in which varied ethnic groups met and mingled. The preeminence of the Middle Atlantic colonies as a source of diverse ideas and items of material culture can be related in part to the presence of a great variety of ethnic groups from Europe. In 1790 the Pennsylvania population was one-third English in origin, one-third German, and one-fifth Scotch-Irish; there were also smaller groups of Swedes, Welsh, and Dutch. Such diversity stood in contrast to the overwhelmingly English character of New England and the English-African population of the Lower South.

In the process of expansion west and southwest from the Pennsylvania–New Jersey hearth, bearers of the Middle Atlantic culture created two more-or-less-distinct subregions—the Upper South and the Lower Midwest. The Upper South was quite different from the adjacent Lower South, to which it has often, and mistakenly, been linked. The Upper South was settled primarily by slaveless yeomen who grew little cotton or other subtropical cash crops. Grains, especially corn and wheat, formed the backbone of the rural economy, supplemented in some areas by hemp and tobacco. The breeding of mules and horses, and the marketing of droves of semiwild hogs, were important. In general, the agriculture was more diversified and less market-oriented than in the Lower South.

Settlement of the Upper South began in the first half of the eighteenth century when small farmers, mainly of Scotch-Irish, German, or English descent, spilled southwestward out of Pennsylvania into the Great Valley and the Piedmont, which formed the back country of Maryland, Virginia, and North Carolina. These pioneers were met by other yeoman farmers, primarily of English descent, who were moving inland from the Tidewater plantation area of the Chesapeake colonies where many had been introduced as indentured servants. The westward expansion of the Upper South began earlier than that of the Lower South, with yeomen penetrating Tennessee and Kentucky even before the Revolution. Later, in the first half of the nineteenth century, most of Missouri and Arkansas was added to the Upper South. In the Atlantic seaboard states, however, the yeomen retreated as the planters of the Lower South pushed inland from their Tidewater base to annex the interior coastal plain and Piedmont of Virginia and to challenge the upper-southern stronghold in North Carolina.

The Lower Midwest was, in many re-

spects, the twin of the Upper South as it was born of the same parent, Pennsylvania. Here, too, agriculture was dominated by the small family farm. However, there was greater attention to livestock fattening, which developed into the present-day Corn Belt, and wheat was more important as a frontier cash crop than was the case in the Upper South. Also, the Lower Midwest acquired many settlers directly from Europe, especially after 1840, which was not true of the area south of the Ohio River.

ORIGINS OF THE ANGLO-TEXANS, TO 1836

The Anglo host culture of Texas is derived almost entirely from two of the three eastern subcultures—the Middle Atlantic, especially the Upper South, and the Lower South. To a very great extent, the peopling of Texas by old-stock Anglos became a spatial contest between upper and lower southerners.

During the initial period of Anglo settlement, from about 1815 to the winning of Texas independence in 1836, the Middle Atlantic subculture, represented mainly by backwoodsmen from the transmontane Upper South, prevailed. Anglo-American settlement in Texas was first accomplished in the far northeastern corner of the province during the period of Spanish rule (Figure 4.2). About 1815, under the impression they were in the territory of Arkansas, small numbers of pioneers began occupying the valley of the Red River, on both the Texas and Oklahoma sides. From the very first, the large majority of the pioneers in the Red River valley were upper southerners, with Tennessee, Kentucky, Arkansas, and North Carolina the leading states of birth and removal. The result was a Middle Atlantic foothold on the northeastern rim of Texas as early as 1820.

Anglo-American colonization in Texas began in earnest in the ensuing decade, when the newly independent Mexican government instituted a policy designed to attract settlers to the province. Contracts

72

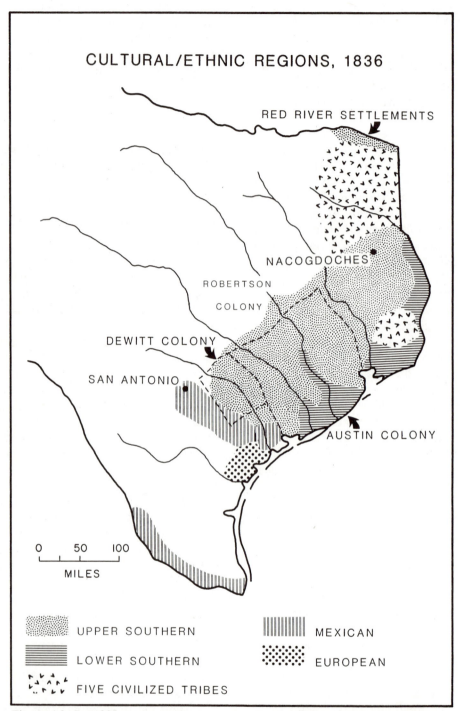

CULTURAL/ETHNIC REGIONS, 1836

RED RIVER SETTLEMENTS

NACOGDOCHES

ROBERTSON
COLONY

DEWITT COLONY

SAN ANTONIO

AUSTIN COLONY

0   50   100
MILES

UPPER SOUTHERN

LOWER SOUTHERN

FIVE CIVILIZED TRIBES

MEXICAN

EUROPEAN

Figure 4.2. By 1836 upper southerners were the dominant Anglo group in Texas, and lower southerners were confined to a border periphery in the southeast. Irish Catholics occupied the Coastal Bend country, and South Texas remained Hispanic.

were made under which vast tracts of land were turned over to certain selected individuals called *empresarios,* who were responsible for introducing specified numbers of settlers onto their grants. The first such contract was made in 1820 with the Austin family, Americans who had acquired Spanish citizenship during an earlier residence in Missouri. The Austin Colony lay in South Central Texas and included the valleys of the lower Brazos and Colorado rivers, an area generally acknowledged by contemporary observers to include the best lands of the province. The colony thrived, boasting a population of nearly 10,000 by 1836. Other *empresarios* also enjoyed some measure of success in attracting Anglo-Americans to South Central Texas, particularly in the DeWitt and Robertson colonies, which bordered the Austin Colony on the west and north.

In each of these three colonies, upper southerners prevailed numerically. Missouri, Kentucky, Tennessee, and Arkansas provided the largest number of settlers, and the principal town of the Robertson Colony was named Nashville in honor of the Tennessee capital. Few slaveowning planters were among the settlers, perhaps because of the antislavery policy of the Mexican government. In the Austin Colony, a small number of planters clustered in the river valleys near the coast, but the interior of the colony was almost exclusively upper southern (Figure 4.2).

Outside the zone of major *empresario* activity, in the eastern border area of Texas, Anglo settlement also occurred during the period of Mexican rule. In the southeastern corner of Texas, a region known as the Atascosita District, Anglos began drifting across the border about 1819 and settling without title to the land. The Atascositans differed from the Red River settlers and the *empresario* colonists in that they were lower southerners or, more exactly, poor whites from the pine barrens of Louisiana, Mississippi, and Alabama.

North of the Atascosita stretched the unpopulated expanse of the Big Thicket, a tangle of dense forest and undergrowth, dotted with swampland, which few white men had seen by the 1820s. But north of the Big Thicket, in the wooded, undulating terrain between the Trinity and Sabine rivers, some small settlements lay strewn in the expanse of forest, and a gradual but sizable influx of Anglo-Americans characterized the Mexican period. By 1835, a population of about 4,200 had accumulated, scattered in colonies such as Bevil, Tenaha, San Augustine, and Nacogdoches. The majority of these East Texans were upper southerners, but many were slaveowning planters from the coastal states who had been attracted by the fertile Redlands area.

Under Mexican rule, then, Texas appeared destined to become, in large part, an appendage of the Upper South and part of the Middle Atlantic subculture. When the war for Texan independence came in 1836, it was largely a contest between a poorly led peasant-soldiery of Mexico and sharpshooting backwoodsmen of the transmontane Upper South led by Tennesseans such as Sam Houston and Davy Crockett. Of the men who fought at the Battle of San Jacinto, almost a quarter had been born in Tennessee, and almost one in ten was a native of Kentucky. Anglo-Texas was little more than Tennessee extended. Lower southerners had gained only small footholds in the coastal fringe of the Austin Colony, the Atascosita District, and the Redlands. Overall, more than 60 percent of all Anglo-Texans in 1836 were natives of states in the Middle Atlantic subculture, about a quarter were lower southerners, and only a tenth were New Englanders.

ANGLO-AMERICAN
IMMIGRATION, 1836–1860

In the period following Texan independence, the immigration of Anglos increased and, to a notable degree, drew more heavily from the Lower South. Legalization of slavery by the Republic produced the first large-scale influx of lower southerners, mainly from the Gulf Coastal Plain states of Ala-

Table 4.1.   Origins of the Immigrant[a]
Free Population in Texas, 1850

Place of Birth	Number	Percentage of Immigrant Free Population
Middle Atlantic subculture	48,900	47
Tennessee	17,692	17
Kentucky	5,478	5
North Carolina	5,155	5
Missouri	5,139	5
Arkansas	4,693	4
Other states	10,743	11
Lower-southern subculture	35,600	34
Alabama	12,040	12
Georgia	7,639	7
Mississippi	6,545	6
South Carolina	4,482	4
Louisiana	4,472	4
Other states	422	1
New England subculture	3,100	3
Europe	12,200	12
Mexico	4,459	4
		100

[a]Excludes all Texas-born
Source: U.S. Census.

bama, Georgia, Mississippi, and Louisiana. By the time of the first federal census in 1850, it was obvious that planters were challenging the upper-southern domination of Texas (Table 4.1 and Figure 4.3). To be sure, natives of Tennessee still constituted the largest single group, but Alabamians ranked a not-too-distant second, and natives of Georgia and Mississippi ranked third and fourth. By the eve of the Civil War in 1860, lower southerners had become just about as numerous as natives of the Upper South. Still more significant was the fact that the upper southerners were lo-calized in one part of Texas and the lower southerners in another.

In brief, the planters from the Lower South, who in 1836 were still confined mainly to a southeastern fringe area, had, with the help of large numbers of new immigrants, expanded from their coastal foothold and taken over large areas of the former upper-southern domain by mid-century. Most of eastern and southeastern Texas was annexed to the planters' "cotton kingdom," and the continuing influx of upper-southern yeomen was directed to the interior. The areal expansion of lower southerners is well revealed by comparing the maps for 1836 and 1850 (Figures 4.2 and 4.3). Meanwhile, large numbers of upper southerners continued to pour into Texas, strengthening the Middle Atlantic domination of the interior portions of the state. The Blackland Prairie and Cross Timbers became solidly upper southern, and a new Appalachia took shape in the Hill Country west of the prairie.

The majority of the Anglo population of mid-nineteenth-century Texas, then, had come in roughly equal proportions from the Upper and Lower South, and Tennessee and Alabama had been the leading contributors. By the outbreak of the Civil War, these two subcultural groups were fairly well localized in distinct parts of the state, separated by a line running roughly from the vicinity of modern Texarkana in the northeastern corner of Texas to San Antonio.

Small numbers of New Englanders and other Yankees also lived in antebellum Texas. Natives of New York were more numerous than those of any other state in seven counties in 1850. However, all those counties had only small Anglo-American populations and were dominated by Europeans or Mexicans. Typically, the Yankees were merchants in the port towns or professional soldiers at posts on the Indian frontier (Figure 4.4). A much greater proportion of them lived in urban areas than was the case with upper southerners, mid-

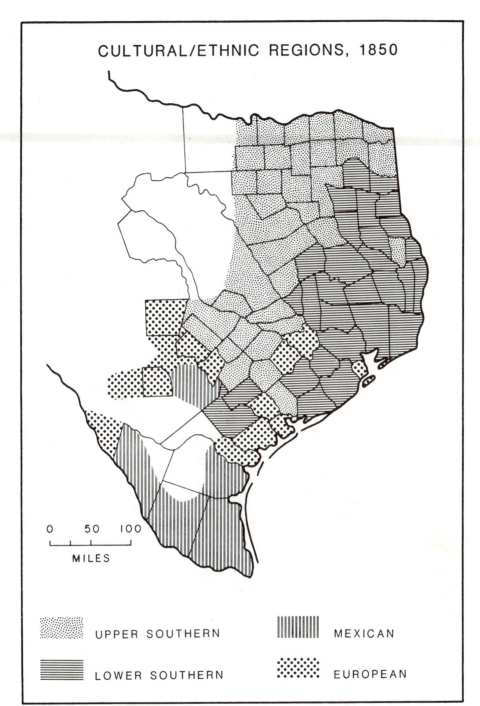

Figure 4.3. Lower-southern immigrants in the decade and a half prior to the mid–nineteenth century expanded their domain to include most of East Texas, and upper southerners occupied interior portions of the state. Large-scale German immigration gave a European flavor to much of South Central Texas. (Source: U.S. Census manuscript schedules.)

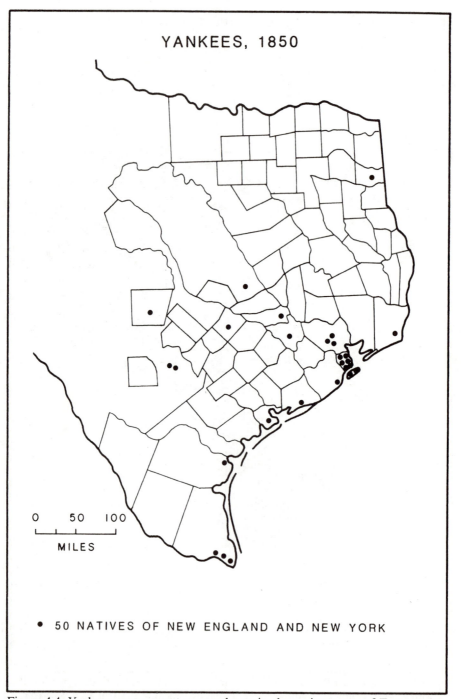

Figure 4.4. Yankees were present as merchants in the major towns of Texas and as military personnel at the frontier forts. (Source: U.S. Census manuscript schedules.)

westerners, or lower southerners. Although the Yankees formed only 3 percent of the immigrant Anglo-American population in 1850, they gained influence out of porportion to their numbers by focusing their efforts in the important mercantile sector of the economy.

POSTBELLUM ANGLO IMMIGRATION

Anglo-American pioneering continued through the remainder of the nineteenth century and well into the twentieth. The Upper and Lower South continued to be, in roughly equal proportion, the dominant source areas, and the Texarkana–San Antonio line between their respective domains did not change noticeably (Figure 4.5). The leading states of prior residence for whites entering Texas between 1860 and 1880 were, in order of importance, Arkansas, Alabama, Mississippi, Tennessee, Missouri, Louisiana, and Georgia. Collectively, the lower-southern states provided 37 percent of the white immigrants; the Middle Atlantic subculture, including the Upper South, 48 percent; and the New England subculture, 2.5 percent.

The Anglo settlement frontier was pushed far to the west, reaching the New Mexico border in successive waves of ranchers and farmers. This expansion was primarily the work of Middle Atlantic settlers, and the greater part of West Texas was joined to their subculture. A partition of sorts occurred, and Middle Atlantic settlers from the Lower Midwest—particularly Illinois, Iowa, and Kansas—became dominant in the northern half of the Texas Panhandle while Middle Atlantic people of upper-southern ancestry occupied most of the remainder of West Texas. Most of these upper southerners came from the central portion of Texas rather than from states farther east (Figure 4.6). The partition between Lower Midwest and Upper South in western Texas is still evident in many facets of that area's culture, economy, and politics.

AFRO-TEXANS

Blacks were present in Texas from Spanish times and the earliest period of American colonization, working as pioneers alongside the white settlers. However, Mexico's opposition to slavery kept the black population very small before the Texas Revolution. In the mid-1830s, only 10 percent of the people in the Austin and DeWitt colonies and 13 percent of the residents in East Texas were black. In Texas as a whole at the time of independence in 1836, perhaps 12 percent of the people were slaves, a proportion very much in keeping with the dominantly upper-southern character of Texas at that time.

A dramatic increase in the black population occurred with the influx of slaveholders from the Lower South after the war of independence. By 1840 the proportion of blacks in the population had risen to one-fifth, and by the time of the Civil War to almost one-third. In thirteen counties of East and Southeast Texas, blacks formed a majority by 1860, even exceeding 80 percent in plantation-dominated Wharton County (Figure 4.7). Their distribution closely paralleled that of the white lower southerners and was clustered east of the Texarkana–San Antonio line.

The black immigrants to Texas had been born primarily in Alabama (18 percent), Virginia (13 percent), Georgia (12 percent), and Mississippi (11 percent). Virginia ranked much higher as a source of blacks than of whites, primarily because of the lively trade in excess slaves from the old tobacco districts of the Chesapeake Tidewater through the New Orleans market. Some Texas blacks arrived directly from Africa in an illegal trade that persisted until the time of Civil War. The census of 1870 revealed 318 blacks of African birth in Texas, a total exceeded only in Louisiana.

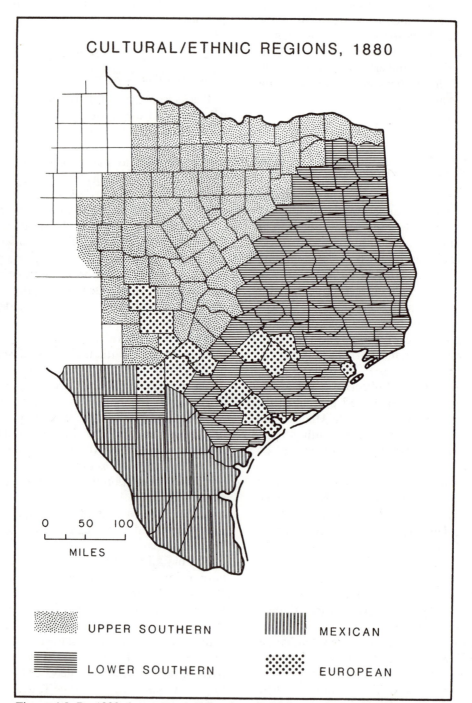

CULTURAL/ETHNIC REGIONS, 1880

0   50   100
MILES

UPPER SOUTHERN MEXICAN

LOWER SOUTHERN EUROPEAN

Figure 4.5. By 1880 the upper-southern domain had expanded to the west, but the old cultural divide between Middle Atlantic and Lower South remained much as it had been in 1850. (Source: U.S. Census and Homer L. Kerr, "Migration into Texas, 1860–1880," *Southern Historical Quarterly* 70 [1966], 184–216.)

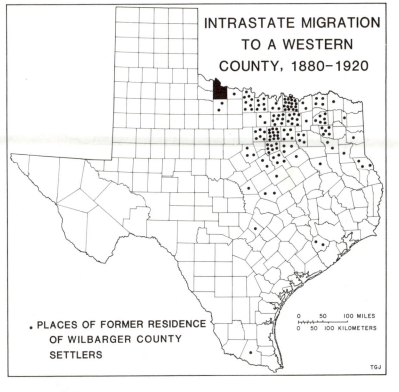

INTRASTATE MIGRATION
TO A WESTERN
COUNTY, 1880-1920

Figure 4.6. Representative of the upper-southern settlement of western Texas is Wilbarger County, which drew most of its population from the older Middle Atlantic stronghold in the Blackland Prairie and Cross Timbers. (Source: Biographical sketches in Charles P. Ross and T. L. Rouse, *Official Early-Day History of Wilbarger County* [Vernon, Tex.: *Daily Record,* 1973].)

• PLACES OF FORMER RESIDENCE
   OF WILBARGER COUNTY
   SETTLERS

0   50   100 MILES
0   50   100 KILOMETERS

TGJ

The abolition of slavery caused a sharp decline in black immigration, and after 1865 the proportion of Afro-Americans in the Texas population began decreasing steadily. Only 6 percent of the immigrants arriving in the period 1865–1880 was black, a proportion that apparently never again rose. Indicative of the virtual halt in black immigration is the fact that by 1880, 71 percent of the Afro-American population was of Texas birth as opposed to less than half of the whites. As a consequence, blacks have formed an ever-smaller part of the state's total population, their percentage sinking by 1960 to the level of 1836 (Table 4.2). During the same period, however, the black population grew through natural increase to total well over 1 million, a growth achieved in spite of large-scale emigration to northern and Pacific states.

In general, the blacks today still live in the same areas where their slave ancestors were introduced. Counties with the highest percentages of blacks lie east of the Texarkana–San Antonio line in the lower-southern cultural region of East Texas (Figures 4.8, 4.9, and 4.10). Even so, the percentages of blacks in those counties have dropped dramatically during the last century, particularly since 1930, mainly as a result of the decline and fall of the share-cropper system. Tens of thousands of blacks have been displaced from the rural areas for that reason, and they have sought refuge in the cities. Migration to urban areas in Texas has, as a rule, led blacks to Houston and Dallas, the two major cities nearest the old plantation districts.

MEXICAN-AMERICANS

The roots of the Hispanic population of Texas reach, of course, into the 150-year

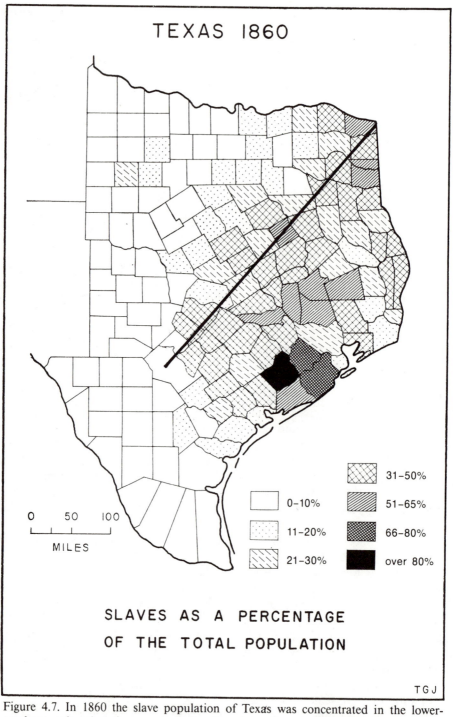

Figure 4.7. In 1860 the slave population of Texas was concentrated in the lower-southern cultural region, east of the Texarkana–San Antonio line (heavy black diagonal line). (Source: U.S. Census.)

Table 4.2.   The Black Population of Texas

Year	Black Population	Percentage of Total Population
1840	15,000	20
1860	183,000	30
1880	393,000	25
1900	621,000	20
1920	742,000	16
1940	924,000	14
1960	1,187,000	12
1980	1,710,000	12

Sources: U.S. Census; Republic of Texas tax lists.

period of Spanish and Mexican colonization, which lasted from about 1680 to 1836. Utilizing four distinct institutions of colonization—mission, *presidio* or military post, *villa* ("civilian town"), and *rancho*—

the Spaniards established several nuclei of settlement, most notably in the San Antonio River valley, the lower Rio Grande Valley, the El Paso area, and the East Texas county of Nacogdoches. The most noteworthy settlement lay in the immediate vicinity of modern San Antonio, where a cluster of five missions, the *villa* of San Fernando de Bexar (1731), a *presidio* (1718), and numerous ranches was established. Spaniards from the Canary Islands were responsible for the establishment of the *villa,* the first civilian settlement in Texas.

Overall, the Spanish colonization of Texas must be judged a failure. When Spanish colonial rule ended in 1821, no more than 5,000 Europeans, Christianized Indians, and racially mixed people lived in Texas. The failure, more than anything else, reflected the low esteem in which Texas was held by Spanish authorities. It was considered a low-quality border province, lacking the gold, silver, and highly civilized

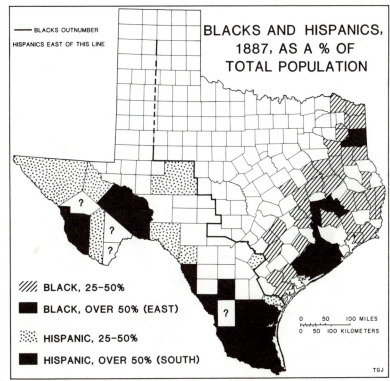

Figure 4.8. Counties for which there is no data are indicated by a question mark. (Source: Texas state census of 1887, found in L. L. Foster, ed., *First Annual Report of the Agricultural Bureau of the Department of Agriculture, Insurance, Statistics, and History, 1887–88* [Austin: State Printing Office, 1889], pp. xliv, 1–249.)

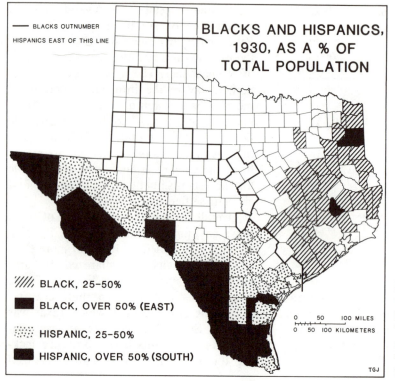

Figure 4.9. Almost no spatial overlap exists between blacks and Hispanics in Texas. Hispanics were identified as persons of "Mexican race." (Source: U.S. Census.)

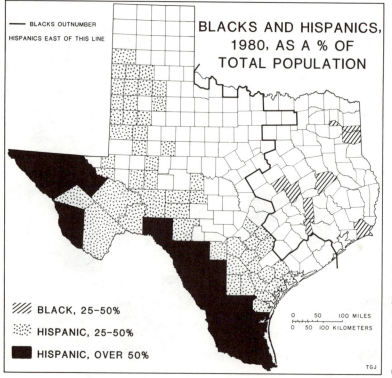

Figure 4.10. The Spanish-surnamed population has grown rapidly since 1930, making South Texas more purely Hispanic and expanding the Hispanic culture region northward. (Source: U.S. Census.)

Indians that attracted Spanish colonial attention. At best, the Spaniards regarded Texas as a buffer zone in which the territorial advances of the French and British could be met and repulsed. Too, the Spaniards were no match militarily for the Apaches and Comanches who regularly attacked the Texas outposts.

The Mexican government fared little better than its Spanish predecessor in attracting Hispanic settlers to Texas between 1821 and 1836. The *empresario* Martín de León was only modestly successful in bringing settlers from Mexico to his Texas colony, which was centered on the town of Victoria on the lower Guadalupe River. Indeed, Anglo-American immigration had reduced the Mexicans to a small minority of the Texas population by the 1830s (Figure 4.2).

By 1850 the Spanish-surnamed population of Texas stood at only about 14,000, roughly 6 or 7 percent of the state's total. Hispanic immigration remained proportionately low in the last half of the nineteenth century, causing the Spanish-surnamed population to fall to only about 4 percent of the Texas total by 1887 (Table 4.3). Locationally very stable, the Hispanic population continued to dominate numerically the Rio Grande counties, but the Hispanic majority in the San Antonio River valley was soon lost, and the old outposts at Nacogdoches and Victoria became tiny ethnic islands in an Anglo sea (Figures 4.3 and 4.5).

The rise of irrigated truck farming in South Texas, beginning about 1910, coupled with the industrialization of the state, produced the first large-scale immigration of Mexicans into Texas. The great majority of the Spanish-surnamed population of Texas is the result of the immigration since 1910, and particularly since World War II. About the middle of the twentieth century, Spanish-surnamed people surpassed Afro-Americans to become the largest minority in Texas. Without question, the most significant ethnic development of the twentieth century in Texas has been the growth and territorial expansion of the Mexican-American population (Figures 4.8, 4.9, and 4.10). If the trend continues, a Hispanic majority in much of Texas is quite possible within forty to fifty years. The cultural, economic, and political effects of this ethnic shift are indeed profound. Perhaps now, more than at any other time in the last century and a half, Anglo-Texans are aware of the borderland status of their state.

THE GERMAN ELEMENT

Collectively, the old-stock Anglo-American, black, and Mexican elements constitute just over 90 percent of the Texas population. Most of the remaining 10 percent consists of persons of European birth or recent European ancestry (Table 4.4).

Table 4.3. The Hispanic Population of Texas

Year	Hispanic Population	Percentage of Total Population
1850	14,000[a]	6.5
1887	83,400[b]	4.1
1930	684,000[c]	12
1949	1,122,000[d]	14
1950	1,028,000[e]	13
1960	1,423,000[e]	15
1970	1,664,000[e]	15
1970	2,060,000[f]	18.4
1980	2,986,000[g]	21

Sources:
[a] Spanish-surnamed population, based on a hand count of U.S. Census manuscripts. The count includes an estimate for the El Paso area, which was not enumerated.
[b] Texas state census of 1887, with adjustments made for counties not enumerated. See Terry G. Jordan, "The 1887 Census of Texas' Hispanic Population," *Aztlán* 12:2 (1981).
[c] U.S. Census, "Mexican race."
[d] "Latin-Americans," based on a socioeconomic survey of scholastics funded by the Rockefeller Foundation.
[e] U.S. Census, "Spanish surname."
[f] U.S. Census, "Persons of Spanish language or surname."
[g] U.S. Census, "Persons of Spanish origin."

Table 4.4. National Origins of Texans, 1980

National Origin	Number of People Wholly or Partially of This National Origin	As a Percentage of Respondents	Number of People Wholly of This National Origin
English	3,083,323	27%	1,639,322
Irish	2,420,367	21%	572,732
Scottish	656,892	6%	55,711
Welsh	60,420	<1%	
German	2,168,947	19%	754,388
Dutch	297,351	3%	45,838
Swedish	121,275	1%	34,687
Norwegian	65,335	<1%	20,875
Danish	35,017	<1%	
Czech	178,932	2%	
Polish	167,465	1%	70,688
French	689,298	6%	152,072
Italian	189,799	2%	78,592
Hispanic	2,763,607	24%	
Subsaharan African	1,361,020	12%	
Asian	121,100	1%	
American Indian	631,277	6%	
TOTAL	11,400,000		

Source: U.S. Census, 1980, Population and Housing Summary Tape File 3A.

The immigration that produced this minority occurred largely between 1830 and 1914 and involved mainly Germans, Slavs, and Scandinavians (Figure 4.11).

By far the largest European element in Texas is German. Perhaps 6 percent of the state's total population is wholly of German birth or ancestry, a proportion that has remained relatively constant since the middle of the nineteenth century. Over 2 million Texans claim at least partial German ancestry, but this figure includes descendants of colonial German settlers that form part of the old-stock Anglo population. The initial German immigration, between 1830 and 1840, was unorganized and resulted in a modest accumulation of settlers in the area between the lower Brazos and Colorado rivers in Fayette, Austin, and Colorado counties. Major German colonization efforts occurred in the 1840s as a result of several organized projects. The Adelsverein,

a society of German noblemen who were interested in overseas peasant colonization, introduced more than 7,000 Germans, mainly Saxons and Hessians, into Texas between 1844 and 1847, and a similar effort led to the immigration of about 2,000 Alsatians. Both of these projects placed German-speaking settlers on the frontier, west and north of San Antonio, in settlements such as New Braunfels, Castroville, and Fredericksburg. Through the remainder of the nineteenth century, large-scale German immigration continued, interrupted only by the Civil War blockade.

The result was a fragmented "German belt" across South Central Texas, from Houston and Galveston on the east into the Hill Country beyond San Antonio and Austin on the west (Figure 4.12). By 1900 almost 200,000 ethnic Germans lived in Texas, forming over 6 percent of the total population. Counties such as Comal, Ken-

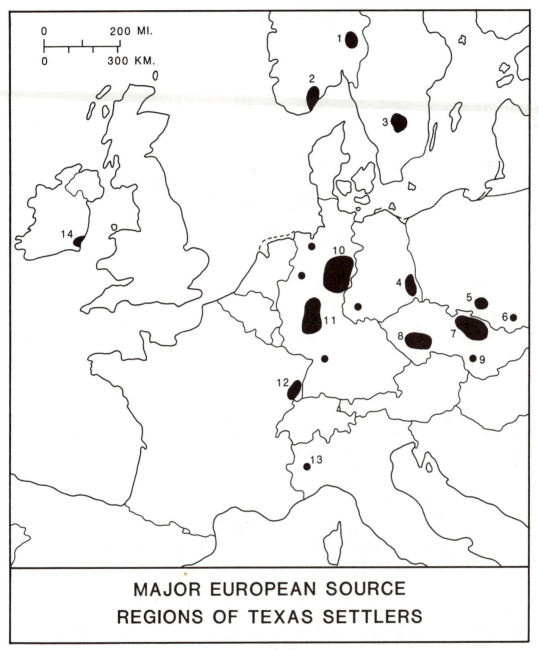

MAJOR EUROPEAN SOURCE
REGIONS OF TEXAS SETTLERS

Figure 4.11. Europeans migrated to Texas from distinct clusters.
Key: 1 = Hedmark; 2 = Aust Agder; 3 = Jönköping (Småland); 4 = Lausitz; 5 = Opole district of Silesia; 6 = Galicia; 7 = northern Moravia; 8 = southern Bohemia; 9 = Myjava district of Slovakia; 10 = Lower Saxony; 11 = Hesse; 12 = Alsace; 13 = Spraco Sano, source of Montague County Italians; 14 = County Wexford.

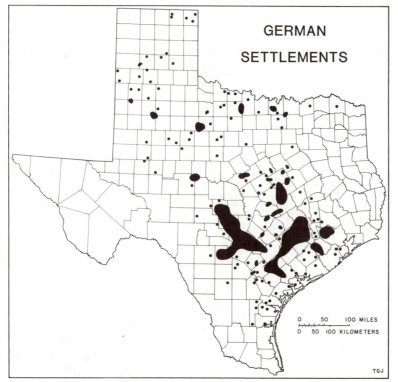

GERMAN
SETTLEMENTS

0   50   100 MILES
0   50   100 KILOMETERS

TGJ

Figure 4.12. Most Germans live in South Central Texas, but ethnic islands are scattered across much of the remainder of the state.

dall, Gillespie, Medina, Austin, and Washington became dominantly German and have retained much of that flavor to the present (Figure 4.13). Germans formed one-quarter to one-third of the populations of Galveston, San Antonio, and Houston by the late nineteenth century, occupying distinctive ethnic neighborhoods. Beyond the major German concentration in South Central Texas lie scores of ethnic islands scattered across much of the remainder of the state (Figure 4.12). These outlying settlements were generally created by second- or third-generation offspring moving out of the German belt or by immigrants from the Midwest.

SLAVIC IMMIGRATION

Texas was also the goal of a substantial and an enduring Slavic immigration, involving mainly Czechs, Poles, Wends, and Slovaks. The state has the largest rural Czech population in the union, mainly in the Coastal and Blackland prairies of Central Texas (Figure 4.14). Even though these people habitually refer to themselves as "Bohemians," four-fifths of their ancestors came from the northern part of Moravia, and most of the rest emigrated from southern Bohemia (Figure 4.11). The first sizable group of Czechs arrived in 1851, and Fayette County was the early focus for their settlement. From there they expanded, with continuing immigration, to dominate some of the best farmland in Texas, and their reputation as excellent agriculturists is widespread. Often they settled among the Germans, sometimes sharing a parish church with them. In numerous Czech brotherhoods and lodge halls, their distinctive Slavic culture is still evident today, in part because their immigration persisted until 1914 which means that some of the Czech-born immigrants are still living.

The oldest Polish colony in the United States, Panna Maria, was founded on Texas soil in 1854. It is the focus of a thriving

OTTO STACKBEIN 4 Mi.
HAROLD STRACKBEIN 5 Mi.
KERMIT CRENWELGE 6 Mi.
ALVIN CRENWELGE 6 Mi.
HARRY WAHRMUND 2½ Mi.
KARL FRIEDRICH 2 Mi.
BERNARD CRENWELGE 4 Mi.
TED MUND 3½ Mi.
EDWIN BRAEUTIGAM 6½ Mi.
CLARENCE STRACKBEIN 6 Mi.
KENNETH MANER 4 Mi.
OTTO SPAETH 2 Mi.
KIRCHNER BROS. 2½ Mi.
SAUER RANCH 4 Mi.
JAMES BAETHGE 5 Mi.
RAYMOND KUHLMANN 9 Mi.
HENRY BAETHGE 5½ Mi.
E. HAHN RANCH 5 Mi.
E. W. BODE 7 Mi.
EUGENE CRENWELGE 6½ Mi.
PETER CRENWELGE 11 Mi.
ALVIN HEIMER 3 Mi.
ANTONIO RODRIGUES 2 Mi.
JOHNNY BECKER 4 Mi.

PRESLEY ARHELGER 12 Mi.
Mrs MARTIN ANDEREGG 1 Mi.
CORWIN ANDEREGG 11½ Mi.
EMIL ANDEREGG 11 Mi.
ERWIN ANDEREGG 9½ Mi.
DAN ANDEREGG 11½ Mi.

WILLIE EVERS 7½ Mi.
KEN PEACOCK 8 Mi.
AMELIO GARZA 6 Mi.
ROY BIERSCHWALE 12 Mi.
GILBERT KADERLI 4 Mi.
REUBIN GEISTWEIDT 6 Mi.
WALTER GEISTWEIDT 6½ Mi.
ARCHIE GEISTWEIDT 5 Mi.
JIM FAUGHT 5 Mi.
HENRY BIERSCHWALE 9 Mi.
JAME HENKE 7 Mi.
DURDEN & WILTROUT 10 Mi.
HARRY BRUSENHAN 2 Mi.
RICHARD KASPER 2 Mi.
JACK EVERS 11 Mi.
HEINZE & MOEHR 7½ Mi.
EDGAR WENDEL 3 Mi.
WALTER SATTLER 4 Mi.
ARNOLD RODE 6 Mi.
ROBERT KORDZIK 7½ Mi.
DENNIS LANGE 3 Mi.
WALTER ITZ 7 Mi.
ROY ITZ 7½ Mi.
BENNO ITZ 7½ Mi.
EDGAR GEISTWEIDT 8 Mi.
NELSON GEISTWEIDT 8 Mi.
WALTER ECKERT 13 Mi.
ERWIN ECKERT 13 Mi.
BEN EVERS 6 Mi.

Figure 4.13. This direction marker, near Fredericksburg in the Texas Hill Country, suggests the dominantly German character of the local population. (Photo: Terry G. Jordan, 1975.)

concentration of Silesian Poles whose ancestors came to Texas from the Opole region, under the leadership of a Catholic priest, to settle in the San Antonio River valley (Figures 4.11 and 4.14). Later, after the Civil War, several settlements of Galician Poles were founded in some of the old plantation districts of East Texas.

In the same year that Panna Maria was founded, hundreds of Wends, or Sorbs, departed their Slavic homeland in the Lausitz region of Germany for Texas (Figure 4.11). Led by a pastor who feared that their ethnic identity and Lutheranism were endangered in Prussia and Saxony, these immigrants established the only Wendish col-

onies in the Western Hemisphere, in the sandy post-oak area of Lee County, Texas (Figure 4.14). From their mother colony of Serbin, or "place where the Wends live," they later spread out to establish a number of smaller ethnic settlements. The irony of Wendish colonization in Texas is that in great measure, they were absorbed by the German population, much as they would have been had they remained in Germany.

Slovaks founded only one agricultural colony in Texas, the settlement of Pakan in Wheeler County in the Panhandle region. Beginning in 1903, a small Lutheran group from the Myjava area of Slovakia purchased lands there from the Rock Island Railroad

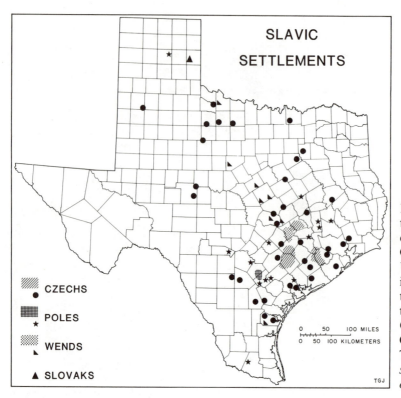

Figure 4.14. Texas contains the oldest Polish colonies and the largest rural Czech population in the United States. Shadings indicate major concentrations; symbols, minor settlements. (Source: Terry G. Jordan, "Population Origin Groups in Rural Texas," *Annals of the Association of American Geographers* 60 [1970], map.)

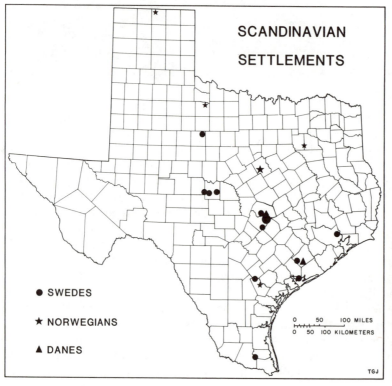

Figure 4.15. Each Scandinavian group has one principal cluster of settlement, indicated by the larger symbols. (Source: Terry G. Jordan, "Population Origin Groups in Rural Texas," *Annals of the Association of American Geographers* 60 [1970], map.)

(Figures 4.11 and 4.14). Some 2,100 Texans listed Slovakian as their mother tongue in 1970.

SCANDINAVIANS

Texas contains the southernmost Scandinavian settlements in the United States. Although not large, these colonies present the unusual situation of Danes, Swedes, and Norwegians living in a subtropical setting.

The first Scandinavians to settle in Texas were the Norwegians. By the middle 1850s, they had established their only major enclave, in the fertile valleys and cedar-covered hills of Bosque County, west of Waco (Figure 4.15). The earliest immigrants came from mountain hamlets in the Aust-Agder province of southern Norway, and they were followed by a large contingent from the eastern shore of Lake Mjøsa in Hedmark, north of Oslo (Figure 4.11).

Swedish immigration, mainly from the province of Jönköping, occurred after the Civil War and was directed to the capital city of Austin and the adjacent Blackland Prairie (Figures 4.11 and 4.15). The catalyst of the migration was a Jönköping Swede, S. M. Swenson, who had come to Texas in the days of the Republic and had become wealthy. He and his family helped bring poor farmers from his home province to Texas under a system of indentured labor, and by 1910, some 10,000 persons of Swedish birth or parentage lived in Texas. Seventy-three percent had come from Jönköping, and 13 percent of those had come from Swenson's home parish of Barkeryd.

The southernmost Danish agricultural colony in the world was established on the table-flat Coastal Prairie at Danevang, "level place where the Danes live," in 1894. This Wharton County settlement is noteworthy for the prosperity and success of its farmers, based on a long tradition of mutual aid.

OTHER EUROPEAN GROUPS

The first European immigrants to establish agricultural colonies in nineteenth-century Texas were Irish Catholics. In the late 1820s and early 1830s, the *empresario* settlements of San Patricio, bearing the name of the Irish patron saint, and Refugio were founded, part of an attempt by Mexico to place a barrier of Roman Catholics in the path of Anglo-American westward expansion. County Wexford in southeastern Ireland was the principal source region of the colonists for these settlements (Figure 4.11). As late as 1850, San Patricio and Refugio counties remained dominantly Irish, but acculturation and intermarriage subsequently destroyed most of the group's identity.

Other European colonies of note include La Reunion, founded by French utopian socialists near Dallas in 1855; Nederland, a Dutch settlement in the coastal marshes of Southeast Texas; and a scattering of small Italian farming colonies in the Brazos Valley and elsewhere, including a cluster of Piedmontese in Montague County (Figure 4.11). The La Reunion French, who included many craftsmen and university-educated people, may have played a formative role in the initial development of Dallas into the cosmopolitan city that it has become.

European Jews also emigrated to Texas, settling primarily in the towns and cities. In antebellum times, the Jews were principally Sephardic and very few in number. They were followed in the 1865–1890 period by numbers of Ashkenazic Germans and still later, between 1890 and 1920, by Ashkenazic Poles and Russians. Over 2,000 Jews immigrated through the port of Galveston alone during the 1907–1914 period. Today, their descendants are concentrated in Houston and Dallas.

LOUISIANA FRENCH

In spite of its proximity to Louisiana, Texas did not acquire a large French-speaking population. The Louisiana French failed to participate massively in the westward expansion and, as a result, did not enter Texas in sizable numbers during the nineteenth century. In this respect they displayed a locational stability similar to that of the Mexican-Americans, and the example of the Louisiana French calls to mind the French Canadians, who took little part in the early settlement of Ontario and the prairie provinces. A French-surname count in Texas revealed a population of only 1,071 in 1850, confined largely to far Southeast Texas, where some settlers of Louisiana-French origin, mainly Cajuns, were engaged in cattle herding on the coastal prairies. A small contingent of Louisiana Creoles settled in the town of Liberty about that time.

Only after the discovery of oil at Spindletop, near Beaumont, around the turn of the century did Cajuns begin moving into Southeast Texas in sizable numbers. Today, about 100,000 Cajuns, black and white alike, live in Texas, mainly in the Beaumont–Port Arthur–Houston area. Telephone directories of that area reveal numerous Broussard, Boudreaux, Richard, Landry, LeBlanc, and Hebert listings, all typical Cajun names. Nowhere, though, do the Cajuns approach majority status in the population.

INDIAN IMMIGRATION

One generally does not think of Indians as having immigrated to Texas, yet the early nineteenth century witnessed a major influx of remnant tribes from the east. The rapid advance of the Anglo-American frontier in the eastern states from about 1775 to the 1820s displaced most of the Indians east of the Mississippi River, and some of the shattered remains of these tribes were shunted west into Texas. Earlier, in the 1680s, unrest in the Spanish colonies of the upper Rio Grande Valley in New Mexico had caused some Pueblo Indians, including the Tigua, to resettle in the El Paso area. In recent years, other out-of-state Indians have migrated to the urban centers of Texas, especially Dallas. Since the native Indians of Texas, such as the Caddo in the east and the Jumano of the far west, were almost entirely exterminated or removed, the present Indian population of the state is the result of these various immigrations.

The migration from the eastern states began before 1800, when some members of the Alabama tribe from the state of that name moved west of the Sabine and took up residence on the Neches River. They were soon followed, in 1807, by their linguistic kin, the Coushatta, with whom they were already thoroughly mixed through intermarriage. By 1809 a Choctaw village had been established in present Red River County, and later a large number of Choctaws settled along the Sabine and Neches rivers. A major immigration of eastern tribes started about 1819 or 1820, composed mainly of Cherokee and associated bands of Shawnee, Delaware, Kickapoo, and Quapaw. The main center for Indian migration was northeastern Texas. The Cherokee, for example, were centered in the area of present Smith, Rusk, Van Zandt, and Cherokee counties, the Shawnee settled on the upper reaches of the Sabine River, and the Kickapoo were located north of Nacogdoches.

The Indian migration continued through the 1820s and into the 1830s, bringing Chickasaw, Seminole, Biloxi, and others to Texas. The immigrant tribes were for the most part peaceful, and their settlements were often quite close to those of Anglo-Americans. For example, the 1835 census of present Shelby County listed 687 whites, 29 black slaves, 164 Choctaws, and 53 Huonna Indians. Indeed, most of the Indian immigrants belonged to the so-called civilized tribes, agricultural Indians from southeastern United States who had taken on many traits of the white culture. They were at least the cultural equals of the pioneer Anglo-Americans in their vicinity, but in the end, they were treated simply as Indians, and nearly all were driven north of the Red River into Oklahoma, a displacement that began in 1839 and took but a few years to complete. The only tribes able to remain permanently in Texas were the Tigua and Alabama-Coushatta, which presently have reservations in the state.

Dallas contains the largest Indian population in Texas, numbering about 10,000

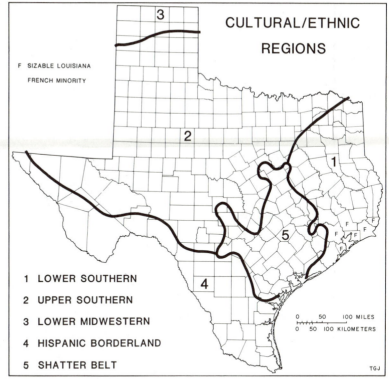

Figure 4.16. The regions represent present-day patterns.

CULTURAL/ETHNIC REGIONS

F SIZABLE LOUISIANA FRENCH MINORITY

1 LOWER SOUTHERN
2 UPPER SOUTHERN
3 LOWER MIDWESTERN
4 HISPANIC BORDERLAND
5 SHATTER BELT

0   50   100 MILES
0   50   100 KILOMETERS

TGJ

in three residential clusters. Choctaws from Oklahoma constitute the largest tribe in Dallas, followed by the Navajo.

CULTURAL/ETHNIC REGIONS

The diverse cultural and ethnic implantations made during the past three centuries produced five clearly distinguishable population-origin regions within Texas (Figure 4.16). East Texas is the realm of lower southerners, whites and blacks alike, with ancestral roots mainly in the coastal plantation states—particularly Alabama, Georgia, Mississippi, and Louisiana. The southern fringe of this region, Southeast Texas, contains a sizable Louisiana-French minority.

In North and West Texas the population is dominantly of upper-southern origin, derived principally from Tennessee, Arkansas, Kentucky, and Missouri. The bewildering mixture of English, Scotch-Irish, Welsh, German, Dutch, and Swedish surnames reflects the ethnic diversity of the colonial Middle Atlantic region, where the earliest American ancestors of these Texans settled, but in Texas they represent a thoroughly amalgamated subculture. The northern Panhandle belongs largely to their Middle Atlantic kinsmen, the lower midwesterners. A fourth region consists of the Hispanic-majority counties of South and Southwest Texas, from Corpus Christi to El Paso. Continued massive immigration from Mexico strengthens and expands this region from one decade to the next, an effect that is heightened by a significant emigration of Anglos from the area, which first became evident in the 1960s. Finally, centered in South Central Texas, is a fifth cultural/ethnic region best labeled the "shatter belt," where a large European population of Germans, Slavs, and Scandinavians is thoroughly mixed with lower-southern whites, blacks, upper southerners, and Hispanos (Figure 4.17).

The multiple peopling of Texas has many

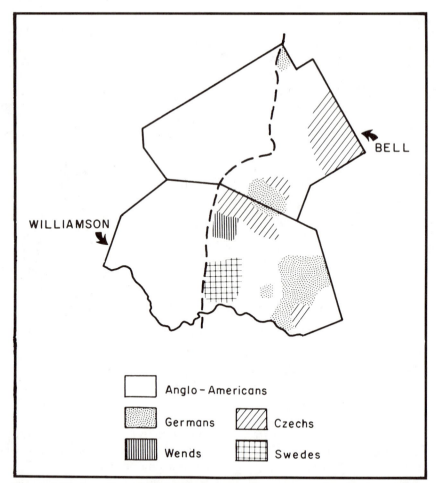

Figure 4.17. A section of the border between the upper-southern region and the shatter belt in Bell and Williamson counties. The boundary (dashed line) follows very closely a physiographic-vegetational border separating the rolling plains of the Blackland Prairie to the east from the forested Hill Country to the west. The ethnic variety of the shatter belt is well illustrated in these two counties. (Reprinted, by permission, from Terry G. Jordan, "The Texan Appalachia," *Annals of the Association of American Geographers* 60 [1970], 417.)

cultural geographical implications, for the regional imprint of the diverse groups is evident in many facets of life. In the following chapter, attention is focused on linguistic patterns.

SOURCES AND SUGGESTED READINGS

Bounds, John H. "The Alabama-Coushatta Indians of Texas." *Journal of Geography* 70 (1971), 175–182.

Glick, Thomas F. *The Old World Background of the Irrigation System of San Antonio.* El Paso: Texas Western Press, 1972.

Hannaford, Jean T. "The Cultural Impact of European Settlement in Central Texas." M.A. thesis, Department of Geography, University of Texas, Austin, 1970.

Jordan, Terry G. "The German Element in Texas: An Overview." *Rice University Studies* 63 (Summer 1977), 1–11.

————. *Immigration to Texas.* Boston: American Press, 1980.

————. "The Imprint of the Upper and Lower South on Mid-Nineteenth-Century Texas."

Annals of the Association of American Geographers 57 (1967), 667–690.

————. "Population Origin Groups in Rural Texas." Map Supplement No. 13. *Annals of the Association of American Geographers* 60 (1970), 404–405 plus folded colored map.

————. "Population Origins in Texas, 1850." *Geographical Review* 59 (1969), 83–103.

Kerr, Homer L. "Migration into Texas, 1860–1880." *Southwestern Historical Quarterly* 70 (1966), 184–216.

Lathrop, Barnes F. *Migration into East Texas, 1835–1860.* Austin: Texas State Historical Association, 1949.

Nostrand, Richard L. "The Hispanic-American Borderland: Delimitation of an American Culture Region." *Annals of the Association of American Geographers* 60 (1970), 638–661.

————. "Mexican Americans Circa 1850." *Annals of the Association of American Geographers* 65 (1975), 378–390. A colored map, serving as a companion to this article, appeared in *Historical Geography Newsletter* 5:2 (Fall 1975), following p. 30.

Spillman, Robert C. "A Historical Geography of Mexican American Population Patterns in the South Texas Hispanic Borderland: 1850–1970." M.A. thesis, Department of Geography, University of Southern Mississippi, Hattiesburg, 1977.

Starczewska, Maria. "The Historical Geography of the Oldest Polish Settlement in the United States." *Polish Review* 12 (Spring 1967), 11–40.

Wilhelm, Hubert G. H. "Organized German Settlement and Its Effects on the Frontier of South-Central Texas." Ph.D. dissertation, Department of Geography, Louisiana State University, Baton Rouge, 1968.

CHAPTER 5

LINGUISTIC GEOGRAPHY

Language is the vehicle of culture, the principal device by which beliefs, practices, and institutions are handed down from one generation to another. In spoken or written form, language provides both communication and identity for cultural groups and subgroups. In Texas, settlers of every origin introduced distinctive forms of speech, and even after a century of mixing and acculturation, many dialects and languages survive. The result is a highly varied linguistic geography, clearly reflecting the human diversity of the state.

ENGLISH DIALECTS

The three old-stock Anglo-American subcultures described in Chapter 4 are each linked to a particular English dialect, an association first documented by the linguistic geographer Hans Kurath. Using lexical evidence as the basis for his classification, Kurath and his students mapped the pattern of dialects on the eastern seaboard and gave the names Northern, Midland, and Plantation Southern to the three principal regional types. Other linguists have built on Kurath's work by studying the traditional speech forms west of the Appalachians. Many, although by no means all, of these linguistic geographers are convinced that Kurath's basic threefold classification remains valid even west of the

Mississippi River. To be sure, subdialects abound, perhaps the most important of which is an oft-cited split between Midwestern and Hill Southern within the Midland dialect (Figure 5.1).

The lexical contrasts between the three

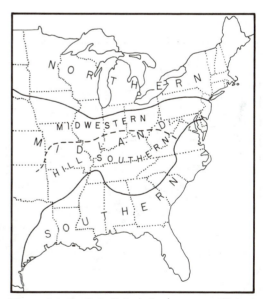

Figure 5.1. English dialects in the eastern United States. Southern is the same as Plantation Southern. (Based on Kurath, *Word Geography*; Tarpley, *From Blinky to Blue John*; and Atwood, *Regional Vocabulary*; see "Sources and Suggested Reading.")

dialects of U.S. English are abundant (Figure 5.2 and Table 5.1). Although many of the words that provide distinctiveness to the dialects are becoming archaic, others still enjoy widespread usage. Reinforcing the lexical regionalism are numerous features of pronunciation that fit the same threefold classification.

Two of the three major U.S. English dialects were introduced into Texas by immigrants from the eastern states. Chief among these was the Midland speech, represented mainly in its Hill Southern variant. Introduced by settlers from the Upper South, Hill Southern is the subdialect often mislabeled as "typically Texan." The Texas speakers of Hill Southern would be quite at home linguistically in East Tennessee or the Ozarks. In Texas, this subdialect occurs throughout a broad zone from central East Texas to the New Mexico border (Figure 5.3). Its speakers can be distinguished by their use of terms such as *chigger, pulley bone, blinkey, quarter till, snake doctor, tank* (for an artificial stock pond), *green beans, dog irons* (for andirons), and *redworm.* As a result of an intensive study of the community of Spicewood in the Texas Hill Country, Carmelita Klipple reported that the primary pronunciation features of Hill Southern speech included (1) clear enunciation of the preconsonantal *r*; (2) an extreme retroflex *r*, articulated with the tip of the tongue curled far back under the hard palate; (3) terminal *r* or initial *h* added to words not requiring them ("yeller" instead of "yellow," "hit" instead of "it"); (4) the occasional loss of initial and terminal consonants ("tol" instead of "told," "onna" instead of "going to"); (5) the occasional loss of medial sounds ("probly" instead of "probably"); (6) the formation of dipthongs ("hyere" instead of "here"); and (7) metathesis ("childern" instead of "children"). Nasality provides a distinctive "twang" to the Hill Southern dialect.

Plantation Southern, by contrast, has gained only a relatively small and tenuous territorial foothold in Texas, east of a line from Texarkana to the mouth of the Col-

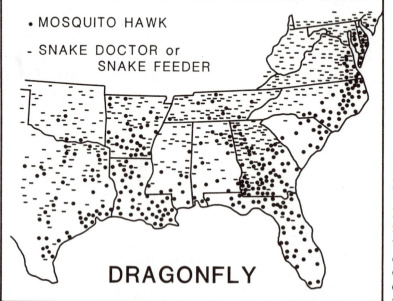

Figure 5.2. Midland and Plantation Southern dialects as revealed in the word for "dragonfly." Each symbol represents a field interview in which the Midland terms *snake doctor* and *snake feeder* or the Plantation Southern term *mosquito hawk* was used. (Based on Hans Kurath, *A Word Geography* [Ann Arbor: University of Michigan Press, 1949], and E. Bagby Atwood, *The Regional Vocabulary of Texas* [Austin: University of Texas Press, 1962].)

Table 5.1. Selected Vocabulary Items in the Three Major Dialects of American English

	Northern Dialect	Midland Dialect	Plantation Southern Dialect
dragonfly	darning needle	snake doctor	mosquito hawk
cottage cheese	pot cheese	smear cheese	clabber cheese
worm in ground	angleworm	redworm	earthworm
food eaten between meals	bite	piece	snack
beans eaten in the pod	string beans	green beans	snap beans
fifteen minutes before the hour	quarter of	quarter till	quarter to

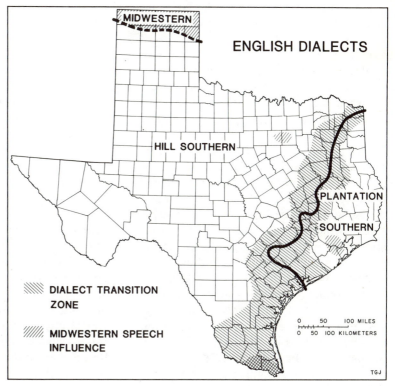

Figure 5.3. Much of the map is based on speculation, since in-depth field studies have not been carried out in most areas. (Based on Stanley A. Arbingast et al., *Atlas of Texas,* 5th ed. [Austin: University of Texas, Bureau of Business Research, 1976].)

orado River. Its lower-southern speakers use terms such as *redbug, pond* (rather than "tank,"), *skeeter hawk, snap beans, peckerwood* (instead of "woodpecker"), *wishbone,* and *snack.* In pronunciation they slur the preconsonantal *r* ("dawk" instead of "dark"); slur the terminal *r* after vowels ("nevah" instead of "never"); omit unstressed initial syllables ("gatuh," instead of "alligator"); and employ certain African tones, pitch patterns, and rhythms.

Black English, widely spoken today in rural East Texas and in cities such as Houston and Dallas by about 80 percent of the Afro-American population, is a variant form or subdialect of Plantation Southern. In addition to the pronunciation features already listed for Plantation Southern, speakers of Black English in Texas also typically omit a terminal *l* and final consonant clusters, render an initial *th* as *d* and a terminal *th* as *f,* lengthen stressed vowels, and omit many medial syllables. They also omit the terminal *s* on third-person singular verb forms ("he go") and add an *s* to many plural forms not requiring it ("feets," "they goes"). Studies in rural East Texas in the 1930s and in the city of Dallas in the 1970s suggest that Black English has survived relocation from country to urban setting without major change.

The zone of contact between Hill Southern and Plantation Southern dialects in Texas is characterized by considerable blending and mixture, so that some linguists are unwilling to draw a dialectal border. Actually, only the northern segment of the contact zone has received intensive study. Although the results were inconclusive, much of the evidence did support the notion of a dialectal border trending northeast-southwest across the region bounded by Texarkana, Marshall, Dallas, and Sherman (Figure 5.4). Other local studies suggest that in the contact zone, Plantation Southern is steadily retreating before Hill Southern, so that in the relatively near future, Plantation Southern may survive only in major urban ghettos. A study in the East Texas town of Nacogdoches, for example, revealed that among whites, the purest Plantation Southern speech was confined to elderly persons and that most of the younger speakers displayed some Hill Southern features.

Also gaining ground in present-day Texas is the Midwestern variant of Midland speech, a subtype best identified as "standard American" or "television-announcer English." Traditionally, the Midwestern subdialect was common only among Anglo-Americans in the northern Panhandle and the lower Rio Grande Valley, where large numbers of settlers from the Midwest arrived in the first two decades of this century (Figures 5.3). Texas Senator Lloyd Bentsen belongs to a Rio Grande Valley family of North Dakotan origin and well illustrates in his speech mannerisms the old-line midwestern element in the state's population. More recently, a massive influx of northerners to Dallas, Houston, and certain other cities since World War II has produced pockets of the Midwestern subdialect in the upper-middle-class and affluent neighborhoods.

SPANISH

In addition to the major English dialects spoken in Texas, numerous linguistic minorities are found (Table 5.2). Without serious challenge, the most important of these is Spanish, spoken in 1970 as a mother tongue by just under 2 million Texans, amounting to 16 percent of the total population of the state and 87 percent of the Spanish-surnamed element. Because of this sizable and growing linguistic minority, Texas will probably become a legally bilingual state in the relatively near future. For some years many highway signs in South Texas have been in both English and Spanish, and public notices in newspapers and election ballots, even as far north as Dallas, now appear in the two languages. Recent court orders also require much more state involvement in bilingual education than heretofore. Nowhere is the status of Texas as a border state more evident than

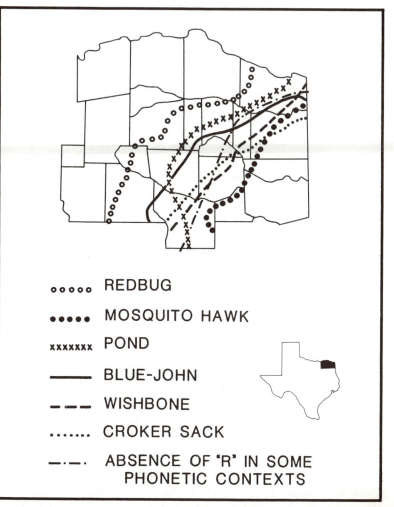

Figure 5.4.
The Hill Southern–Plantation Southern dialectal border in Northeast Texas. In each case the word or pronunciation shown is the Plantation Southern form, used east of the isogloss. This "bundle" of isoglosses provides strong support for the concept that East Texas differs linguistically from the remainder of the state. (Based on data in Fred Tarpley, *From Blinky to Blue John* [Wolfe City, Tex.: University Press, 1970].)

○○○○○ REDBUG

●●●●● MOSQUITO HAWK

xxxxxxx POND

——— BLUE-JOHN

— — — WISHBONE

······· CROKER SACK

—·—· ABSENCE OF "R" IN SOME
PHONETIC CONTEXTS

in the storm of controversy that surrounds the rise of Spanish to the position of a second legal language. The linguistic issue is the present focus and flash point of the 150-year-old cultural conflict between Anglo and Hispano.

Traditionally, the English-Spanish contacts were confined mainly to South Texas, where the population of Mexican origin and ancestry was concentrated. Daily work contacts between Anglo employers or foremen and Hispanic laborers produced a pidgin, locally known as Border Spanish or Tex-Mex. It consists of a small vocabulary, primarily but not exclusively Spanish, and can still be heard on the ranches and truck farms of South Texas. Increasingly, though, Anglo-Texans are confronted with speakers of standard Mexican Spanish. A large proportion of the Hispanic population is bilingual, but a substantial part, consisting mainly of the recently arrived immigrants, speaks only Spanish. Incredible as it seems, in light of Texas's border location and frequent contacts with Mexico, the overwhelming majority of Anglo-Texans

Table 5.2. The Most Common Mother Tongues in Texas

Language	1910[a]		1970[b]		1980[d]	
	Number of Speakers	% of Population	Number of Speakers	% of Population	Number of Speakers	% of Population
English	?	?	8,316,021	74.0	10,221,830	78.0
Spanish	234,179	6.0	1,793,462	16.0	2,484,188	19.0
German	177,430	4.5	237,572	2.0	84,369	.6
French	8,707	.2	90,902	1.0	47,612	.3
Czech	41,080	1.0	64,938	.6	?	?
Polish	13,694	.4	29,047	.3	10,597	.08
Italian	14,568	.4	25,894	.2	10,940	.08
Yiddish	4,980	.1	10,803	.1	?	?
Swedish	12,110	.3	8,797	.08	?	?
Chinese	?	?	6,499	.06	21,796	.2
Total Non-English	532,088	14.0	2,879,395	26.0	2,813,189	22.0
Unable to Speak English	193,597	8.0[c]	?	?	?	?

[a]The 1910 figures include only the foreign-born whites and the first-generation American-born whites.

[b]In 1970 "mother tongue" was defined as the language spoken in the household of the respondent when he or she was a child, with preference given to non-English languages.

[c]Whites over ten years of age.

[d]The 1980 question was "does this person speak a language other than English at home?" It was directed to all persons five years of age or older.

Sources: U.S. Census.

know no Spanish at all. It is possible, in the public schools and universities of Texas, for a student to graduate without ever having learned the Spanish language. Anglo-Texans seem to have chosen Belgium or Canada rather than Switzerland as their ethno-linguistic model, and the seeds of linguistic conflict and possible partition have thus been sown.

Even so, two major languages cannot exist side by side for over a century without exerting influence on one another. Perhaps the mot obvious result is that the Hill Southern speech of the western half of Texas has adopted numerous Spanish loanwords. Many such lexical borrowings relate to stock raising or farming and seem to have entered the Hill Southern vernacular by way of Border Spanish. Examples include remuda (a group of saddle horses), toro,

ranch, lariat, bronc, morral (feed bag), and acequia (irrigation ditch). Others describe physical environmental features or foods, such as mesa, arroyo, resaca (dry river channel), and frijoles. Most of these Spanish loanwords have not reached east of a line from Matagorda Bay to the eastern base of the Panhandle, a limit clearly marked by a "bundle" of loanword isoglosses (Figure 5.5).

FRENCH

The mother tongue of some 91,000 persons in 1970, French ranks a distant second behind Spanish among the Romance languages in Texas. The large majority of Francophones, some 65 percent of them, live as a minority group in the southeastern corner of Texas, mainly in the cities of

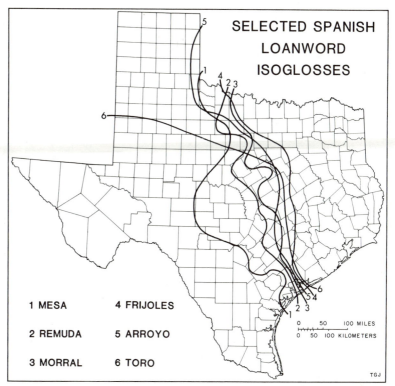

SELECTED SPANISH LOANWORD ISOGLOSSES

1 MESA 4 FRIJOLES

2 REMUDA 5 ARROYO

3 MORRAL 6 TORO

Figure 5.5. In each case, the Spanish loanword is used in the Hill Southern English dialect west or south of the isogloss. (Based on data in E. Bagby Atwood, *The Regional Vocabulary of Texas* [Austin: University of Texas Press, 1962].)

Houston, Beaumont, and Port Arthur. Both whites (79 percent) and blacks (21 percent) are included, and the large majority identify themselves as Cajuns of Louisiana ancestry or birth. Nearly all are bilingual and highly acculturated, with the result that French lacks the vitality of Spanish and seems destined to die out in the near future.

Despite their minority position in Southeast Texas, speakers of Louisiana French did succeed in implanting some loanwords into the Plantation Southern English dialect of the region. These include bayou, pirogue (small boat), cush (corn meal), banquette (sidewalk), lagniappe (baker's dozen), and others (Figure 5.6).

GERMAN

The third-ranking mother tongue in Texas, spoken by nearly a quarter of a million people in 1970, is German (Table 5.2). Implanted during the mass immigra-

tion of Germans to South Central Texas in the period 1840–1890, the language has proved remarkably durable, particularly considering the prejudice directed against Texans of German descent during the two world wars (Figure 5.7).

The characteristics and ultimate fate of the German language in Texas are representative of all foreign tongues introduced directly from Europe and can serve as an example. One feature shared by virtually all of the European immigrant languages is a tendency to preserve features that have become archaic in the Old World. The Texas Germans employ many words, such as *Knabe* ("boy"), that have long since fallen out of common usage in Germany. Too, the Texans are unaware of the reformed spelling introduced in Central Europe in the late nineteenth century, so they render words such as *Teil* and *Ratskeller* as *Theil* and *Rathskeller* (Figure 5.8). A second trait causing Texas German to differ from its

Figure 5.6. Both loanwords mean "something extra" or "baker's dozen." "Pilón" is borrowed from Spanish and used west and south of the isogloss; "lagniappe" comes from Louisiana French and is heard east of the isogloss. Each dot symbol represents one field interview. The respective zones of importance of the Spanish and French languages in Texas are nicely illustrated by these two loanwords. (Based on data in E. Bagby Atwood, *The Regional Vocabulary of Texas* [Austin: University of Texas Press, 1962].)

Figure 5.7. The German language employed in a street name in Fredericksburg, Texas. *Ufer* means "stream bank," and Ufer Street runs alongside a creek. (Photo: Terry G. Jordan, 1961.)

Figure 5.8. Use of archaic German spelling in the village of Kendalia, Kendall County. (Photo: Terry G. Jordan, 1961.)

European prototype is the tendency of people to coin new German words for inventions that occurred after the migration. Thus "airplane" in Texas German is *Luftschiff* instead of the correct *Flugzeug,* a difference heightened by the fact that in European German, *Luftschiff* means "dirigible blimp."

Too, Texas Germans, under the influence of frontier democracy and the English language, abandoned the polite personal pronouns that are still important in Germany and preserved only the familiar forms. At the same time, large numbers of English loanwords have been adopted into German speech, often without the speakers' being aware that a correct German word exists.

The loanwords are provided with gender and German verb endings, often with almost comical results. Examples include *das Rop* ("the rope," instead of *das Seil*), *greasen* ("to grease," instead of *schmieren*), *aufrounden* ("to round up"), *fixen* ("to fix"), and *der Pickupwagen* ("the pickup truck").

Few, if any, German monoglots remain in Texas, but the English spoken by this ethnic group remains highly distinctive because of the phonetic and structural influences of German. *W* sounds are rendered as *v,* and *th* becomes *d.* German loanwords such as schrank (closet) are not uncommon, and literal translations abound ("he is a pretty man"). German word order often prevails ("he went the corner around"), and

Table 5.3. Selected Generic Placenames in the United States

Origin	Generic Placename	Meaning	Texas Examples
Northern dialect	-center	town	Hale Center (Hale Co.)
	-corners	small settlement	Four Corners (Montgomery Co.)
	-notch	mountain pass	(none present)
	-brook	creek	(none present)
Midland dialect	-burg	town	Forestburg (Montague Co.)
	-run	creek	Pleasant Run (Dallas Co.)
	-gap	mountain pass	Indian Gap (Hamilton Co.)
	-hollow	elongated flat valley	Stillhouse Hollow (Bell Co.)
	-knob	rounded hill	Pilot Knob (Denton Co.)
	-fork	tributary stream	Salt Fork (Young Co.)
	-branch	small tributary stream	Bee Branch (San Saba Co.)
	-cove	small oval valley	Copperas Cove (Coryell Co.)
Plantation Southern dialect	-store	small settlement	Pauls Store (Shelby Co.)
	-gully	small stream valley	Cedar Gully (Harris Co.)
	-bayou	sluggish stream	Double Bayou (Chambers Co.)
	-baygall	marshy, thickety place where bay trees and gallberry grow	Deserter Baygall (Hardin Co.)
	-island	grove of trees in a prairie	High Island (Galveston Co.)
Spanish	loma-	hill	Loma Alto (Val Verde Co.)
	mota-	hill	Mota Negra (Kenedy Co.)
	arroyo-	normally dry stream course	Arroyo Segundo (Presidio Co.)
	mesa	flat-topped hill	Burro Mesa (Brewster Co.)
German	-burg	town	Fredericksburg (Gillespie Co.)
	-heim	village	Hochheim (DeWitt Co.)
	-berg	hill or mountain	Kreuzberg (Kendall Co.)
	-thal	valley	Schoenthal (Comal Co.)
French	-ville	town	Castroville (Medina Co.)
	-prairie	grassy area	Round Prairie (Robertson Co.)
Unknown or disputed origin	-mott	grove of trees in a prairie	Blue Mott (Victoria Co.)
	-draw	normally dry stream course	Crooked Draw (Edwards Co.)

Germanlike English words are preferred to non-Germanic synonyms ("forest" instead of "woods").

Precise parallels to the linguistic situation of Texas German exist in Czech, Polish, Swedish, Norwegian, and other languages introduced in the nineteenth century from Europe. For example, linguists have come from Poland to study the archaic Silesian dialect spoken by some Texas Poles, a dialect that has died out in the Old World. The various European immigrant languages in Texas also share the probability of an unavoidable and imminent death. Few will survive to the year 2000, and linguistic acculturation seems certain. A few loan-words, such as fest and kolache, may survive as reminders of the European languages in Texas, but little else.

PLACENAMES

Another facet of the linguistic geography of Texas lies in the names placed on the land at the time of settlement. Bearers of each culture and subculture had their own distinctive array of placenames (Table 5.3). Once implanted, these terms generally tend to be more durable than the languages and dialects that produced them, with the result that placenames may well provide a permanent index to linguistic diversity.

Of particular interest to cultural geographers are generic placenames, those that describe what kind of place is being named. In the toponyms Greenville and Elm Fork, for example, the generic parts are -ville and -fork, indicating that the first place is a town or city and the latter, a tributary stream. The specific element in these two names, Green- and Elm-, merely indicates which specific town or stream is being described. In addition to the foreign languages, each of the three major dialects of U.S. English can be linked to a particular array of generic placenames.

Many typical Midland and Plantation Southern placenames occur in Texas, roughly demarking the zones of upper- and lower-southern settlement. In the upper-southern realm in interior Texas, topographic generic names that include hollow, cove, gap, and knob are abundant, as are stream names that include branch and fork (Figures 5.9, 5.10, and 5.11). Lower-southern counties in East Texas, by contrast, are dotted with Plantation Southern generic placenames, particularly island (meaning a grove of trees in a prairie), bayou, and gully (Figure 5.12).

Various ethnic minorities also succeeded in implanting generic placenames in Texas. The Hispanic borderland is dotted with toponyms such as mesa, arroyo, mota (small hill), and cerro (Figure 5.11). The Anglo-Texan use of the placename "pass" in place of "gap" in some hilly and mountainous regions is possibly derived from the Spanish paso (Figure 5.10). From the Germans came generics such as -heim, -burg, and -thal, as in Bergheim (mountain home), Frelsburg, and Schoenthal (pretty valley).

GENERIC PLACENAME PROBLEMS

Certain other generic toponyms occurring in Texas are more difficult to interpret and have uncertain cultural/ethnic roots. In this category are draw, a widely used Texas name for an intermittent stream (Figure 5.12), and mott or motte, a generic employed in the area around Corpus Christi in the names of groves (Figure 5.13).

Since the latter toponym, mott, may be the only example of a generic that occurs exclusively in Texas, and because its origins are disputed, we will use it as an example of the problems that are sometimes encountered in attempting to understand the linguistic geography of the state. In Texan vegetational terminology, mott means a copse or small stand of trees on a prairie, a clump of trees in a prairie, a small thicket of bushes or trees, or a grove of trees. Mott occurs in Texas both in the vernacular and as a generic placename suffix. Some linguists have traditionally considered it to

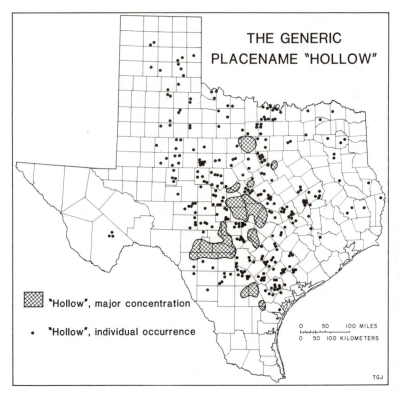

Figure 5.9. The distribution of "hollow" is closely linked to the zone of hill-southern settlement. The term describes an elongated, narrow, flat valley and is derived from the Midland dialect. (Based on Stanley A. Arbingast et al., *Atlas of Texas,* 5th ed. [Austin: University of Texas, Bureau of Business Research, 1976].)

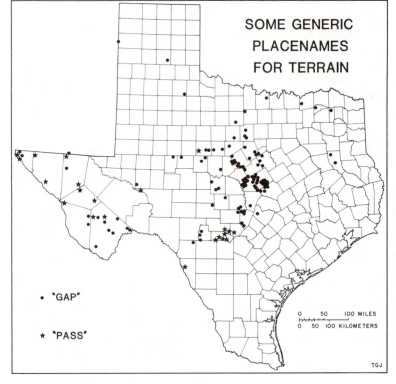

Figure 5.10. Both of these generic placenames are used in the names of mountain passes. "Gap" comes from the Midland dialect, and "pass" may be derived from the Spanish *paso.* (Based on Stanley A. Arbingast et al., *Atlas of Texas,* 5th ed. [Austin: University of Texas, Bureau of Business Research, 1976].)

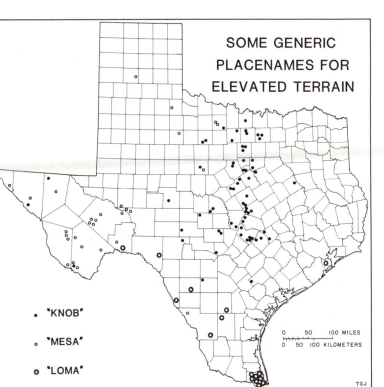

Figure 5.11. "Knob" is a Midland term, and "mesa" and "loma" are generic toponyms borrowed from Spanish. (Based in part on Stanley A. Arbingast et al., *Atlas of Texas,* 5th ed. [Austin: University of Texas, Bureau of Business Research, 1976].)

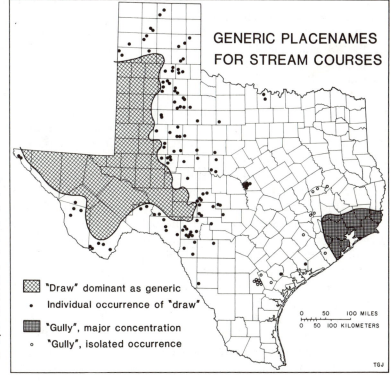

Figure 5.12. "Gully" is a Plantation Southern generic term used to describe a small stream valley, and "draw" is a West Texas toponym of uncertain origin applied to intermittent streams and their valleys. (Based on Stanley A. Arbingast et al., *Atlas of Texas,* 5th ed. [Austin: University of Texas, Bureau of Business Research, 1976].)

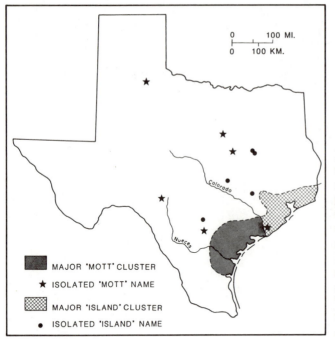

Figure 5.13. Toponymic regionalization of "mott(e)" and "island" as generic vegetational terms. Both of these generic placenames mean a grove of trees in a prairie. "Island" is a Plantation Southern name apparently derived from the parallel usage of *île* in Louisiana French, and "mott" is probably Irish or Mexican in origin. (Based on Terry G. Jordan, "The Origin of 'Motte' and 'Island' in Texan Vegetational Terminology," *Southern Folklore Quarterly* 36 [1972], 121–135.)

be a modified Spanish loanword, in the same category as lariat, ranch, bronc, and many others. The Spanish word *mata* has been proposed as the parent of the Anglo-Texan word mott. There are, however, a number of other plausible origins for the word, and mott may not be derived from Spanish at all.

An important clue to the origin of mott may be revealed by its spatial distribution in Texas. As a generic placename ending, it occurs mainly in the Coastal Prairie adjacent to the Gulf of Mexico, particularly in the Coastal Bend country from the lower Colorado River southwestward beyond the Nueces (Figure 5.13). The eastern boundary of the toponymic mott is rather sharply drawn, for only one example has been found east of the lower Colorado. Mott placenames are only occasionally found in the interior prairies of Texas. In several instances, rural communities in Texas have been named for a nearby mott, as in Long Mott, a Calhoun County hamlet, and Elm Mott, a growing suburb of Waco in Central Texas. The term is much more widespread

in the vernacular than as a placename suffix. E. B. Atwood has mapped its usage in folk speech, concluding that mott is concentrated as a vernacular term "mostly in the Corpus Christi area," though it "has spread to a considerable portion of South Central and Southwest Texas."

Additional assistance in determining the origin of mott can be gained by ascertaining, as nearly as possible, the place and date of its first usage in the vernacular. The earliest known written reference to mott dates from the 1840s. George Wilkins Kendall, a native of New Hampshire and resident of New Orleans who was newly arrived in Texas, wrote that the word "mot" was used by Texans to describe small clumps of woods in a prairie. Kendall first encountered the term in the south-central part of the state, near or within the present zone of major mott usage, and it was obviously new to him. The famous Texas adventurer "Big Foot" Wallace, describing his experiences of the mid-1830s, spoke of "mots of wild cherry and plum trees," but his account was not written until the 1870s, and it is impossible to know when mott became a part of his vocabulary. In 1846, the traveler William A. McClintock, a native and resident of Kentucky, saw "here and there a 'motte' of thorns and brambles" near the Aransas River near the Gulf Coast, within the area where mott usage is most common today. McClintock's account is the first known written reference in which one of the two correct spellings of the word is employed. Still later, in 1857, William H. Emory, a native of Maryland who was taking part in the U.S.-Mexico border survey, referred to "clumps of post-oak called *mots*" in Texas. He apparently first encountered the term in the Coastal Prairie near Matagorda Bay, and it was obviously not previously known to him. The written evidence suggests, then, that mott probably entered the Anglo-Texan vernacular during the 1830s and that one of the current spellings was used at least by the mid-1840s, if not earlier.

In addition to the commonly assumed Spanish origin, there are a number of other possible explanations for the Texan mott. Similar words are found in French, English, and Erse. In modern French, *motte* means clod, ball of earth, mound, or a slight elevation, either natural or artificial, and none of those definitions are close enough to the Texan meaning to excite further interest. The Louisiana-French use of *île* to mean grove further damages any claim for direct French origin of the Texan mott, as does the absence of French colonization in the zone of mott concentration. It is true that the French explorer La Salle visited that part of the Coastal Prairie of Texas in the late 1600s, but no placenames of any sort were left behind by his ill-fated expedition.

The French word *motte* was introduced into English speech as a result of the Norman invasion, and the spelling and meaning survived the transplanting intact. The first meanings listed for mott, or motte, in any English dictionary are "clod," "clump," "hillock," and "a type of palisaded mound common in prehistoric Europe," all of which virtually duplicate the definitions of the French parent word. It is true, however, that the preferred English version is *mote,* pronounced with a hard *o* and meaning height, eminence, or hill. The use of motte/ mott to mean a clump of trees in a prairie follows only as a secondary definition, accompanied by the remark that this latter usage is found only regionally in the United States. It is conceivable that the Texan mott was derived from the English noun mottle, which means a colored spot or an appearance like that of having colored spots, blotches, or cloudings. Related words include mottled and motley. To describe groves of trees in a prairie as mottles would be quite in keeping with the meaning of the word. There are, however, some serious difficulties involved in accepting an English or Anglo-American origin of the Texan mott by way of mottle, not the least of which are the altered spelling and pronunciation. It is not common for the *l* sound to be lost through contraction in English. Furthermore, it is difficult to explain why Anglo-Americans would have developed this word only in parts of Texas, for they encountered groves of trees in the prairies along the entire perimeter of the American frontier, from Minnesota to Texas. In short, it seems unlikely that the Texan mott was derived directly from English motte or mottle. This supposition is further strengthened by the absence of mott as a placename or vernacular term in Louisiana, the former home state of many of the Anglos who settled the Texas Coastal Prairie.

As suggested above, the generally accepted theory for the origin of the Texan mott is that it is derived from the Spanish *mata.* In Castilian Spanish, that word can mean a piece of ground covered with trees of the same species, copse, orchard, a young live oak tree, and canebrake. Even more promising are the Mexican-Spanish meanings for *mata,* which include a group of trees in the middle of a prairie and a hill or a forest that is small or of limited extent. So convincing is this evidence that the Spanish-origin theory has been accepted by the Texas linguistic expert E. B. Atwood and the editor of the *American Heritage Dictionary of the English Language,* among others.

However, certain difficulties are involved in accepting that theory, and plausible alternative explanations exist. First, the most convincing meaning of Mexican-Spanish *mata,* a group of trees in the middle of a prairie, is found in *southern* Mexico, the part of that country farthest removed from Texas. In Texas, *mata* normally refers to canebrakes, as in Matagorda (big cane). Second, many Spanish words ending in *a* were absorbed into the Anglo-Texan vernacular, including reata, acequia, resaca, remuda, and hacienda, but only rarely with the loss of pronunciation of the final *a,* such as would have occurred had *mata* been the basis for mott. Moreover, Anglo-Texans typically flattened the sound of the Spanish *a* in loanwords, as in ranch, dally rope, savvy, cavvieyard, and wrangler, a modification that did not occur if mott was derived from *mata.* Also worth noting is the fact that *mata* is invariably a prefix when used in Spanish placenames, but in Texas, mott is always a suffix. Almost none of the Texan motts have a Mexican-Spanish prefix. Even around the city of Victoria, founded by the Mexicans on the Coastal Prairie in the mid-1820s, there are names such as Sutton Mott, Kentucky Mott, and Blue Mott, which suggest non-Mexican origin. The only exception detected so far is Alazan Mott in Kleberg County, but its Arabic-Spanish prefix was derived from nearby Alazan Bay by Anglo-Texans. In short, the transition from *mata* to mott does not parallel the changes or lack of changes in spelling and pronunciation observed in other words traditionally thought to have been borrowed from Spanish that turn out not to be explainable in terms of English phonological interference on Spanish.

Still, the temptation to accept the Spanish *mata* origin might remain compelling if no attractive alternatives existed. The zone of mott concentration on the Coastal Prairie is today peopled not only by descendants of Anglo-Americans and Mexicans, but also by persons of Irish, German, Czech, Danish, Swedish, and Polish ancestry. Of these diverse European minority groups, only the Irish were present as early as the 1830s, when mott presumably entered Texas English. The Irish colonists settled in Texas in the late 1820s and early 1830s at the encouragement of the government of Mexico, which sought to impose a human barrier of Catholic Europeans in the path of the westward expansion of potentially disloyal Protestant Anglo-Americans. The major Irish settlements founded were San Patricio and Refugio, both of which lay in the zone of present mott concentration. The Irish quickly spread out from these villages, scattering through much of present-day Refugio, Aransas, and San Patricio counties. As late as 1850, persons of Irish birth or parentage constituted the largest single ethnic group in these counties, accounting for almost 50 percent of the population. By contrast, Spanish-surnamed individuals were only one-sixth as numerous as the immigrant Irish in those counties in 1850.

Since the Irish settled in a largely unpopulated region between clusters of Anglo and Hispanic settlements, it stands to reason that they were the people responsible for naming many of the environmental features of the area. Only some of the streams, bays, and other prominent features had been named previously by the Spaniards. The adoption of cattle ranching by many of the Irish settlers in the 1830s caused them to spread out and become familiar with the vegetational features of the surrounding area, and the cattle often found refuge from the heat of summer in the shade of motts.

The leading European source area of the Irish immigrants was County Wexford, situated in the east of Ireland in the coastal region south of Dublin. Perhaps some of the colonists had at least a partial knowledge of Erse, or Irish Gaelic, the ancestral Celtic tongue of the Irish, but English was the mother tongue for all of them. The eastern location of County Wexford meant that the Anglo-Norman influence from England had been strong over the centuries.

Significantly, there are many mottes or motes in County Wexford and other parts of Ireland. To be sure, these are mottes in the traditional British English sense, defined as man-made mounds dating from antiquity. According to the geographer A. R. Orme, an expert on Ireland, the motte or mote is a 20–40 ft (6–12 m) high, steep-sided, artificial mound of earth topped by a 30–100 ft (9–30 m) wide summit flat originally defended by a timber palisade and blockhouse. Most of these mottes were established as fortifications in the late twelfth and early thirteenth centuries, at a time when Anglo-Norman efforts to conquer Ireland reached a peak. The use of the word mote or motte in Ireland can be attributed to the French spoken by these Norman invaders, and it has survived in the vernacular English of the Irish. The word, modified as *móta,* also entered the vocabulary of Celtic Erse.

Once accepted into the Irish vernacular, the term subsequently came to mean any artificial mound, including some that predated the Norman invasion. Graves of chieftains and other hallowed places came to bear the name, and perhaps by such association numerous Norman mottes came to be venerated. In addition, various Irish saints sometimes ascended such mounds to speak to the gathered peasantry, lending the mottes a special religious significance. For these reasons, the mottes were generally not tilled or grazed, with the result that in time, the artificial slopes and summits became covered with trees (Figure 5.14). In later times, particularly in the 1600s, some landlords deliberately had trees planted on mottes. Significantly, the forested mottes were among the few timber-covered places anywhere in Ireland, for the countryside had become almost completely deforested.

Figure 5.14. A mott in Ireland. (Photo: Courtesy of Anita Pitchford; used with permission.)

The mottes stood as islands of timber, rising impressively from the surrounding fields, pastures, and meadows, and were visible for many miles. To be sure, some of the mottes remained devoid of trees and were covered only by grass, but there is no doubt that a significant number of them were tree covered in the early 1800s when the Wexford emigrants left for Texas. The numerous mottes found in Wexford, especially in the south along the Slaney and Barrow valleys, surely made a lasting impression on the superstitious peasants of the area.

The evidence reveals, then, that the term *motte* was used in parts of nineteenth-century Ireland, including Wexford, to describe mounds that were often, if not always, tree covered. Confronted with oak groves that rose impressively from the table-flat Coastal Prairie of Texas, the Wexford emigrants could quite understandably have employed the word mott to describe them. Indeed, the similarity becomes almost compelling when one considers that some of the Texan motts occupy slightly raised ground, small natural mounds and salt domes that abound on the otherwise level coastal plain. An example is Lund Motte, which occupies a low height overlooking Tres Palacios Bay in the Coastal Prairie of western Matagorda County. Still further evidence supporting an Irish origin of the Texan motts can be detected in certain of the placename prefixes, as in the case of O'Leary Motte in Refugio County. In addition, it is perhaps significant that an accepted spelling of the Texan mott duplicates one spelling of the proposed Norman-English-Irish parent word.

Another possible Irish origin is offered by the Erse word *mothar,* which means a clump of brush, a thicket, or an area of thick brushwood. Wexford was one of the most Anglicized parts of Ireland, and the Celtic language had probably passed out of use there even by the 1820s, when the Texas migration began. Also, the *th* sound in Celtic and English speech tends to be persistent and is rarely hardened to a *t* by native speakers of those languages, as would

have been necessary if *mothar* "mothered" mott. Still, it is a possibility that should not be overlooked. At the very least, we can say that the Irish were preconditioned by their own vocabulary to accept the Spanish word.

People who are disinclined to accept an Irish origin for the word mott should consider Spanish words other than *mata* as the possible parent. Of particular interest is the Spanish word *mota,* equivalent to the French *motte,* meaning mound, hummock, or an eminence of low altitude that rises above a plain. Unlike *mata* and its "grove" meaning, *mota* has been widely used in Texas as a generic placename, especially in Kenedy and Brooks counties on the southern fringe of the core area of mott usage. There one finds numerous hillocks with names such as Mota Verde, Mota Casa, Mota del Tacon, and Mota Negra. A variety of other names, such as La Mota Ranch and San Pedro de las Motas, appear in the same general area. Some of these *mota*s are tree covered and surrounded by prairie or brush country.

The linguistic geography of Texas, then, is both complex and incompletely interpreted. The wide varieties of dialects and languages, words, pronunciations, and toponyms are revealing and occasionally confusing. Their cataloging and interpretation have only just begun. When completed, the linguistic analysis will no doubt produce results that will confirm the highly complex cultural diversity of the state.

SOURCES AND SUGGESTED READINGS

Atwood, E. Bagby. *The Regional Vocabulary of Texas.* Austin: University of Texas Press, 1962.

Gilbert, Glenn G. *Linguistic Atlas of Texas German.* Marburg, West Germany: N. G. Elwert Verlag, 1972.

Gilbert, Glenn G., ed. *Texas Studies in Bilingualism: Spanish, French, German, Czech, Polish, Sorbian, and Norwegian in the Southwest.* Berlin: Walter de Gruyter & Co., 1970.

Hancock, Ian F. "Texas Gullah: The Creole English of the Bracketville Afro-Seminoles." In *Perspectives on American English,* ed. J. L. Dillard, pp. 305–333. The Hague: Mouton Publishers, 1980.

Herman, Lewis, and Herman, Marguerite. "The East Texas Dialect." In *American Dialects,* pp. 109–124. New York: Theatre Arts Books, 1947.

Hill, Robert T. "Descriptive Topographic Terms of Spanish America." *National Geographic Magazine* 7 (1896), 291–302.

Jordan, Terry G. "The Origin of 'Motte' and 'Island' in Texan Vegetational Terminology." *Southern Folklore Quarterly* 36 (1972), 121–135.

————. "Traditional English Dialects" and "Selected Generic Place-Names." In Stanley A. Arbingast et al., *Atlas of Texas,* pp. 33–37. 5th ed. Austin: University of Texas, Bureau of Business Research, 1976.

Klipple, Carmelita. "The Speech of Spicewood, Texas." *American Speech* 20 (1945), 187–191.

Kubesch, Lillian. "Dialects of South Colorado County, Texas." M.A. thesis, Sam Houston State University, Huntsville, Texas, 1963.

Kurath, Hans. *A Word Geography of the Eastern United States.* Ann Arbor: University of Michigan Press, 1949.

Norman, Arthur M. Z. "Migration to Southeast Texas: People and Words." *Southwestern Social Science Quarterly* 37 (1956), 149–158.

————. "A Southeast Texas Dialect Study." *Orbis* 5 (1956), 61–79.

Price, Armstrong. "Place Names in Texas." *Texas Geographic Magazine* 8:2 (1944), 31–34.

Rosenquist C. M. "Linguistic Changes in the Acculturation of the Swedes in Texas." *Sociology and Social Research* 16 (1932), 221–231.

Stanley, Oma. *The Speech of East Texas.* American Speech Reprints and Monographs, no. 2. New York: Columbia University Press. 1937.

Tarpley, Fred. *From Blinky to Blue John.* Wolfe City, Tex.: University Press, 1970.

Walsh, Harry, and Mote, Victor L. "A Texas Dialect Feature: Origins and Distribution." *American Speech* 49 (1974), 40–53.

West, Robert C. "The Term 'Bayou' in the United States: A Study in the Geography of Place Names." *Annals of the Association of American Geographers* 44 (1954), 63–74.

Wheatley, Katherine E., and Stanley, Oma. "Three Generations of East Texas Speech." *American Speech* 34 (1959), 83–94.

SOURCES OF QUOTATIONS

Emory, William H., *United States and Mexican Boundary Survey,* House of Representatives, 34th Cong., 1st sess., Executive Document no. 135 (Washington, D.C.: Cornelius Wendell, 1857).

Kendall, George Wilkins, *Narrative of the Texan Santa Fé Expedition* (London: Wiley & Putnam, 1844).

McClintock, William A., "Journal of the Trip Through Texas and Northern Mexico in 1846–1847," *Southwestern Historical Quarterly* 34 (1930–1931), 20–37, 141–158, 231–256.

Wallace, William A. A., and Duval, John C., *The Adventures of Big-Foot Wallace* (Lincoln: University of Nebraska Press, 1966).

CHAPTER 6

THE GEOGRAPHY OF RELIGION

In terms of religion, Texas has a pronounced internal regionality. The essential feature of the state's religious geography is a division between north and south, between the British-based Calvinism of the Bible Belt and the diversity of the Catholic/Lutheran southern borderland (Figure 6.1). Without serious challenge, the northern half of Texas belongs religiously to the Anglo host culture, with its Afro-American subsidiary, perpetuating a heritage of British dissenter Protestantism enlivened by the frontier experience.

THE BIBLE BELT NORTH

Curiously, the Anglo-Texan culture does not reveal internal religious differences along the old subcultural divide between the Lower South and the Middle Atlantic. This is not to say that the three Anglo subcultures of the East lack a religious expression. Traditionally, for example, Presbyterianism was stronger in the upper-southern region, a heritage of the Scotch-Irish immigrants to the Middle Atlantic colonies, and the Episcopal Church was closely identified with the wealthy planters of the Tidewater districts. In the last century or so, however, a rapid spread of the Southern Baptist faith has tended to unite the Upper and Lower South, both in Texas and the South as a

whole. In this way, the Middle Atlantic subculture, religiously characterized by thorough diversity, has been pushed out of the Upper South and has shrunk to a narrow belt confined mainly to the Lower Midwest (Figure 6.2). In Texas, the religions of the Middle Atlantic subculture claim only a tenuous foothold in the northern Panhandle and perhaps in cities such as Dallas (Figure 6.3).

The Middle Atlantic's loss has been the Lower South's gain. From a base in the Gulf-Atlantic coastal plains, a lower-southern religious complex has spread—mainly in the twentieth century—to reach the Ohio River, providing a cultural unity to the South far surpassing the unity once offered by the institution of slavery. The hallmark of the religious South is a Baptist absolute majority accompanied by sizable Methodist, Presbyterian, and Church of Christ minorities, as well as smaller representations of a variety of other fundamentalist groups.

Such is the largely undifferentiated religious character of Anglo northern Texas today (Table 6.1). From the Sabine River in the east to the New Mexico border, a Baptist-dominated Bible Belt prevails (Figure 6.4). A greater contrast to the remainder of Texas could scarcely be imagined.

115

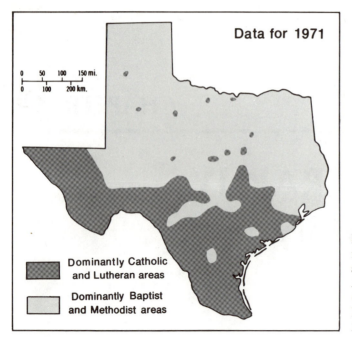

Data for 1971

0 50 100 150 mi.
0 100 200 km.

Dominantly Catholic
and Lutheran areas

Dominantly Baptist
and Methodist areas

Figure 6.1. Religions north and south in Texas. (Source: Terry G. Jordan and Lester Rowntree, *The Human Mosaic: A Thematic Introduction to Cultural Geography,* 1st ed. [San Francisco: Canfield Press, 1976], p. 254, used with permission.)

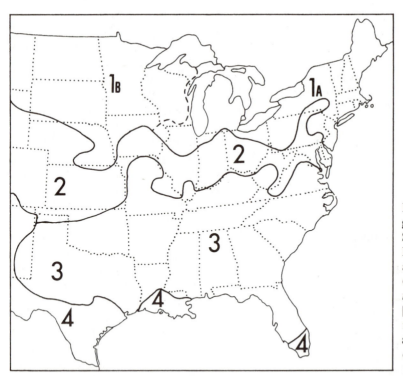

1B
1A
2
2
2
3
3
4
4
4

Figure 6.2. Religious regions of the eastern United States, 1971. (Based on Douglas W. Johnson et al., eds., *Churches and Church Membership in the United States, 1971* [Washington, D.C.: Glenmary Research Center and National Council of Churches of Christ, 1974].)

Key: 1 = North—traditional Puritan-based faiths, upon which was superimposed nineteenth- and twentieth-century immigration, leading to dominance by Roman Catholicism (1A) and Lutheranism (1B); 2 = Middle Atlantic—highly diverse, no single denomination claiming as much as half of the church-going population, Methodism the leading denomination; 3 = South—Baptists make up the largest denomination, accounting for half or more of the church-going population with sizable Methodist, Presbyterian, and Church of Christ minorities; 4 = Catholic Borderland—Roman Catholic majority rooted mainly in Mexican, Cuban, and French ethnic groups.

117

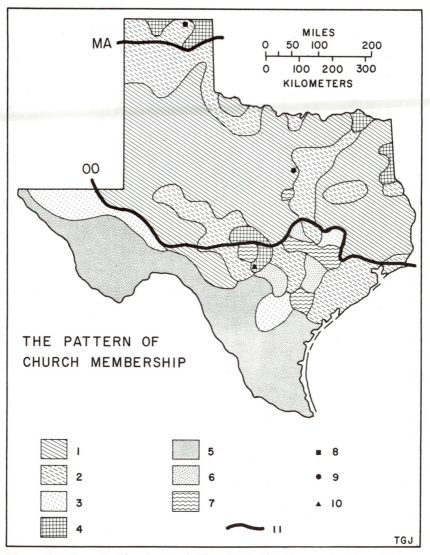

Figure 6.3. Source: *Churches and Church Membership in the United States*
(New York: National Council of the Churches of Christ in the United States,
1956–1958).
Key: 1 = Southern Baptist absolute majority, Methodist minority; 2 = Southern Baptist
simple majority, large Methodist minority; 3 = Southern Baptist simple majority, large
Catholic minority; 4 = Methodist majority, usually with large Baptist minority; 5 =
Roman Catholic absolute majority; 6 = Roman Catholic simple majority, with large
Lutheran and Reformed minority; 7 = Lutheran majority, usually with Catholic minority;
8 = Mennonite enclave; 9 = Seventh-Day Adventist large colony; 10 = traditional
agnostic, anticlerical sentiment; 11 = Major religious borders; OO = Odessa-Orange
line; MA = southern border of Middle Atlantic religious subculture.

Table 6.1. Selected Religious Denominations in Texas (total adherents)

	1950	1971	1980
The Bible Belt North			
Baptist	1,371,000	2,475,000	2,847,000
Methodist	640,000	857,000	1,021,000
Church of Christ	—	—	355,000
Presbyterian	136,000	216,000	207,000
Episcopal	101,000	176,000	175,000
Disciples of Christ	125,000	118,000	120,000
Assembly of God	77,000	—	162,000
Mormon	12,000	43,000	68,000
Church of the Nazarene	14,000	36,000	39,000
Seventh-Day Adventist	8,000	18,000	23,000
Church of God (Cleveland, Tenn.)	4,500	11,500	16,000
The Catholic/Lutheran South			
Roman Catholic	1,402,000	2,012,000	2,340,162
Lutheran	147,000	249,000	264,000
Evangelical and Reformed (United Church of Christ)	12,500	22,000	21,000
Unity of the Brethren (Moravian)	—	4,000	—
Other			
Jewish	51,000	80,000	30,000

Sources: Churches and Church Membership in the United States (New York: National Council of Churches of Christ in the United States, 1956–1958); Douglas W. Johnson et al., eds., *Churches and Church Membership in the United States, 1971* (Washington, D.C.: Glenmary Research Center and National Council of Churches of Christ, 1974); and Bernard Quinn et al., eds., *Churches and Church Membership in the United States, 1980* (Atlanta: Glenmary Research Center, 1982).

Figure 6.4. Traditional church structures of the Bible Belt, in the northern half of Texas, are modest frame structures. The usually white chapels are generally steepleless and often have two separate doors, one for each sex, as exemplified by the upper photograph, taken in Collin County. Black churches, such as the Nacogdoches County example in the lower illustration, often have small twin steeples, an architectural feature perhaps derived from the "high church" Anglican slaveowners of the Carolina low country in colonial times. (Photos: Terry G. Jordan, 1980 and 1978.)

Figure 6.5. These two imposing rural Gothic churches stand, like sentinels guarding a frontier, almost exactly on the major religious border in Texas, visually announcing entry into the Catholic/Lutheran south. The upper illustration is of Holy Trinity Catholic Church, a Czech/German parish in Williamson County; the lower shows the German Catholic church at Westphalia in Falls County. (Photos: Terry G. Jordan, 1960 and 1966.)

THE CATHOLIC/ LUTHERAN SOUTH

The southern perimeter of the Bible Belt is formed by a line running from near Odessa to Orange. South of this line, Roman Catholicism and Lutheranism of Latin American and continental European origins are the prevalent denominations.

Clearly, Mexican Catholicism is the dominant religious force in this region. For three centuries, from the time of the earliest Spanish missions, the borderland has had a strong Mexican Catholic flavor, still exemplified today by the exquisite architecture of the surviving eighteenth-century missions, abundant shrines to the Virgin of Guadalupe, and pilgrimage sites of local importance such as the shrine of Our Lady of San Juan of the Valley. Religious acculturation of the Hispanic Catholics has progressed very slowly. Of the Mexicans in Texas about 1980, only 50,000 were Baptists in 627 parishes, and only 16,000 were Methodists in 97 churches, accounting for no more than 2.5 percent of the total Hispanic population.

In the nineteenth century, central European Catholicism was introduced alongside the older Mexican variety and today claims nearly all of the Texas Poles and Cajuns, about three-fourths of the Czechs, and one-fourth of the Germans as members. Their grand Gothic cathedrals jut into the South Central Texas sky, announcing yet another Catholic tradition (Figure 6.5).

The continental European Reformation was also introduced into Texas by the nineteenth-century immigrants. Lutheranism is abundantly represented, accounting for the great majority of the Norwegians, Danes, and Wends; about 55 percent of the Germans; and just over half of the Swedes (Figure 6.6). Moravianism claims more adherents in Texas than in any other state and finds its base in one-fourth of the Czech population. The United Church of Christ (reformed) survives among a minority of the German Texans.

Catholicism's sizable majority south of the Odessa-Orange line in fact conceals considerable religious diversity. A good case in point is provided by the Germans of the Texas Hill Country. Each succeeding river valley in the German-settled portion of the hills brings the visitor into a different religious realm: the Llano Valley in the north, settled by stern, ascetic converts to Methodism escaping the corruption of their drinking, dancing fellow Germans; the Pedernales Valley, centered on Fredericksburg, peopled by hard-working, fun-loving Lutherans and Catholics; and the upper Guad-

Figure 6.6. This rural church at New Sweden in Travis County represents the Lutheranism of southern Texas. Its spire is visible for many miles in the surrounding Blackland Prairie. (Photo: Terry G. Jordan, 1961.)

alupe Valley, the only major stronghold of rural Texan agnosticism, occupied by unchurched ranchers descended from university-educated political refugees (Figure 6.7).

The religious split between north and south in Texas finds many expressions. Among these are voting tendencies, ecclesiastical architecture, beverage preferences, and the traditional burial practices. In many localities, the religious cultures of both north and south are present. This is true not only along the Odessa-Orange religious divide, but also where outliers of one of the cultures lie imbedded in the domain of the other. Such localities offer an opportunity for geographers to observe, over short distances, the striking religious regionality that characterizes the state as a whole. A two-county area in North Texas, where small outliers of Catholic/Lutheran South Texas thrive, islandlike, in an Anglo Bible Belt sea, is used as a sample study to illustrate the religious geography of Texas at large.

A NORTH TEXAS MICROREGION

North Texas, represented in the sample study by the counties of Cooke and Denton, as well as adjacent parts of Grayson, Collin, and Wise, is in many respects a Texan microcosm, containing within its confines great environmental and cultural contrasts (Figure 6.8). The remnants of once impenetrable forests stand beside expanses of open prairie, and sons of central European immigrants are neighbors of descendants of southern American backwoodsmen. To understand the two fundamentally different religious cultures that were implanted in this area, one must first know something about the local patterns of physical environment and settlement.

The most striking environmental feature of North Texas is the sharp vegetational contrast between woodland and grassland. The greater part of the area was originally grass covered, including the Blackland Prai-

rie in the east and the Grand Prairie in the west. Both were tall-grass prairies underlaid by rich dark soils. Only streambank strips of forest and scattered groves relieved the pristine monotony of these undulating blacklands. The two expanses of open prairie were held asunder by a narrow, hilly belt of oak forest, the East Cross Timbers, stretching from the Red River southward across North Texas (Figure 6.8). George W. Kendall, a nineteenth-century observer, described the East Cross Timbers as "an immense natural hedge," an apt verbal portrait of this 10-mi- (16-km-) wide strip of small post oaks and blackjack oaks that bisects the prairies. Its red-orange and yellow soils are mainly sands and clays, much less fertile than those of the adjacent blacklands but easier to work. When the first white settlers entered the East Cross Timbers in the mid-nineteenth century, they found a densely wooded land, in places made virtually impenetrable by a tangle of briers, wild grapevines, plum thickets, sumac, and Virginia creeper. Environmentally, then, North Texas offered two contrasting worlds. The cultural patterns implanted in the course of a half century of immigration accentuated rather than diminished these differences.

The first group of settlers to enter the area were old-stock Anglo-Americans, who brought with them a backwoods, upper-southern culture. Their immigration began in the 1840s and lasted through the 1890s. These upper southerners were already a thoroughly amalgamated group by the time they reached Texas, though their ultimate origins were diverse. The modest gravestones in their bare-earth, cedar-studded cemeteries bear surnames reflecting the mixture of English, Welsh, Scotch-Irish, and German peoples that, long before and far to the east, had blended to form the highland-southern people—surnames such as Gentry, Wakefield, and Oxford; Jones, Williams, and Davis; McLeod, McElhannon, and McKitrick; Eddleman, Crubaugh, and Foutch. Most of these Texas settlers were by birth and place of removal

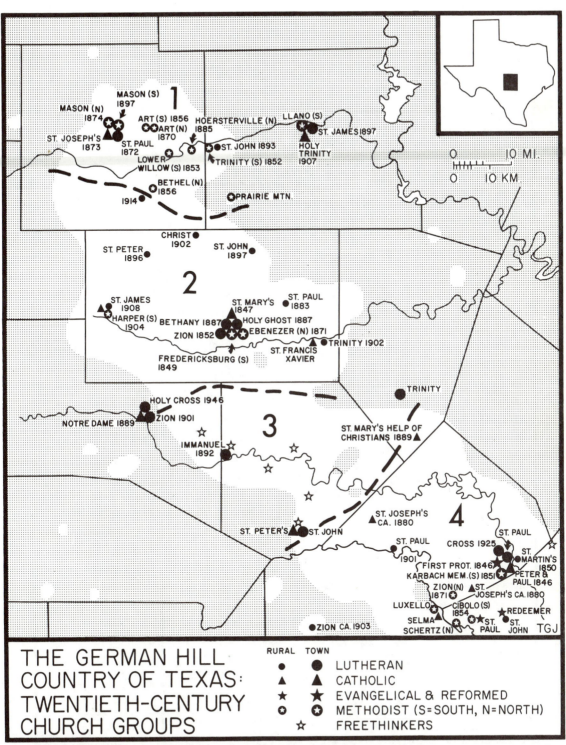

Figure 6.7. Source: Terry G. Jordan, "A Religious Geography of the Hill Country Germans of Texas," in Frederick C. Luebke, ed., *Ethnicity on the Great Plains* [Lincoln: University of Nebraska Press, 1980].)
Key: 1 = Llano Valley Methodists; 2 = Pedernales Valley Lutherans/Catholics; 3 = Upper Guadalupe Valley agnostics; 4 = Comal County Catholics/Reformed/Lutherans.

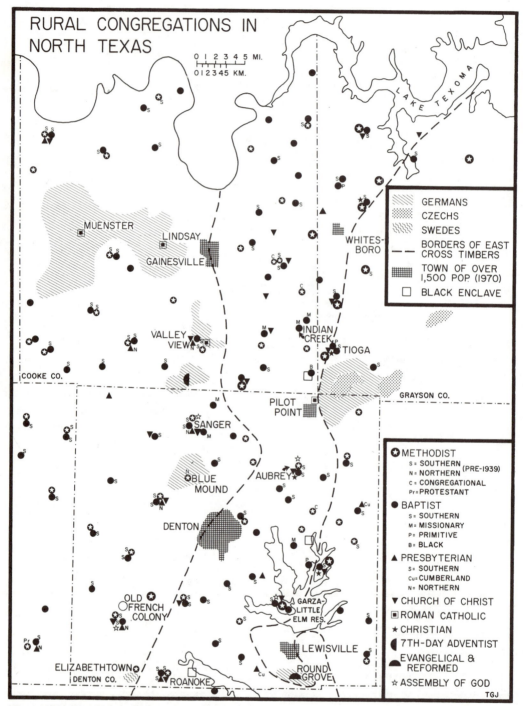

Figure 6.8. The North Texas sample study region.

from Missouri, Kentucky, and Tennessee. More exactly, the principal source regions, in order of importance, seem to have been Central and West Missouri, South Central Kentucky, and Middle Tennessee.

The goal of most of the Anglo settlers prior to about 1870 was the Cross Timbers belt, which became almost exclusively an upper-southern domain. There was seemingly no antigrassland prejudice on the part of the upper-southern backwoodsmen as they often chose to settle the margins of the small, sandy prairies that dotted the East Cross Timbers. Indeed, many migrants from the Upper South claimed lands in and adjacent to the groves and stream-bank forests in the Blackland and Grand prairies, but they generally shunned settlement on the open prairie, leaving it as a hunting preserve and cattle range.

In time, some of the children of upper-southern pioneers began moving out onto the open prairies of North Texas, but large expanses of open grassland were left thinly occupied into the 1880s and 1890s. These stretches of prairie were destined to belong in part to quite different people, in particular, midwesterners and Europeans. Midwestern Anglo-Americans, principally from Illinois and Indiana, were immigrating to North Texas even as early as 1850, and they continued to come throughout the remainder of the nineteenth century. Over 17 percent of the immigrants to Grayson County between 1865 and 1880, and over 10 percent of those immigrating to Cooke and Denton counties, were from Illinois, Indiana, and Kansas, with additional numbers from northern Missouri.

Although the vanguard of the midwestern immigration was composed largely of old-stock Anglo-Americans, the ethnic character of this human stream changed considerably in the later decades of the nineteenth century and the first years of the twentieth. The new element was European born, largely German, and composed mostly of people who had resided for a decade or more in the Midwest. To these was added a sizable group of Euro-peans from settlements in South Central Texas. In rapid order, German prairie colonies were founded at Muenster (1889) and Lindsay (1891) in Cooke County, at Round Grove (1885) and Blue Mound (1876) in Denton County, and near Pilot Point (1892) straddling the Grayson-Denton line (Figure 6.8). Once established, these colonies continued to draw settlers for a decade or two. The arrival of other European ethnic groups, particularly Czechs and Swedes, added to the diversity on the North Texas prairies.

In this way, different cultural groups were implanted in North Texas, establishing two major cultural realms: that of the Upper South, centered in the Cross Timbers, and that of the Midwest and Europe, concentrated on the open prairies (Figure 6.9). The Cross Timbers became an area of poor, Populist-voting farmers, who eked out a near-subsistence-level living with only a crop of peanuts, the yield of a small patch of cotton, or the produce of a small truck garden to sell. The prairie folk, by contrast, became prosperous wheat and cotton farmers, shifting after World War II toward commercial dairying. Their political allegiance was most often Democrat, frequently Republican, but never Populist. It was almost as if Kansas or Wisconsin had been placed alongside southern Appalachia.

Religious Denominations

The North Texan subcultures are quite distinct with regard to religion. People of southern Anglo-American stock are usually fundamentalist Protestants, mainly southern Baptists, with a large Methodist minority and ample representation of the Church of Christ, Assembly of God, the Christian Church, and several Presbyterian groups (Figure 6.8). A strong individualistic strain is reflected in the presence of splinter groups such as the Congregational Methodists. Several churches are nondenominational, and at least one Baptist congregation—the only rural black group surviving in the area—has no outside affiliations.

These southern churches were also im-

Figure 6.9. The German Catholic settlement of Muenster in Cooke County, with its Gothic spire towering over the wheat fields. (Photo: ca. 1950, courtesy of the *Texas Almanac*; used with permission.)

planted on the blackland prairies, but a quite different religious order prevailed there. Prairie Protestant churches occasionally have northern affiliations. Indeed, membership in the northern Presbyterian church in Denton and Cooke counties exceeded the combined number of adherents to southern and Cumberland Presbyterianism for a long time. The colony of midwestern Germans at Blue Mound is a Northern Methodist congregation, belonging formerly to a German-speaking conference of that church. The Blue Mound Colony also supported a Lutheran church for a time. Even more unusual are the rural congregation of German Seventh-Day Adventists on the prairie southwest of Valley View in Cooke County and a German Evangelical and Reformed group, now part of the United Church of Christ, at Round Grove in Denton County.

By far the most significant exotic religious element brought to the North Texas prairies was Roman Catholicism, which was introduced largely by German immigrants from Catholic colonies in the Midwest, especially Iowa. Large, thriving Roman churches are found at Muenster, Lindsay, and Pilot Point. These churches have served as the principal cultural rallying points for the minorities of North Texas and serve as a partial shield against assimilation. Most ethnic groups have clung stubbornly to their churches while most of the Anglo midwesterners have accepted southern churches. The Swedes, who were never numerous enough to support a Lutheran church, have been completely assimilated, but other European groups retain some distinctiveness.

The House of Worship

The cultural-religious contrasts in North Texas are nowhere more evident than in the appearance of the church buildings. On one extreme is the austere, southern folk church of the rural Cross Timbers, a one-room, white frame structure generally lacking even a rudimentary steeple (Figure 6.10). Wooden benches are arranged on either side of a single aisle, which leads to a door in the gable end opposite the pulpit, and a wood-burning stove stands between the preacher and his flock (Figure 6.11). Four square-topped, unadorned windows, covered with curtains, admit light from both sides, and another window is situated behind the pulpit. The entire structure is slightly raised on sandstone blocks. Baptists, Methodists, Church of Christers, and Presbyterians all built these humble chapels in the Cross Timbers, and all are as alike as peas in a pod. The frame chapels are usually on the order of 20–30 ft (6–9 m) wide and 30–50 ft (9–15 m) long. All in all, the Cross Timbers folk churches are splendid expressions of the stern fundamentalism of the area, of sects teaching that the way to hell is broad and that to heaven, narrow. Cross Timbers religion is not meant to be a comfortable experience; no beauty or grandeur is provided for the eye to behold, and few physical comforts are present to distract or lull the faithful, though evaporative coolers have found a place on the windowsills of most chapels.

Figure 6.10. The Indian Creek Missionary Baptist Church, Cooke County. Steepleless white frame structures such as this, with front doors in one gable end and four square-topped, clear-glass windows on each side, are the dominant type of Anglo rural church building in the eastern Cross Timbers and all of northern Texas. The church was built about 1875 of imported pine lumber and the congregation was active until the early 1970s. See also Figure 6.11. (Photo: Terry G. Jordan, 1973.)

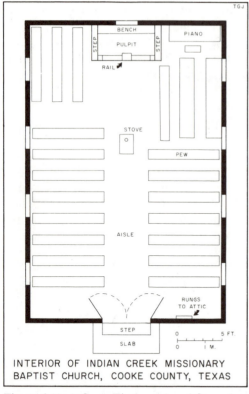

INTERIOR OF INDIAN CREEK MISSIONARY
BAPTIST CHURCH, COOKE COUNTY, TEXAS

Figure 6.11. A Cross Timbers chapel floor plan.

These chapels also express, in the simplest possible terms, the British dissenter Protestant view of a church structure as merely a place of assembly, not God's abode. Here in the Cross Timbers, the British term "chapel goers" still has validity. Indeed, the Old World prototypes of these chapels are to be found in the dissenter districts of Great Britain (Figure 6.12).

And yet in spite of their humble character, many of these structures cost much time, effort, and money to build. Construction of the Indian Creek Church (Figure 6.10) required that its builders purchase imported pine lumber and haul it 30 mi (50 km) overland in ox-drawn wagons from the nearest railhead in the mid-1870s. Typically, such churches were the first rural structures of any description in the Cross Timbers to be of frame rather than of log construction.

In startling contrast are the Romanesque and Gothic cathedrals built by German

Catholics on the North Texas prairie. In this sense, the Cooke County placename Muenster is unintentionally appropriate. Although derived from the Westphalian capital city, the original German meaning is cathedral or minster. For many years the prairie town boasted just that, a splendid red brick Gothic structure with a tower visible for many miles into the surrounding countryside (Figure 6.9). Lindsay is similarly endowed. Only 17 mi (27 km), as the North Texas crow flies, separate the Indian Creek Missionary Baptist Church from St. Peters Catholic Church in Lindsay, but it could just as well be 1,700. A greater contrast could scarcely be imagined than that between the rustic simplicity of the Indian Creek church and the grandeur of Lindsay's cathedral.

The church in Lindsay is the finest surviving example of German architecture in the North Texas area (Figure 6.13). The church building dates from 1918 and is best described as a Romanesque cathedral, far grander than one would expect in a small parish. Its structure is faithful to the Old World Romanesque style in almost every detail, from its red brick walls and red tiled roof to its finely counterbalanced tower and nave and round-topped windows. In the interior, an alternation of round and square pillars flanks the congregation, and the walls and ceiling are decorated in a Romanesque riot of color (Figure 6.14). The only deviation from the prescribed style is the use of hand-painted decoration, simulating colored tiles. Real tile was too expensive for the people of the parish to afford, but the hand painting is a splendid substitute. Filling out the interior are numerous pieces of typical Catholic statuary. The building is abundantly festooned with statues of saints, German-inscribed stained-glass windows, bas-relief murals, carvings, and other miscellaneous symbolism.

This architectural excessiveness on the North Texas prairie is a clear-cut manifestation of the dramatic religion it represents. Its incongruity illustrates Catholicism's overwhelming impact on community

Figure 6.12. A Methodist chapel on the Lleyn Peninsula of Wales, Great Britain, exemplifying the Old World prototype of the southern Anglo-American folk chapel. Compare it to the chapels shown in Figures 6.4 and 6.10. (Photo: Terry G. Jordan, 1974.)

Figure 6.13. A Romanesque church building, St. Peters Catholic Church, with its cemetery, in the German town of Lindsay, Cooke County. The counterbalanced tower and nave, red brick construction, and red tiled roof are all Romanesque traits. (Photo: Terry G. Jordan, 1974.)

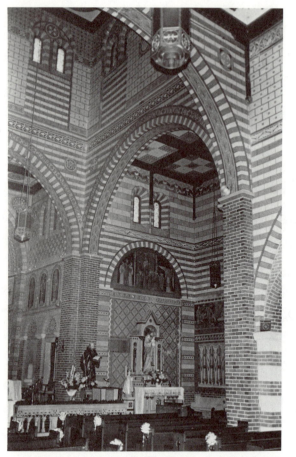

Figure 6.14. Interior of St. Peters Catholic Church in Lindsay. In almost every detail, the decoration is faithful to the central European Romanesque prototype. (Photo: Terry G. Jordan, 1976.)

consciousness. The Lindsay church reflects the desire for a holy place, not just a meeting hall. St. Peters Church would be in place in a German market town with a population of several thousand, yet it is situated in a small Texas town of 500 souls, only 9 mi (14.5 km) from the still-larger Catholic church in Muenster. Even non-Catholics entering the Lindsay cathedral are awe-struck, sensing the air of ritual mystery and communion miracle that the church conveys. Here on the prairie, Christianity is elaborate, here the appeal is to the senses.

The contrasts between the church buildings of the East Cross Timbers and the German Catholic prairie settlements extend beyond architectural style, size, and ornateness. Invariably, the Catholic churches are situated in towns, even if, as at Pilot Point, this means that they are on the periphery of a German-settled area. Typically, they are flanked by a complex of other buildings, such as a parish hall, a school, a rectory, and assorted shrines and grottoes. In Lindsay, an elaborate stone shrine representing the grotto of the Holy Virgin at Lourdes, France, stands directly behind the church. The chapels of the East Cross Timbers, by contrast, are often, or even usually, isolated in pastoral surroundings rather than in towns, and the only other structures present are two wooden outhouses—segregated by sex and distance from each other and by a cold winter's walk from the church—and perhaps a brush-arbor tabernacle for revival meetings.

Landscapes of the Dead

The cemetery is also an integral part of the religious landscape of North Texas, and considerable differences exist among the graveyards of the various church groups in the area. In general, the contrasts parallel those observed for church structures.

The southern folk cemetery of North Texas is distinguished principally by bare earth, with all grass and weeds removed (Figure 6.15). Perhaps this vegetative "scraping" was a reflection of a desire to keep grazing livestock out of the burial grounds, though nearly all Anglo cemeteries are now fenced in. The tradition may also date back to the time when many grave markers were wooden, prompting removal of the grass to prevent fires from destroying them. The origins of this scraping are seemingly not British; instead, the custom is apparently a surviving African tradition. On each grave, the earth is heaped in an elongated mound, both to mark the location and to drain rainwater. The mounding of graves is a British custom and is frequently seen in England. Often the mounds in Texas are decorated with objects such as broken glass, dishes, or shells, which also serve to

Figure 6.15. Bare-earth, mounded southern folk cemetery, typical of the Bible Belt northern half of Texas, including the eastern Cross Timbers. (Photo: John Henry Kothmann, 1978; used with permission.)

protect the mound from raindrop erosion and hinder weed growth (Figure 6.16). The placement of glass, dishes, and shells on graves can be observed in West Africa, and the Texas custom is possibly derived from there. Shells have also been placed on graves in Europe ever since prehistoric times as part of the worship of a life-restoring, mother-fertility goddess. In the Cross Timbers, shells are gathered in freshwater creeks and then boiled to remove dirt and discolorations.

Traditionally, the tasks of removing the grass, building the grave mounds, and decorating the mounds with shells and other objects were performed twice each year, in spring and early autumn, on communal "decoration days." This custom is fading away, and maintenance is now often done by hired workers. The spring decoration day has become mainly a social gathering or reunion rather than a day for work.

The bare-earth graveyards are studded randomly with native cedars (junipers), evergreen symbols of eternal life imported to America in colonial times from the northwestern and central parts of Europe and seemingly traceable to pre-Christian custom. Typically, these cedars have spread with the prevailing winds to dot abandoned fields in the surrounding countryside, and the presence of a cemetery in the East Cross Timbers is often announced by a scattering of cedars as much as a quarter mile (.4 km) distant. Other favorite cemetery plants among the Anglos are iris—symbolic of spring and of Christ's journey into Jerusalem—and crepe myrtle. Rose bushes and nandenas are often present, and occasionally bluebonnets, wild violets, or other planted flowers decorate the graves.

Southern Anglo cemeteries are unsanctified and generally are not adjacent to churches. Even those that are associated

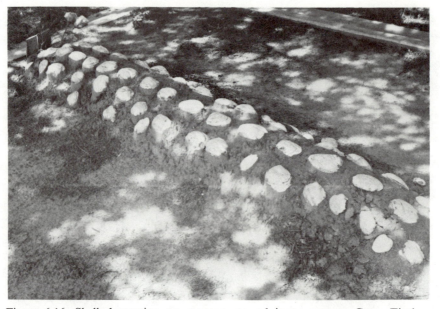

Figure 6.16. Shell decoration on a grave mound in an eastern Cross Timbers cemetery. (Photo: Terry G. Jordan, 1974.)

with particular congregations are sometimes situated as much as half a mile (three-quarters of a km) away from the church building. No particular religious advantage is attached to burial in church-related cemeteries. Many private family cemeteries are found situated in field corners or on hillsides on land originally settled by the family. In the only multidenominational cemetery observed, Baptists are buried in the south end and are separated by a wide open strip from Cumberland Presbyterians in the northeast corner. Each multifamily cemetery is divided into individual family plots.

Gravestones are modest in size, and epitaphs are short and to the point. Many mounded graves have no markers at all. The oldest markers were wooden, and few of them survive. They were succeeded by crudely hewn slabs of native ferrous sandstone, locally called ironstone, upon which was scratched a minimum of information about the deceased (Figure 6.17). Those, in turn, gave way to commercially manufactured stones in a variety of modest

styles. Invariably, the feet of the deceased person lie to the east, as in England, so that he or she might arise from the grave on Judgment Day and be facing Jerusalem. Inscriptions, however, are almost always on the west side of the tombstone.

Family tragedies are not explained in any detail on the tombstones. Rather, the curious passerby is given only hints of what happened, and the imagination must take full rein to reconstruct the unhappy events. In a rural Cross Timbers cemetery in Denton County, for example, a stone marked simply "Hattie Settle" is flanked on each side by three smaller stones inscribed "Hattie's baby." Short verses often appear, such as the hope and plea that a deceased child "budded on earth to bloom in heaven," but biographical data are usually meager. At most there will be a cursory mention of war service, a reminder that the person was "a lifelong Baptist" or a member of the Masons or some other brotherhood, a plaintive cry that he was "murdered," or a fond remark that she was "a loving mother." Birthplaces and dates of migration of the Anglos are hardly ever revealed, perhaps reflecting the American backwoodsman's compulsive mobility and lack of attachment to place. The silence of the stones on the subject of origins seems to say, "It is of no consequence where I was born; my people moved often and we had no roots."

The German Catholic dead of the North Texas prairies rest in a quite different setting, one that bespeaks German orderliness, regimentation, attention to family history, and feeling of community. In Lindsay's typical German Catholic cemetery, the stones are lined up in neat straight rows, like soldiers standing in rank (Figure 6.13). The surface is grass covered and carefully manicured, unbroken by grave mounds and not enclosed by a fence. Husband and wife are permitted to be buried next to one another, but there are no family plots, and the grave sites are otherwise determined by chronological sequence of death. Private family cemeteries are unknown in the Catholic colonies. Children are buried in special rows, distinguished by smaller stones, and fallen soldiers are likewise clustered. Adult markers are usually large and impressive, crowned with stone crosses, and a few are made of metal. Many inscriptions are in the German language, some carved in Teutonic Gothic script, and "hex signs" often flank the epitaph (Figure 6.18). The almost military effect conveyed by the arrangement of the cemetery is further heightened by sentinel-like stations of the cross lining the perimeter of the yard. Even the cedars, present in two of the three Catholic cemeteries, are lined up in neat order rather than strewn about as in the southern Anglo graveyards. All in all, the German Catholic cemetery is a maintenance man's dream, and it speaks to the outsider of order, of a people who desire symmetry and value geometric orderliness.

The German Catholic markers reveal a lot more about the deceased's life and character than do the Anglo markers. Immigrants often are identified by place of birth, and epitaphs list even the person's village

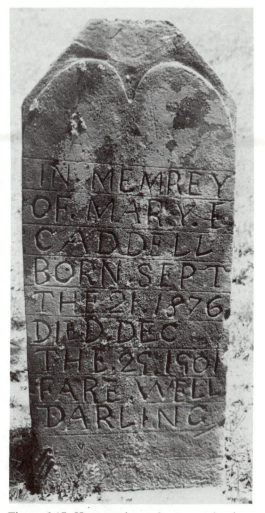

Figure 6.17. Homemade sandstone marker in a rural Denton County graveyard, typical of the folk tombstones of the eastern Cross Timbers. (Photo: Terry G. Jordan, 1980.)

of origin. Such information might best be regarded as symptomatic of a profound homesickness that was never cured, a resistance to being buried in the Texas earth without a parting cry admonishing the passerby, "Do not forget that I was a German, that these alien prairies are no proper resting place for me." Thus we read in the Pilot Point cemetery, in a German already corrupted by English spelling, "Here rests the virtuous young woman and farmer's daughter Rosina Maier, Born 25 Feb. 1882

Figure 6.18. An exquisite hand-carved German tombstone, complete with hex signs, in the German area of South Central Texas. (Photo: Terry G. Jordan, 1978.)

in Auggenbach in Bavaria." Such heartfelt Teutonic cries, intelligible with each passing generation to fewer and fewer kinsmen-descendants, will soon be almost meaningless hieroglyphic scratchings.

The German Catholic graveyards of North Texas invariably lie adjacent to the church complex in town, almost in the shadows of the Romanesque and Gothic towers (Figure 6.13). Although the Catholic immigrant farmers were persuaded to abandon the Old World pattern of clustered farm-village settlement in Texas, they returned to it in death, for the Catholic cemeteries not only lie in the towns, but also resemble villages, lined up as regularly as any central European *Strassendorf.* Let the Anglos scatter their graves across the countryside in family cemeteries and rural church graveyards; the German Catholics demand instead clustered communities of the deceased.

To traverse rural North Texas, then, is to witness not only environmental contrasts, but also pronounced differences in the traditional religious way of life. Catholic Germans came and built holy places and cathedrals on the Texas prairie, a far cry from the humble Cross Timbers board chapels. Europe seems ages removed from the woodland religious landscape, but its imprint is still vivid there on the prairies. And so it is throughout Texas—two religious cultures in juxtaposition, a twofold religious geography.

SOURCES AND SUGGESTED READINGS

Jordan, Terry G. "Church Membership, 1971." In Stanley A. Arbingast et al., *Atlas of Texas,* p. 32. 5th ed. Austin: University of Texas, Bureau of Business Research, 1976.

_____ . "Forest Folk, Prairie Folk: Rural Religious Cultures in North Texas." *Southwestern Historical Quarterly* 80 (1976), 135–162.

_____ . "A Religious Geography of the Hill Country Germans of Texas." In Frederick C. Luebke, ed., *Ethnicity on the Great Plains,* pp. 109–128. Lincoln: University of Nebraska Press, 1980.

_____ . "'The Roses So Red and the Lilies So Fair': Southern Folk Cemeteries in Texas." *Southwestern Historical Quarterly* 83 (1980), 227–258.

_____ . *Texas Graveyards: A Cultural Legacy.* Austin: University of Texas Press, 1982.

_____ . "The Traditional Southern Rural Chapel in Texas." *Ecumene* 8 (1976), 6–17.

Morgan, George R. "Man, Plant, and Religion: Peyote Trade on the Mustang Plains of Texas." Ph.D. dissertation, Department of Geography, University of Colorado, Boulder, 1976.

Newman, William M., and Halvorson, Peter L. *Atlas of Religious Change in America.* Washington, D.C.: Glenmary Research Center, 1978.

_____ . *Patterns in Pluralism: A Portrait of American Religion.* Washington, D.C.: Glenmary Research Center, 1980.

Shortridge, James R. "Patterns of Religion in the United States." *Geographical Review* 66 (1976), 420–434.

Sopher, David E. *Geography of Religions.* Englewood Cliffs, N.J.: Prentice-Hall, 1967.

Tatum, Charles E., and Sommers, Lawrence M. "The Spread of the Black Christian Methodist Episcopal Church in the United States, 1870 to 1970." *Journal of Geography* 74 (1975), 343–357.

Zelinsky, Wilbur. "An Approach to the Religious Geography of the United States." *Annals of the Association of American Geographers* 51 (1961), 139–167.

SOURCES OF QUOTATIONS

Kendall, George Wilkins, *Narrative of the Texan Santa Fé Expedition* (London: Wiley & Putnam, 1844).

CHAPTER **7**

POLITICAL GEOGRAPHY

In voting patterns, ideologies, political systems, and laws, the state of Texas reveals its diverse cultural origins and borderland status. Rarely have the people of Texas been of one mind politically, and even the legal system that governs them reflects a conflict of cultures and internal contradictions.

Perhaps no facet of human endeavor is more revealing of cultural heritage than a free vote of the people on some controversial matter. Sectionalism is the rule rather than the exception in U.S. politics, and Texas has long displayed many of the fundamental political divisions that characterize the country at large. One major facet of this sectionalism, the contrast between plantation South and border South, has greatly influenced Texas politics.

UPPER VERSUS LOWER SOUTH

The old-stock Anglo-American population of Texas, though predominantly southern in origin, has, almost from the very first, been divided by some very basic political differences. In Texas at least, the "solid South" has been more a political illusion than a reality. Repeatedly, for over a century, the basic cultural contrast between people from the hills of the Upper South and those from the plantation states of the Lower South has found political expression and has provided the basis for a deep-rooted sectionalism, a cleavage along the old Texarkana–San Antonio line.

As the United States drifted toward civil war in the months following Lincoln's election in 1860, a political dichotomy rooted in the issue of secession became apparent in the South. The secession movement originated in the Lower South, and by the end of January 1861, the only states that had severed ties with the Union—South Carolina, Georgia, Florida, Alabama, Mississippi, and Louisiana—lay in the coastal plantation belt. Popular sentiment in these lower-southern states ran very strongly in favor of secession, even to the point of near unanimity in some districts. In the Upper South, by contrast, the people were about evenly divided on the secession issue. This lack of consensus can be seen in the fact that only two of the four transmontane upper-southern states, Tennessee and Arkansas, left the union (and even they delayed action until the late spring of 1861), and the other two—Kentucky and Missouri—did not secede. The mountainous western portion of Virginia, also unmistakably a part of the Upper South, rejected the secession decision of plantation-dominated eastern Virginia and reentered the Union as West Virginia.

137

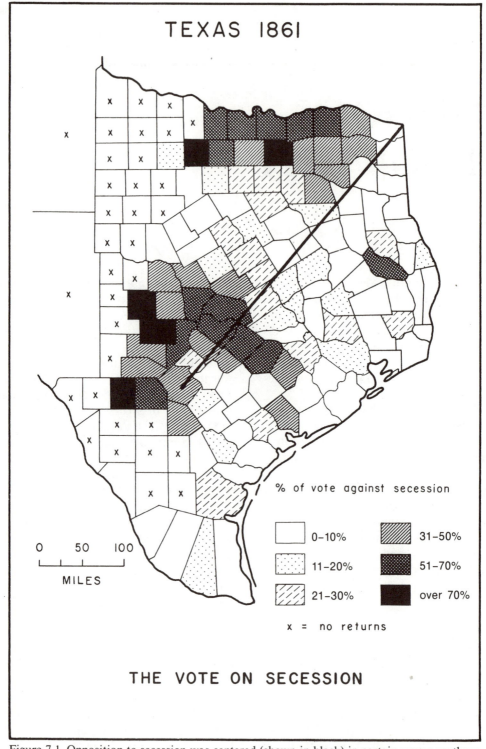

TEXAS 1861

% of vote against secession

- 0–10%
- 11–20%
- 21–30%
- 31–50%
- 51–70%
- over 70%

x = no returns

0   50   100

MILES

THE VOTE ON SECESSION

Figure 7.1. Opposition to secession was centered (shown in black) in certain upper-southern and German counties, west of the Texarkana–San Antonio line. (Source: E. W. Winkler, ed., *Journal of the Secession Convention of Texas, 1861* [Austin: State Library, 1912].)

The issue, then, revealed two different sections: a strongly secessionist Lower South and a politically divided Upper South. This same contrast developed within Texas. In East and Southeast Texas, no notable opposition to secession arose, but in the interior counties, with predominantly upper-southern populations, the issue was hotly debated. The clearest possible expression of this political cleavage was provided by the state's secession referendum held in February 1861. The results revealed that the electorate in lower-southern counties east of the Texarkana–San Antonio line voted very heavily for secession and the people of the upper-southern interior were about evenly divided (Figure 7.1). Overall, only 12 percent of the East Texas electorate opposed withdrawal from the Union, but in counties with upper-southern roots 46 percent opposed it. In twelve different interior counties populated by upper southerners, antisecession majorities, some rather sizable, were recorded. Obviously, many Texans from the Upper South followed their Tennessean governor, Sam Houston, in supporting the Union. In several counties of North Texas, a petition was circulated demanding the separation of that district from Texas and its reentry into the Union as a new state.

In the century and a quarter since the secession issue first demonstrated the east-west division in Anglo-Texas, the upper-southern–lower-southern split has again and again appeared. Early in the twentieth century, the issue of women's suffrage revealed that the division was still viable. The only states that failed to ratify the constitutional amendment extending the vote to women lay in the old coastal southern-plantation zone, and even though Texas ratified the amendment, opposition was very strong in East Texas. Most congressional representatives from eastern and southeastern districts of Texas voted against a resolution favoring women's suffrage that passed in the U.S. House of Representatives in the spring of 1919. More recently, the coastal southern states also failed to ratify the Equal Rights Amendment. Clearly, some element in the lower-southern subculture fosters opposition to female rights.

The third-party presidential candidacy of Alabama Governor George Wallace in 1968, running on the American Independent Party ticket, provides another splendid example of the political distinctiveness of the Lower South. Nationwide, nearly all of the counties carried by Wallace lay in the lower-southern states. Included were several tiers of counties in East Texas, the westernmost appendage of the Lower South (Figure 7.2). Similarly, support for the States' Rights Party in 1948 was strongest in East Texas (see figure, "Selected third-party presidential results," in section on "Texas-German Political Behavior" below). The revived Ku Klux Klan of the 1960s and 1970s also found its greatest strength in East and Southeast Texas.

MIDWESTERNERS

Internal political diversity and sectionalism within the old-stock Anglo-American population are further heightened by the distinctive voting tendencies of people of midwestern descent. The northern part of the Texas Panhandle is the section that has been the most influenced by midwestern immigration. Both ancestry and livelihood tie the wheat farmers of the northern Panhandle more closely to Kansas or Iowa than to the remainder of Texas or the South. They even perceive themselves to be residents of the Midwest.

Not surprisingly, then, voters in the northern Panhandle constitute one of the few Republican strongholds in Texas. Political scientist Douglas Weeks concluded that the Panhandle contains the largest contiguous block of counties "in which the Republican Party makes its best showing," a pattern that has held true ever since grain farmers displaced cattle ranchers in the first two decades of this century (Figure 7.3).

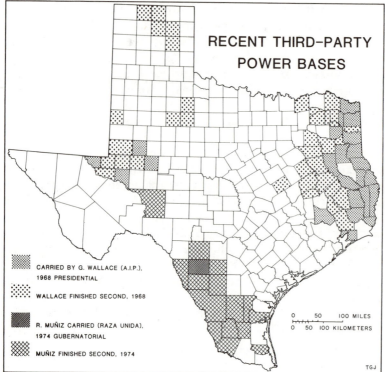

RECENT THIRD–PARTY
POWER BASES

CARRIED BY G. WALLACE (A.I.P.),
1968 PRESIDENTIAL

WALLACE FINISHED SECOND, 1968

R. MUÑIZ CARRIED (RAZA UNIDA),
1974 GUBERNATORIAL

MUÑIZ FINISHED SECOND, 1974

0   50   100 MILES
0 50 100 KILOMETERS

TGJ

Figure 7.2.

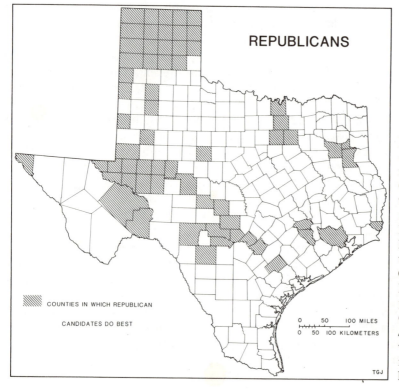

REPUBLICANS

COUNTIES IN WHICH REPUBLICAN

CANDIDATES DO BEST

0   50   100 MILES
0 50 100 KILOMETERS

TGJ

Figure 7.3. The Republican Party traditionally found its strength in the German counties and in the Panhandle where many midwesterners settled. More recently, the party has acquired support in the urban areas. (Based on O. Douglas Weeks, "Texas: Land of Conservative Expansiveness," in *The Changing Politics of the South,* ed. William C. Havard [Baton Rouge: Louisiana State University Press, 1972].)

BLACKS IN
TEXAS POLITICS

Since about 1950, the electoral section-alism rooted in the old-stock Anglo-American population has been further complicated by the emergence of the blacks as a political force. Traditionally denied access to the ballot box by the poll tax, the white-only primary, and a variety of other barriers, the blacks acquired noteworthy political power only after World War II. Since the black population is heavily concentrated in East Texas, the major result of their political activity has been to heighten the electoral distinctiveness of the lower-southern counties.

Studies carried out in the 1960s and

1970s revealed that Texas blacks tended to bloc-vote for Democratic candidates, were ideologically the most liberal group in the state's population, were somewhat less likely to register or turn out to vote than whites, and displayed the highest political alienation level of any group of Texans (Table 7.1). Bloc votes of over 90 percent for liberal Democrats such as Lyndon Johnson, Adlai Stevenson, and Ralph Yarborough are not unusual.

To some degree, the rise of East Texas blacks as liberal Democratic voters has simply reinforced a trait long evident in the lower-southern white population. The People's Party, or Populist movement, in the 1890s found much of its strength among the "poor white" farmers in Piney Woods

Table 7.1. Political Contrasts Between Blacks, Mexican-Americans, and Anglos

	Blacks	Mexican-Americans	Anglos[a]
% perceiving themselves to be "liberal," 1969	47	30	18
% perceiving themselves to be "conservative," 1969	14	23	40
% perceiving themselves to be "highly alienated" politically, 1969	52	36	25
% voting straight-party Democrat, 1969	53	35	16
% usually voting Republican, 1969	3	2	21
% identifying themselves as Democrats, 1969	90	86	53
% identifying themselves as independents, 1969	4	8	19
% registered to vote, Harris County, 1967	47	—	57
% of registered voters actually voting in the Harris County primaries, 1966	35	—	39
% voting for Democratic presidential candidates in Harris County, 1952	94	—	42

[a]"Anglos include all nonblacks and non-Mexicans.
Sources: Chandler Davidson, *Biracial Politics: Conflict and Coalition in the Metropolitan South* (Baton Rouge: Louisiana State University Press, 1972), and Clifton McClesky and Bruce Merrill, "Mexican-American Political Behavior in Texas," *Social Science Quarterly* 53 (1973), 785–798.

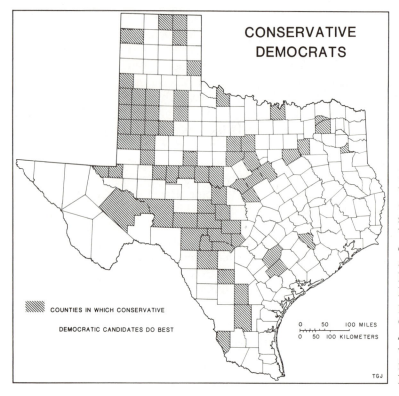

Figure 7.4. The conservative wing of the Democratic Party has been strongest in Central and West Texas among people of upper-southern birth or ancestry. (Based on O. Douglas Weeks, "Texas: Land of Conservative Expansiveness," in *The Changing Politics of the South,* ed. William C. Havard [Baton Rouge: Louisiana State University Press, 1972].)

East Texas counties such as San Augustine, Sabine, Nacogdoches, and Walker. The People's Party, rooted almost exclusively in the old-stock Anglo-American population, also drew strength from some of the poorer upper-southern hill counties of interior Texas, but its main strength lay in the Piney Woods. After the fall of the Populist movement, East Texas poor whites gravitated to the liberal wing of the Democratic Party. In the crossroads stores and on the idlers' benches of the sandy eastern counties, their present-day descendants can still be heard lamenting the fate of the "little man" and the ascendant position of the "fat cats" and coal strippers. Upper-southern Texans, by contrast, do not have much of a liberal tradition and generally support the conservative Democrats (Figure 7.4).

The uneasy, if natural, coalition of blacks and poor whites makes the lower-southern stronghold in East Texas the major power base of liberal Democrats (Figure 7.5). The coalition fails to be effective only if, as in

the case of the Wallace candidacy, populism is linked to racism, or if the liberal candidate happens to be black.

SOUTH TEXAS

South Texas has always been a distinctive political region within the state. Its unique character is rooted in the Hispanic culture and in the traditional economic relationship between Anglos and Mexicans. Until very recently, the politics of South Texas operated within the context of the semifeudal *patrón* system, in which county bosses commanded powerful political machines. In a speech made by Jim Wells, one of the legendary South Texas bosses of the late nineteenth and early twentieth centuries and for whom a county in the region is named, the statement was made that "the Mexican naturally inherited from his ancestors from Spanish rule the idea of looking to the head of the ranch—the place where

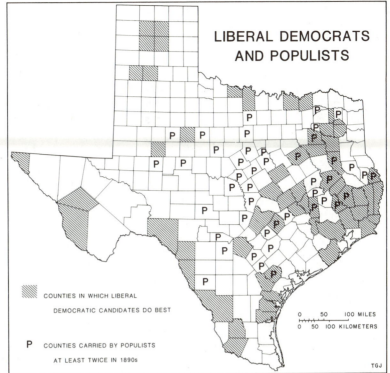

LIBERAL DEMOCRATS
AND POPULISTS

COUNTIES IN WHICH LIBERAL
DEMOCRATIC CANDIDATES DO BEST

P   COUNTIES CARRIED BY POPULISTS
AT LEAST TWICE IN 1890s

0   50   100 MILES
0   50   100 KILOMETERS

TGJ

Figure 7.5. The liberal wing of the Democratic Party and its Populist predecessor have traditionally been strongest in East Texas among small farmers of lower-southern birth or ancestry, particularly poor whites in the sandy counties. More recently, East Texas blacks and border-county Mexican-Americans have joined the liberal Democratic coalition. (Based on O. Douglas Weeks, "Texas: Land of Conservative Expansiveness," in *The Changing Politics of the South,* ed. William C. Havard [Baton Rouge: Louisiana State University Press, 1972], and Roscoe C. Martin, *The People's Party in Texas* [Austin: University of Texas, 1933].)

he lived and got his living—for guidance and direction." In the latter half of the nineteenth century, the Mexican landed aristocracy of South Texas was largely displaced by Anglos, but the older, colonial Hispanic *patrón-peón* relationship endured. Anglo ranch owners controlled county politics through the votes of their Mexican employees. Typically, the *patrón* paid the poll tax of his workers, permitted illegal aliens to vote, and marked the ballots for illiterate or non-English-speaking employees. In some cases, he tampered with vote tabulations.

In exchange, the *peón* received from the *patrón*, generation after generation, job security, favors, and assistance in time of illness or disability. An analogy to the feudal system or the Mafia is not far-fetched, and the bosses even bore the honorific title of

don. In making the transition to the modern era, bosses have handed out jobs in the irrigated market gardens, on county highway crews, or in the food-processing factories, in addition to the traditional ranch employment.

Centered in the counties of Cameron, Hidalgo, Starr, Willacy, Duval, Kenedy, and Kleberg, the *patrón* system was important to some degree in most of South Texas. Challenged by progressives and reformers, among whom were included many midwesterners who settled in the Rio Grande Valley after 1910, some vestiges of the system nonetheless survive today. In some thinly populated ranching counties, the *patrón* still delivers the vote in the traditional manner. For the most part, though, a rather different political order now prevails in South Texas. The great majority of Mexican-Americans now function as independent voters, and most municipal and county offices are held by people with Spanish surnames. Even as early as the 1920s, all officeholders in Zapata County were of Mexican origin, but that was probably more a reflection of the fact that the landowner *patrónes* there were also Hispanic than a harbinger of true democracy.

The real political awakening of the Mexican element in South Texas occurred in the 1960s, when, in a bitter struggle, control of the local government of Crystal City in Zavala County was wrested away from the Anglo minority. One product of the Crystal City episode was the birth of the Raza Unida, possibly the only ethnic political party in U.S. history (Figure 7.2). Ramsey Muñiz, running for governor on the Raza Unida Party ticket in 1974, carried only Zavala County, the party's place of origin, but he finished second in most other counties of South Texas.

Most Raza Unida successes have been on the local and county levels, and the party is now in decline. The great majority of Mexican-Americans vote Democratic, and the most purely Hispanic counties along the Rio Grande are the only ones in Texas that have never failed to provide majorities for the Democratic presidential candidates in the twentieth century. Even so, compared to the Texas black, the Mexican-American is less liberal, more conservative, less alienated, and much less likely to vote a straight Democratic ticket (Table 7.1). Zapata County, probably the most traditional Mexican county in Texas, consistently supports conservative Democratic candidates, but the majority of the Mexican-dominated counties provide part of the liberal Democratic power base. Counting Democrats of both persuasions and members of the Raza Unida, more than 700 elected Spanish-surnamed officials held office in Texas by 1971. Impressive as this figure sounds, it still represents the lowest per capita representation among the state's three major ethnic groups.

TEXAS-GERMAN POLITICAL BEHAVIOR

The Texas political mosaic also reflects the presence of European ethnic minorities, particularly Germans. Ten predominantly German counties in South Central Texas—Austin, Comal, DeWitt, Fayette, Gillespie, Guadalupe, Kendall, Lee, Medina, and Washington—have consistently displayed a political individuality ever since the immigrant ancestors of the present inhabitants began participating in the political process.

The most fundamental political trait of the Texas Germans is conservatism, which is rooted both in their prosperity and in a Saxon peasant tradition derived from the fatherland. In a state where conservatism is the norm, the Germans constitute the extreme. Lacking the populism of the Anglo poor or the liberal Democratic ties of the Mexicans and blacks, the Germans are consistently and almost unanimously conservative. A small liberal minority of "Forty-Eighter" political refugees and intellectuals, which flourished among the Texas Germans in the mid-nineteenth century, was long ago absorbed and extinguished, leaving behind only a few reminders, such as the only Texas monument to Union Civil War dead (Figure 7.6).

One major expression of the Germans' conservatism has been their loyalty to the Republican Party throughout the twentieth century. Their deep attachment to Republicanism dates to about 1896, when the party acquired its conservative image. Recognizing that Texas is basically a Democratic state, the Germans normally vote in the Democratic primary, supporting the conservative candidates. In the November elections, the Germans back the conservative Democrat if no Republican is on the ticket. In more than one statewide election, the conservative Democratic margin provided by the ten German counties has caused the liberal candidate to lose. Among the conservative Democrats who owed their victory margin to the Texas

Figure 7.6. Monument to the Union dead in the small German town of Comfort, Kendall County. No other Union monuments exist in Texas. Local Germans, many of whom were university-educated intellectuals, organized a pro-Union volunteer unit and sought to reach Mexico and the North. Confederate militia intercepted them, killing or capturing most of the force at the Battle of the Nueces in 1862. The inscription reads, in German, "loyal to the Union," and the names of the dead appear on other sides of the monument. (Photo: Terry G. Jordan, taken on the occasion of the centennial anniversary of Texas secession, 1961.)

Germans were W. Lee O'Daniel, in the U.S. Senate special election of 1941, and Price Daniel, in the Democratic gubernatorial primary in 1956.

A classic example of the conservative Republican preference of the Texas Germans occurred in the 1978 election for U.S. senator, which pitted liberal Democrat Robert Krueger against Republican John Tower. Krueger, a Texas German descended from the earliest settlers of New Braunfels, was unable to carry any of the German counties, not even his home county of Comal. Ideology overcame the natural affinity of German voters for candidates with Teutonic surnames and violated the friends-and-neighbors principle, one of the time-honored spatial concepts of political science (Table 7.2). The Krueger loss in his home county and surrounding districts is even more astounding in light of the fact that people with Spanish surnames, who generally supported him, constitute a quarter or more of the local population. The German rejection of one of their own was almost total.

An equally astounding result was produced in the 1960 presidential election in German-dominated Gillespie County, centered on Fredericksburg. Lyndon Johnson, the Democratic vice-presidential candidate, was a *native* and *resident* of Gillespie County. His running mate, John F. Kennedy, was, in common with about one-third of the Germans in Gillespie County, Roman Catholic. Yet the Republican Nixon carried the county with a 76 percent majority (Table 7.2).

Another political trait of the Texas Germans has been their persistent loyalty to certain individuals, generally men they perceive to be strong, decisive leaders. Theodore Roosevelt, for example, was immensely popular among them, and they followed him, even on the third-party Bull-moose ticket in the presidential election of 1912. His portrait continued to hang in some Texas-German homes as late as the

1950s. Jim ("Pa") Ferguson, scandal-ridden governor of Texas in the World War I era, was another strong leader who always claimed the German vote. He had initially attracted the Germans through his opposition to prohibition and the Ku Klux Klan, and they continued to support him even after he was impeached for corruption.

A lingering attachment to Germany has also played a role in the politics of Texas Germans. Woodrow Wilson became their archfiend for taking the country to war against Germany, and Progressive Robert La Follette of Wisconsin, whose liberal ideology and French surname were anathema to the Germans, nonetheless received their support in his third-party Progressive bid for the presidency in 1924 because he had earlier opposed the U.S. entry into World War I (Table 7.2 and Figure 7.7). Similarly, W. Lee O'Daniel's opposition to lend-lease aid for Britain in 1939 and 1940 contributed to the winning margin he built up in the German counties in the special election for the U.S. Senate in 1941. By the 1950s, this attachment to Germany had weakened to the extent that Dwight Eisenhower, leader of the Allied military conquest of the Third Reich, attracted almost unanimous support from the Texas Germans. Eisenhower was no doubt aided by his German surname and conservative Republican affiliation.

The Germans' Republican preference, coupled with their tendency to support "maverick" candidates on third-party tickets, has caused them, historically, to be generally on the losing side in Texas elections (Table 7.2). Only recently has Texas become a true two-party state, permitting the German element to become part of an increasingly successful conservative Republican power bloc. In the 1978 governor's race, for example, conservative Republican Bill Clements defeated middle-of-the-road Democrat John Hill by forging a coalition of middle-class urbanities, Germans, Panhandle midwesterners, oil-field residents,

Table 7.2. The Voting Record of a Dominantly German-American County

Year	Vote	Gillespie County	Remainder of Texas
		(% of votes cast)	
1861	In favor of secession from the Union	4	74
1912	President, for Theodore Roosevelt (Bullmoose)	67	9
1924	President, for Robert La Follette (Progressive)	58	7
1940	President, for Wendell Willkie (Republican)	87	19
1948	Primary, U.S. Senate, for Lyndon Johnson	14	50
1954	Primary, Governor, for Allan Shivers (Conservative Democrat)	90	53
1960	President, for Kennedy-Johnson (Democratic)	24	51
1970	Governor, for Paul Eggers (Republican)	60	46
1976	President, for Gerald Ford (Republican)	74	48
1978	U.S. Senate, for Robert Krueger (Democrat)	32	49

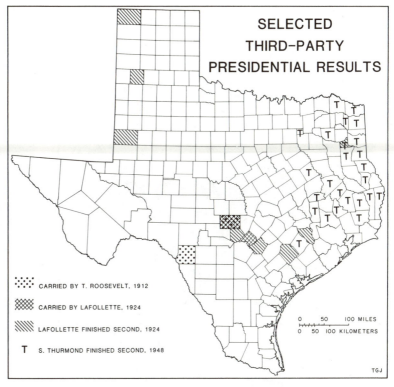

Figure 7.7. The support for third-party presidential candidates Theodore Roosevelt on the Bull-moose ticket in 1912 and Robert La Follette on the Progressive ticket in 1924 was concentrated in the German counties of South Central Texas. Strom Thurmond's States' Rights candidacy in 1948 fared best in East Texas, the old lower-southern stronghold.

and even one South Texas Mexican *patrón*ship. Texas Germans now belong to what may be an emerging Republican majority, part of the political mainstream at last. The important point is that it is the remainder of the Texans, not the Germans, who have changed. Their inherent Saxon conservatism survives intact.

THE ALCOHOL ISSUE

Perhaps no other political issue has so divided Texas or so clearly revealed a political cleavage within the state as prohibition. Essentially it has been a contest between the Bible Belt northern half of Texas and the Catholic/Lutheran southern part (Figure 7.8). Local-option laws—under which each county, precinct, or municipality can accept or reject the sale of beer, wine, distilled spirits, and liquor by the drink—provide a splendid vehicle for political sectionalism. The result has been a pattern that parallels the distribution of

the major religious denominations (Figure 6.1). The conflict zone at present is the Bible Belt, where proliquor forces endeavor to create more and more "oases" where liquor may be purchased, sometimes by incorporating mobile-home parks or municipal enclaves (Figure 7.9).

Traditionally, though, the "wet-dry" battle was fought on the statewide level. In the nineteenth and early twentieth centuries, leaders of the temperance movement campaigned repeatedly to make alcoholic beverages illegal in the entire state. One referendum followed another, invariably revealing the north-south split. In ethnic terms, the antialcohol forces were based in the old-stock Anglo-American population, aided by the Norwegians (whose ancestors had come to Texas with temperance leader Johan Reierson), the Swedes (many of whom had converted to Methodism), and the Danes. Aligned against them, on the wet side, were the Mexicans, Germans, Czechs, Poles, and Cajun French. A typical election

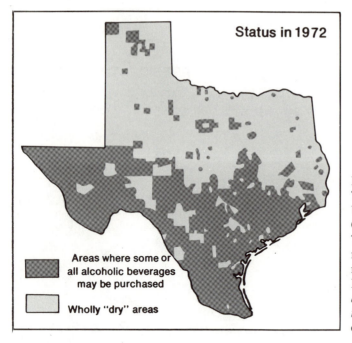

Figure 7.8. Map of "wet" and "dry" Texas. The legal sale of alcoholic beverages is concentrated in the Catholic/Lutheran southern half of Texas, and the Bible Belt north remains largely dry. (Copied, with permission, from Terry G. Jordan and Lester Rowntree, *The Human Mosaic: A Thematic Introduction to Cultural Geography,* 1st ed. [San Francisco: Canfield Press, 1976], p. 254.)

Figure 7.9. An indication of the wet-dry issue in North Texas. When the owners of a rural weekend property development attempted to legalize the sale of alcoholic beverages for the benefit of their Dallas-based clientele, the local Bible Belt Calvinists rose as one to smite "demon rum." The area remains dry today. (Photo: Terry G. Jordan at Indian Creek in Cooke County, election day, 1972.)

result in a German district, for example, was the 1887 vote in Gillespie County, where the wets won 1,186 to 59, a result almost exactly duplicated in 1914 when the margin was 1,220 to 80. Another great statewide election fight over the sale of alcohol occurred in 1970, when the wet forces in the south narrowly passed a constitutional amendment that legalized local-option liquor by the drink in restaurants and private clubs.

Interestingly, the manufacturing and distribution of illegal whiskey is heavily concentrated in dry northern Texas, in the same Bible Belt counties where the prohibitionist sentiment is based (Figure 7.10). The old southern pattern of voting dry and manufacturing wet certainly holds true for the old-stock southern portion of Texas. Blacks and whites alike, mainly of lower-southern ancestry, are engaged in the moonshine industry. As might be expected, illegal stills are most common in the thickly forested East Texas counties, but some have even been discovered on the open expanses of the High Plains. The industry finds its support in the southern folk preference for homemade corn whiskey and the populist hatred of government taxation.

POLITICAL CULTURE REGIONS

The preceding discussion of electoral sectionalism within Texas can be summed up in a map of political regions (Figure 7.11). These regions reflect, to a considerable degree, the cultural/ethnic patterns described in Chapter 4. Lower-southern, upper-southern, midwestern, German, and Mexican-American cultures each find a political expression. The Panhandle midwestern region is characterized by traditional Republican strength, paralleled by conservative Democratic sentiment. In East Texas, the lower-southern region has found political distinctiveness in strongly secessionist and prohibitionist stands, opposition to women's rights, support for populism and the liberal Democrats, a greater

Figure 7.10. The manufacture of moonshine whiskey is concentrated almost entirely in the legally dry counties of the Bible Belt northern half of Texas, particularly in the Piney Woods. (Sources: *Annual Report* of the Texas Liquor Control Board, 1939–1969, and *Annual Report* of the Texas Alcoholic Beverage Commission, 1970–1979.)

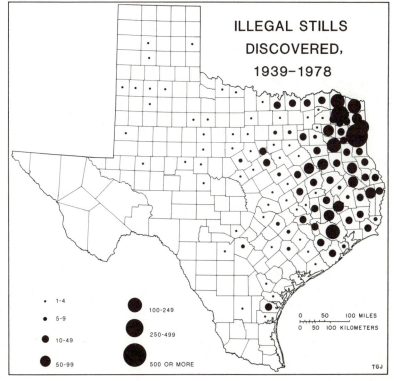

ILLEGAL STILLS DISCOVERED, 1939–1978

1-4
5-9
10-49
50-99
100-249
250-499
500 OR MORE

0   50   100 MILES
0   50   100 KILOMETERS

TGJ

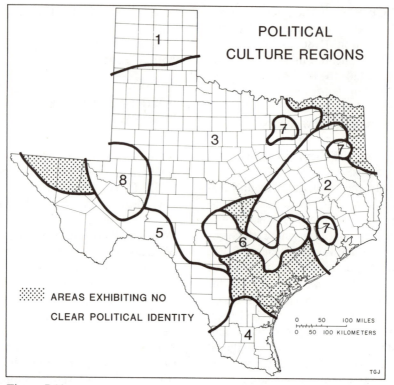

Figure 7.11.
Key: 1 = Panhandle midwestern traditional Republican; 2 = lower-southern Populist and liberal Democratic; 3 = upper-southern conservative Democratic; 4 = Hispanic traditional *patrón* system; 5 = Hispanic liberal Democratic and Raza Unida; 6 = German traditional Republican and conservative Democratic; 7 = suburban conservative Republican; 8 = Permian Basin oil field conservative Republican.

tendency to support third-party populist or racist candidates of the States' Rights and American Independent parties, and the illegal manufacture of whiskey. The upper-southern counties, in an extensive belt from the Blackland Prairie west to New Mexico, provide the main power base of the conservative Democrats. The Hispanic borderland is divided into two political regions, including (1) the focus of the traditional *patrón* system in far South Texas, where a number of huge ranches survive, and (2) the liberal Democratic/ Raza Unida region in Southwest Texas, a product of the Hispanic political awakening of the 1960s. In South Central Texas, the German counties form an ultraconservative bastion of traditional Republican and con-

servative Democratic power. On more than one occasion, the relatively small German region has decided statewide elections in favor of the conservative forces. The German counties have strongly opposed prohibition, the Ku Klux Klan, and populism. Of more recent origin are regions of conservative Republican strength in suburban areas and in the huge Permian Basin oil field.

LEGAL SYSTEMS

The internal diversity of ideology, party preference, and voting behavior is compounded and intensified by the state's legal system, which has had to accommodate two very different heritages. In effect, Texans are governed by a system descended from a "shotgun marriage" of English common law and Hispanic law. The latter system, based largely on the ancient and medieval traditions of Roman law and Islamic law, was implanted in Texas in the seventeenth century under Spanish rule and survived intact until 1840, when the newly independent Republic of Texas introduced English common law, a system with deep roots in the traditions of Germanic peoples.

Confusion might not have resulted had the leaders of the Republic simply replaced Hispanic law with common law, but instead they attempted a grafting. The constitution of the Republic provided that all laws already in use "and not inconsistent with this constitution" would remain in force. Subsequent constitutions have had similar provisions. The legal ambiguities and confusion that have resulted have provided employment for thousands of lawyers in the last century and a half and promise to do so for generations of barristers yet unborn.

This overlay of two very different legal systems has produced the greatest amount of confusion and litigation in the areas of land and water law. Fully 15 percent of the land area of Texas was granted to private individuals before 1836 under Hispanic law. One reason for not simply discarding Hispanic law was the desire to safeguard these Spanish and Mexican land titles, many of which were held by Anglo-Americans. The remainder of the public domain in Texas has passed into private hands under English common law, tinged only slightly by such Hispanic features as the use of the *vara* as the standard unit of linear measure.

Hispanic law and common law have very different traditions concerning water rights. Land grants made in Texas under Hispanic law were of three types: *de agostadero*, large ranching grants permitting only a "right of thirst" for livestock; *de temporal*, grants for dry farming; and *de riego*, small grants for irrigation farming, including deed rights to the necessary water. Only holders of *de riego* property had the legal right to divert water from a stream onto their land. Moreover, this diversion was to occur only as part of an organized irrigation system, governed by the local authorities. English common law, by contrast, guarantees riparian rights. Under this system, the owner of the banks of a stream is entitled to use a reasonable amount of that stream's water for any purpose. A collision of the two traditions was inevitable.

In the border county of Hidalgo, on the Rio Grande, the huge Valmont Plantations began drawing water from the river to irrigate citrus, cotton, and other crops. The county water control board protested, claiming that Valmont was taking water without proper authorization, free of charge. Valmont's lawyers argued in court that riparian rights under common law entitled the enterprise to irrigate. Attorneys for the water control board countered with the charge that the land owned by Valmont had originally been of the *de agostadero* type under Hispanic law and did not entitle the owner to use water for irrigation. Ultimately, the courts ruled that land grants made under Hispanic law remained subject to that tradition and that grants made under English common law possessed riparian rights. In this manner, a jigsaw legal geography was imposed upon the state. Valmont Plantations found itself under the jurisdiction of the county water control board and henceforth had to pay for the right to irrigate.

In many other facets of the complicated Texas legal structure, Hispanic law prevails over common law. The concept of community property in marriage, under which the wife owns half of all property, is of Hispanic origin and is much more favorable to women than common law. In Texas, Hispanic law also makes it more difficult to disinherit children, exempts certain property from confiscation if taxes are delinquent, and entitles the state to offshore mineral rights that would otherwise belong to the U.S. federal government.

Legally and electorally, then, Texas presents a vivid mosaic, a distinct and multiple sectionalism. Ethnic and cultural contrasts are at the root of much of this diversity. In addition, however, forms of livelihood are partly related to the political patterns, as in the small, sandy-land farmers' support for populism and liberal Democrats. Such agricultural contrasts within Texas are discussed in the next chapters.

SOURCES AND SUGGESTED READINGS

Davidson, Chandler. *Biracial Politics: Conflict and Coalition in the Metropolitan South.* Baton Rouge: Louisiana State University Press, 1972.

Dobkins, Betty E. *The Spanish Element in Texas Water Law.* Austin: University of Texas Press, 1959.

McClesky, Clifton, and Merrill, Bruce. "Mexican-American Political Behavior in Texas." *Social Science Quarterly* 53 (1973), 785–798.

McKay, Seth S. *Texas Politics, 1906–1944, with Special Reference to the German Counties.* Lubbock: Texas Tech Press, 1952.

Madla, Frank L. "The Political Impact of Latin Americans and Negroes in Texas Politics." M.A. thesis, St. Mary's University, San Antonio, Texas, 1964.

Martin, Roscoe C. *The People's Party in Texas.* Bulletin no. 3308. Austin: University of Texas, 1933.

Peirce, Neal R. "Texas: Land of the Monied 'Establishments.' " In *The Megastates of America: People, Politics, and Power in the Ten Great States,* pp. 495–563. New York: W. W. Norton, 1972.

Shelton, Edgar G., Jr. *Political Conditions Among Texas Mexicans Along the Rio Grande.* San Francisco: R & E Research Associates, 1974.

Shockley, John S. *Chicano Revolt in a Texas Town.* Notre Dame, Ind.: Notre Dame University Press, 1974.

Smyrl, Frank H. "Unionism in Texas, 1856–1861." *Southwestern Historical Quarterly* 68 (1964), 172–195.

Weeks, O. Douglas. "Texas: Land of Conservative Expansiveness." In *The Changing Politics of the South,* ed. William C. Havard, pp. 201–230. Baton Rouge: Louisiana State University Press, 1972.

————. "The Texas-Mexican and the Politics of South Texas." *American Political Science Review* 24 (1930), 606–627.

CHAPTER 8

AGRICULTURAL GEOGRAPHY

The versatility of agricultural activity in Texas is encouraged by the great variety of environmental regions and by the assortment of cultures. From the time of the early Indian tribes, such as the Caddo of northeastern Texas and Jumano of the upper Rio Grande floodplain, agriculture has been practiced by varied peoples in diverse environmental settings. Certainly the vast areas of flat land and fertile soils, coupled with a long growing season, have inspired Texans to engage in agriculture in nearly every portion of the state (Figure 8.1). At the same time, the contrasts in environment have encouraged agricultural diversity, as have the several contributions of the Spaniards, Mexicans, blacks, Anglos, Orientals, and Europeans to farming and herding. Through hard work, trial and error, luck and ingenuity, invention and innovation, the different cultures have collaborated to establish agricultural productivity as the nucleus and agricultural diversity as the hallmark of the Texas economy. The agricultural geography of the state is perhaps best presented by describing the major regional types (Figure 8.2).

ANIMAL INDUSTRY

LIVESTOCK RANCHING

According to the stereotyped view of Texas, ranching is *the* type of agriculture,

and the traditional importance of this livestock raising system in the state has been very great. Texas received, prior to 1850, implantations of both a Hispanic ranching system, derived mainly from Mexico, and a creolized herding culture—of British, African, and Spanish origin—from the American South. The Hispanic and southern systems of open-range herding fused to produce the colorful cattle ranching culture that briefly dominated the Great Plains and subsequently evolved into the modern, fenced-range type that still prevails in much of the state. In the Hill Country and on the Edwards Plateau, Mexican, German, Anglo, and British influences combined to produce a distinctive ranching economy based on sheep and goats (Figure 8.2).

The continuing importance of livestock ranching is suggested by the fact that in 1980, Texas, as in many previous years, continued to lead the nation in the number of cattle, sheep and lambs, Angora goats, and beef cows that calved. In a typical year during the decade of the 1970s, livestock and related products accounted for slightly more than 50 percent of the income paid to Texas farmers and ranchers. Of this, some 38 percent was from meat animals, 5.5 percent from dairy products, and 6.2 percent from poultry and related products. In 1979 the sale of livestock products brought Texans more than $6 billion, accounting for more than 60 percent of all income paid to farmers and ranchers, and

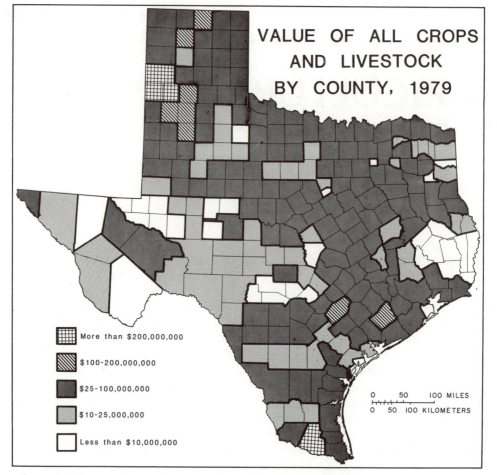

Figure 8.1. Source: Texas Crop and Livestock Reporting Service.

livestock ranching accounted for most of this income.

Cattle Ranching

On January 1, 1981, there were 13,700,000 head of cattle and calves in Texas, and 11,550,000 of them were range animals. Every county in Texas produces some cattle, and at the time of the 1981 survey, all counties had at least 4,000 head, and only eighteen counties counted fewer than 10,000 head. Cattle are raised in every physical region. Hudspeth County, located in the desert region of far western Texas, had 23,000 head, and Cass County, in the humid, subtropical Piney Woods, had 44,000 head. Brazoria County, on the Coastal Prai-

rie, housed 67,000 head; Sherman County, in the northern High Plains, counted 93,000; Kimble County, on the Edwards Plateau, had 25,000 head; and Lamb County, located in the South Plains (Llano Estacado) was home to 66,000 cattle. Even in the three largest urban counties—Harris, Bexar, and Dallas—there was an aggregate of 139,000 cattle in January 1981 (Figure 8.3). The distribution of cattle across Texas was even enough that the ten largest producing counties accounted for only 12.9 percent of all cattle. The distribution of beef cattle generally conforms to the availability and carrying capacity of the range grasses. Therefore the greatest concentration of range cattle occurs in the counties of the Black-

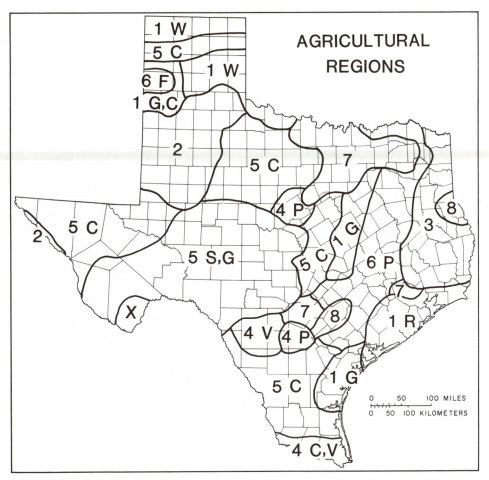

Figure 8.2.

1 = commercial grain farming: W = wheat, R = rice, G = grain sorghum, C = corn
2 = neoplantation: commercial fiber farming
3 = neoplantation: woodland plantation
4 = market gardening: C = citrus, V = vegetables, P = peanuts
5 = livestock ranching: C = cattle, S = sheep, G = goats
6 = livestock fattening: F = feedlots, P = pasture fattening
7 = dairying
8 = poultry raising
X = no appreciable agriculture

land and Coastal prairies, where water is abundant, and forage is not only luxuriant, but nutritious as well. The density of animals per unit area declines proportionally as available forage diminishes toward the west and northwest across the state.

It is probable that the early Spanish explorers who crossed the Rio Grande brought with them some cattle and sheep for food, just as they brought horses for transportation, but records were not kept until the late 1600s, when the mission system spread across southern and eastern Texas. Each mission reserved land for cattle, sheep, horses, and mules in addition to parcels of land set aside for cultivation. The larger missions, especially those that formed the San Antonio complex after 1724, were capable of supporting numerous small perimeter ranches that radiated in all directions from the main mission. A similar pattern developed around Mission La Bahia

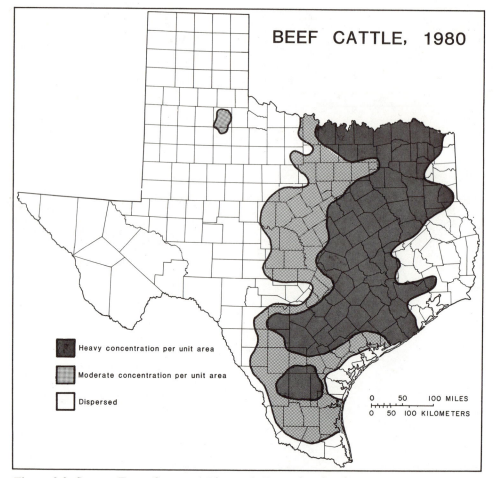

Figure 8.3. Source: Texas Crop and Livestock Reporting Service.

del Espiritu Santo, which ultimately became the settlement of Goliad, the county seat of Goliad County, in 1749.

After 1750 numerous Spanish cattlemen moved their herds into the Rio Grande, Nueces, and San Antonio valleys. Tomas Sanchez located his herd near Laredo, and Enrique de Villareal developed his Rincon del Oso Ranch on 400 sq mi (1,036 sq km) granted to him along Corpus Christi Bay. Blas Maria de la Garza Falcon's Rancho Santa Petronilla was also near Corpus Christi. Antonio Gil Ibarbo located large herds in East Texas around Nacogdoches. In the 1740s seventeen ranching families settled north of the Rio Grande, and by 1750 many of these were among the first

to move their herds to the Coastal Prairie between the Nueces and Guadalupe rivers. Meanwhile, the settlements of Dolores and Laredo on the Rio Grande became headquarters for many other Spanish ranches. The herds of Andalusian cattle grew in number, became increasingly less domesticated, and by 1820 ranged as thousands of wild cattle in the Brush Country of southern Texas.

While the Spanish were introducing their cattle of Iberian ancestry into Mexico and southern Texas, the early colonists from northwestern Europe were introducing their breeds of cattle to eastern North America and evolving an open-range cattle culture in South Carolina. Their descendants brought cattle herds to East Texas during the 1820s, spreading along the Coastal Prairie, Blackland Prairie, and Piney Woods (Figure 8.4). The Texas cattle herds increased to the degree that in the mid-1830s, the estimated cattle population in the Department of Brazos and Nacogdoches had risen to over 75,000 head. The multiethnic character of early Texas cattle ranching is suggested by the diverse origins of the major stockmen. James Taylor White (Leblanc), a Cajun from Louisiana, owned the largest herds east of the Trinity River by 1830, though he was soon rivaled by the "red-bone" Ashworths—South Carolinians of mixed white, black, and Indian ancestry. Thomas O'Connor, an Irishman from Wexford County, became the leading rancher in the Coastal Bend country north of Corpus Christi in the 1840s, and the German Klebergs later helped build the famous King Ranch in South Texas.

After the Civil War, cattle ranching exploded westward to occupy most of the semiarid portion of Texas, particularly the grasslands of the Great Plains (Figure 8.5). Many foreigners, particularly the British, invested millions of dollars in the range

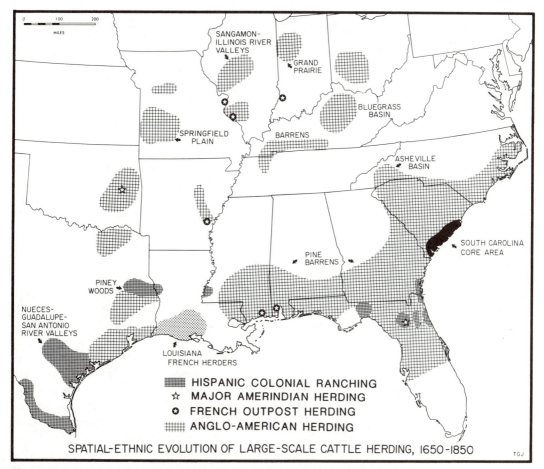

Figure 8.4. Texas cattle ranching represents a blending of Hispanic, British, French, and African traits. Colonial South Carolina served as the nucleus of a British-African cattle culture that was ultimately introduced into Texas by southerners coming from the east. (Reprinted, by permission, from Terry G. Jordan, *Trails to Texas* [Lincoln: University of Nebraska Press, 1981], p. 40; copyright © 1981 by the University of Nebraska Press.)

Figure 8.5. Hereford cattle on a ranch near the town of Canadian in Hemphill County. (Photo: Texas Highway Department.)

cattle industry as they set about to purchase as many ranches as possible. Of the thirty-seven British ranches developed on the Great Plains, seventeen were in Texas. Some of these were the Prairie Cattle Company; the Capitol Freehold Land and Investment Company, which bought the XIT Ranch; Matador Ranch; Spur Ranch; Francklyn; Rocking Chair; the JA Ranch of Charles Goodnight; and Mifflin Kenedy's Los Laureles. Between 1875 and 1890, British investment in the cattle industry amounted to more than $40 million, but the investors received only $15 million in return. They invested heavily and lost heavily, but the Texas cattle industry was totally revamped as a result of the British influence. The British helped make ranching a business. They kept good records, introduced pure-bred livestock to upgrade herds, fenced and cross-fenced ranges, improved water supplies through the introduction of the wind-mill, and required better range management. After 1890 many of the later West

Texas ranches were subdivided and sold to farmers and smaller-scale ranchers, and the traditional range cattle industry gradually evolved into the present system. The Texas cattle inventory of 1900 revealed 9,428,196 head of cattle, valued at $163,228,904. It was not until 1963 that the cattle census totaled more than 10 million head, and 1975 was the peak year, with 16.6 million head reported. The 13.7 million head in Texas on January 1, 1981, had a value of $5 billion.

In West Texas, the cattle ranching industry retained its multiethnic character. Not only was ranch ownership divided among various European and American groups, but also the work force, the cowboys, came from varied cultural backgrounds. Southern Anglos, blacks, and Hispanos alike rode the western range by 1880, again reflecting the creolized character of Texas cattle ranching (Figure 8.6).

The range cattle industry in Texas was the nucleus around which the economy of

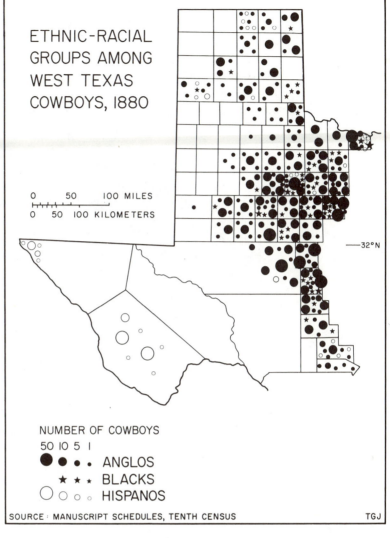

ETHNIC-RACIAL
GROUPS AMONG
WEST TEXAS
COWBOYS, 1880

0   50   100 MILES

0   50   100 KILOMETERS

—32°N

NUMBER OF COWBOYS
50 10 5 1
● ● • · ANGLOS
★ ★ ⋆ BLACKS
○ ○ ○ ○ HISPANOS

SOURCE: MANUSCRIPT SCHEDULES, TENTH CENSUS   TGJ

Figure 8.6. The figure shows the spread of the cattle industry and the ethnically diverse nature of its work force by 1880. (Reprinted, by permission, from Terry G. Jordan, *Trails to Texas* [Lincoln: University of Nebraska Press, 1981], p. 145; copyright © 1981 by the University of Nebraska Press.)

the state developed, and it represented a source of wealth for anyone who had the fortitude to meet the fickle environment and uncertain markets head on and turn one year's financial reversal into the next year's profit. The industry encompassed all of the physical regions of Texas, enticed all of the state's cultures to participate, and perhaps was the thread of unity that linked the early border province together.

Sheep and Goat Ranching

Credit for the introduction of sheep and goats into Texas belongs to the Spaniards,

and it was they who founded the sheep ranching industry that thrived in the Laredo area as late as the 1880s. The ranching system that endured, however, lay further north, on the Edwards Plateau and in its eastern fringe, the Hill Country (Figure 8.7). There, New Englanders, midwesterners, Germans, Mexicans, and Britishers introduced a distinctive system of mixed ranching, based largely on sheep and goats, between about 1845 and 1890. Reflective of this diverse heritage, the largest sheep and goat ranches in the region were developed near Kerrville by, respectively, an

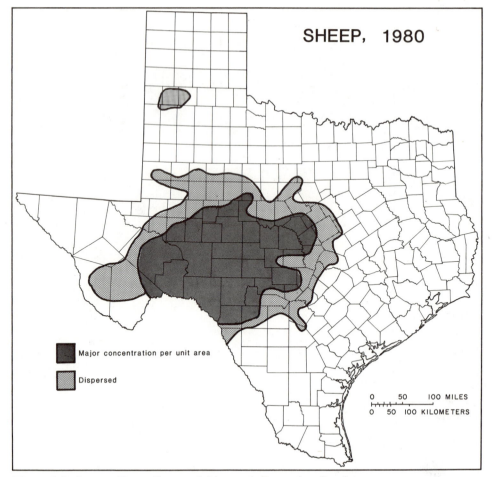

Figure 8.7. Source: Texas Crop and Livestock Reporting Service.

Alsatian, Charles Schreiner, and a German, Adolph Stieler.

By 1900 the Edwards Plateau had assumed its dominant position as the focus of wool and mohair production (Figure 8.8). On January 1, 1981, Texas led the nation with 2,360,000 sheep and 1,380,000 goats. Two-thirds of the goats were located in ten counties of the Edwards Plateau, and most of the goats were the Angora breed (Figure 8.9). Mohair production in Texas approaches 10 million lbs (4,535 t) per year, and wool production is near 20 million lbs (9,070 t) per year.

LIVESTOCK FATTENING

Traditionally, many Texas range cattle were shipped at maturity to the Corn Belt and other out-of-state fattening areas, but this pattern began to change after the Great Depression, when much of eastern Texas was converted from field crops to lush cattle pasture. More recently, there has been a spectacular increase in the number of feedlot operations for livestock fattening. By the early 1970s, Texas had surpassed Iowa to lead the nation in livestock fattening. Most of the activity is concentrated in the High Plains, where considerable amounts of irrigated grain sorghum and corn are produced. More than half of the feedlot activity of Texas occurs in eight counties of this region, with Deaf Smith and Parmer counties accounting for nearly one-fourth of that activity (Figure 8.2). On January

Figure 8.8. Sheep ranch near Marathon in Brewster County. (Photo: Texas Department of Agriculture.)

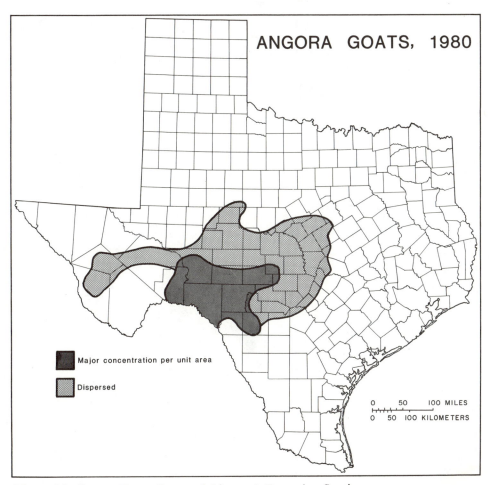

Figure 8.9. Source: Texas Crop and Livestock Reporting Service.

1, 1981, there were 11,600,000 million head of cattle in feedlots in the United States, and nearly 2 million of them were in Texas feedlots. Since 1970, an average of more than 4,500,000 head of cattle has been marketed annually from Texas feedlots (Figures 8.10 and 8.11).

Although much less intensive than the feedlots of the High Plains, the East Texas pasture system is regionally important. The major concentration is on the Blackland Prairie and in the Post Oak Belt, extending into the northern Piney Woods. Landholdings are not large, but the carrying capacity of the range, largely planted to Coastal Bermuda grass, is greater than elsewhere in Texas. More than 5 million head of beef

cattle are pasture fattened for market in the eastern region, usually with dietary supplements of grains, cottonseed meal, and high-protein feed.

DAIRYING

At the end of the nineteenth century, when the population of Texas was largely rural, nearly every farm in the state had at least one cow to provide the family with milk and related dairy products. Occasionally a farmer might milk several cows, marketing whole milk, cream, and butter to customers in nearby settlements, and it was common for urban families to keep a milk cow and a few chickens. As the pop-

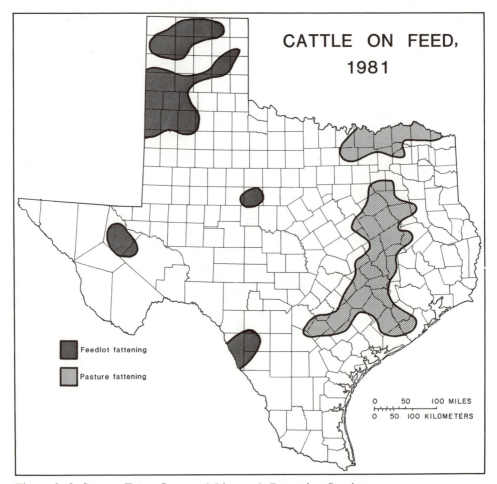

Figure 8.10. Source: Texas Crop and Livestock Reporting Service.

Figure 8.11. Randall County feedlot. (Photo: William M. Holmes, 1981.)

ulation of urban Texas continued to increase, so did commercial dairying. By 1945 more than 4 billion lbs (1,814,000 t) of milk were being marketed annually, and since 1960 improved feeding techniques and more-sophisticated equipment have resulted in an annual per cow production of more than 10,000 lbs (4,540 kg), resulting in a milk flow of more than 3 billion lbs (1,360,500 t). More milk was produced by 320,000 milk cows in 1981 than 556,000 cows produced in 1964.

On January 1, 1981, there were 12,000 commercial dairying operations in Texas, and most of them were located near major urban centers. The traditional dairy center is Hopkins County, and that county and Erath, Wise, Cooke, Johnson, Comanche, Parker, Franklin, and Wood counties constitute the Dallas–Fort Worth milkshed (Figure 8.12). The impact of urban sprawl is reflected in the fact that as recently as 1966, urban counties such as Harris, Bexar, Dallas, Tarrant, and El Paso ranked among the leading dairy areas in the state. Virtually all of the milk produced in Texas is marketed through local milk cooperatives for Texas consumption (Figure 8.13).

POULTRY RAISING

The poultry industry of Texas is confined to highly localized portions of Central and East Texas (Figure 8.14). Gonzales County east of San Antonio is outstanding for its commercial production of not only eggs and broilers, but turkeys as well. Otherwise the broiler industry is mostly confined to East Texas, and turkey production is distributed through Central and South Central parts of the state (Figure 8.15). Egg production is more widely dispersed, illustrating an urban orientation. Counties near or including large urban centers—such as Denton, Caldwell, Brazos, Bexar, Fayette, and Garza—are important egg producers outside the broiler region. In recent years the annual value of the poultry industry to Texas has exceeded $400 million.

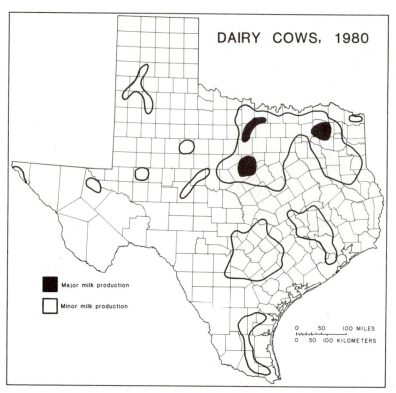

DAIRY COWS, 1980

Major milk production

Minor milk production

0   50   100 MILES
0 50 100 KILOMETERS

Figure 8.12. Source: Texas Crop and Livestock Reporting Service.

Figure 8.13. Dairy cows on a Franklin County dairy farm. (Photo: Texas Highway Department.)

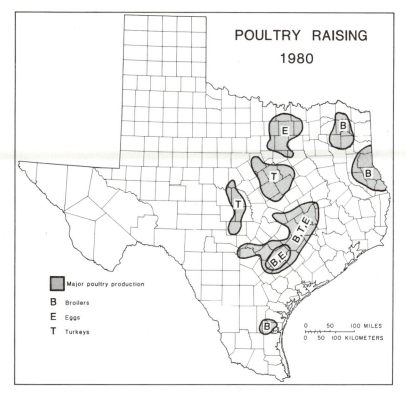

POULTRY RAISING
1980

Major poultry production

B Broilers
E Eggs
T Turkeys

0   50   100 MILES
0 50 100 KILOMETERS

Figure 8.14. Source: Texas Crop and Livestock Reporting Service.

Figure 8.15. Turkey farm near Cuero in DeWitt County. (Photo: Texas Highway Department.)

CROP FARMING

Although the colorful livestock industry has traditionally overshadowed the exploits of cultivators in popular literature and people's perception of Texas, Texas farmers have proved their capability to produce a great array of farm crops. The production of field crops in Texas, like the pastoral economy mentioned earlier, is the result of multiethnic input in virtually every environmental setting in the state. With productive land ranging from Gulf Coast marshland to the High Plains and from the Piney Woods to irrigated desert, the crop versatility of Texas is impressive.

Crops were introduced into East Texas in pre-Columbian times, and the earliest European explorers found thriving corn and bean gardens among the Caddo and some other eastern woodland tribes. The Spaniards, who established complicated ditch irrigation systems at San Antonio, El Paso, and several other settlements, were largely responsible for introducing cultivated crops into South Texas and the far western part of the state. They also began dry farming in a number of places. Southern Anglo-Americans and blacks, who immigrated en masse after about 1820, established a thriving crop agriculture, based in part on the plantation system. In time, the southern Anglos, joined by a midwestern minority, moved to the High Plains.

By 1920 most of the arable land was under cultivation. The resultant variety was great, ranging from tropical and subtropical crops such as cotton and citrus to the hearty middle-latitude grains. Crop production was not only diverse and regionalized, but also of great volume (Table 8.1 and Figure 8.16). In 1980 Texas ranked only behind California in total annual value of agricultural products.

PLANTATION AGRICULTURE

The traditional plantation system in the American South was characterized by large land units, hand labor, slavery, and specialization in cotton, sugarcane, and other subtropical cash crops. Ranching provided the main economic focus of the Texas frontier in the nineteenth century, and plantation agriculture prevailed in the eastern part of the state. By the time of the Civil War, Texas, because of its plantations, ranked as one of the major cotton states, and smaller amounts of sugarcane were raised on plantations along the lower Brazos and Colorado rivers near the coast.

As early as 1829, Stephen F. Austin observed that cotton, along with beef, tallow, pork, and mules, constituted the nucleus of the exports from Texas. In 1833 a Mexican official estimated that the province's exports amounted to about $500,000, with cotton accounting for more than one-half of the total. The cotton-slavery complex rapidly expanded westward during the 1840s, and by mid-century 58,072 bales of cotton were produced in Texas, a ratio of 1 bale per slave. By 1860 the slave population of Texas exceeded 180,000, about 30 percent of the total population, and cotton production amounted to 431,463 bales, or 2.4 bales per slave. Cotton and slavery were virtually synonymous in the state (Figures 4.7 and 8.17).

The abolition of slavery caused great

Table 8.1. Value of Selected Texas Crops, 1979

Crop	Value
Cotton	$1,005,000,000
Grain sorghum	626,940,000
Wheat	538,200,000
Corn	370,440,000
Hay	328,865,000
Vegetables	270,122,000
Rice	238,000,000
Soybeans	117,208,000
Fruits and nuts	69,000,000
Other grains	32,500,000
Sugar beets and cane	20,600,000

Source: Texas Crop and Livestock Reporting Service.

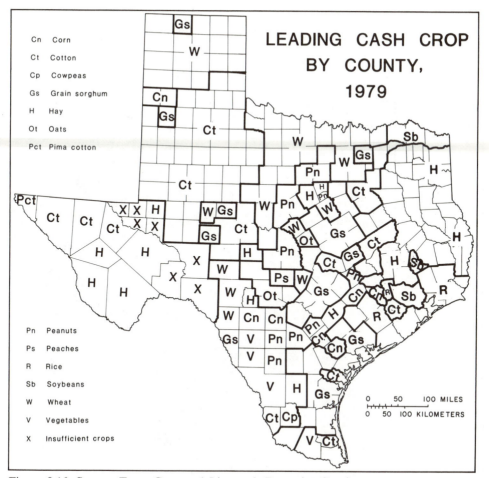

Figure 8.16. Source: Texas Crop and Livestock Reporting Service.

changes in the Texas plantation system, but it survived. Under slavery, large fields had been worked by gang labor, but after abolition, the plantation owners divided their fields into individual sharecropper farms. The former slaves were moved from their old living quarters near an owner's house and placed in sharecropper huts on each tenement farm. In this way, the settlement landscape was greatly altered, but the land-ownership pattern remained much the same.

After about 1930 another great change came to plantation agriculture in Texas, as in most of the Lower South. Hand labor was replaced by machines, and sharecroppers were displaced. Large fields similar to those of the slavery period reappeared, but

the labor force was much smaller, consisting only of machine operators. The resultant mechanized operations are known as neo-plantations.

Commercial Fiber Farming

Through the sharecropper and neoplantation systems, commercial cotton cultivation has survived in Texas to the present. After a brief decline in production immediately after the Civil War, cotton resumed its rise among Texas crops. The fertile Blackland Prairie, where very little cotton was planted before 1860, became a part of the Cotton Belt in the 1870s. By 1880 Texas had become the leading cotton producing region in the world, and there

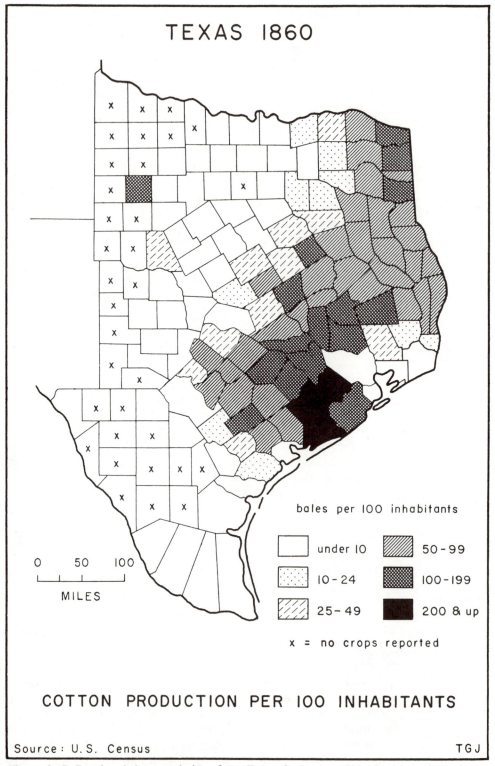

Figure 8.17. Reprinted, by permission, from Terry G. Jordan, "The Imprint of the Upper and Lower South on Mid-Nineteenth-Century Texas," *Annals of the Association of American Geographers* 57 (1967), 678.

have been only two years since 1878 in which Texas failed to produce at least 1 million bales. In many years during the past century Texas produced one-third of all commercial cotton produced in the United States and one-fourth of the world's total. By 1890 the westward expansion of dry-farmed cotton reached its semiarid boundary, and there was no further expansion for nearly half a century until irrigation became established in the South Plains, the Pecos Valley, and South Texas.

In the 1920s the formative phases of the southern High Plains irrigated cotton culture were established in Lubbock, Hale, Lamb, and bordering counties as drillers tapped the groundwater of the Ogallala formation, which increased the agricultural potential of the region. The South Plains had attained cotton supremacy in Texas by 1940 and has retained its position as the outstanding upland cotton producing region in the world since World War II. In 1979 one-fourth of all cotton produced in Texas was grown in the region around Lubbock (Figure 8.18).

The value of cotton to the present-day Texas economy is illustrated in Table 8.1. In 1979 cotton was a $1-billion crop and amounted to more than 10 percent of the total value of agricultural production in the state. This figure includes some $12 million worth of American Pima cotton, a highly specialized long-staple variety

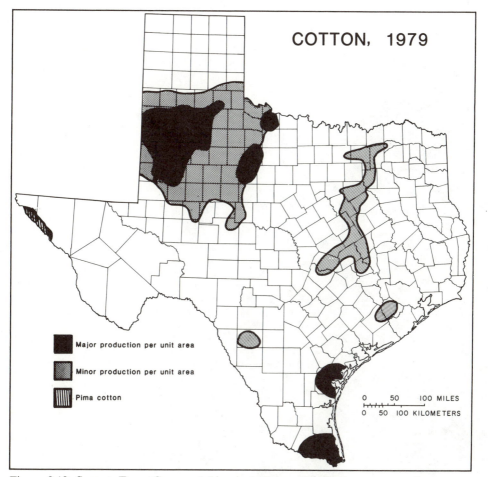

Figure 8.18. Source: Texas Crop and Livestock Reporting Service.

raised mainly on the Rio Grande floodplain in El Paso and Hudspeth counties and to a lesser extent in Reeves and Pecos counties. Virtually all cotton in Texas is presently harvested by machinery, following the neo-plantation pattern (Figure 8.19).

Woodland Plantations

An even more common modern succes-sor of the antebellum slave-cotton agricul-ture is the so-called woodland plantation. In this form of the neoplantation, the old fields were planted to pine, and the entire agricultural operation shifted to the pro-duction of forest products. The result is one of the most startling reversals in the state's land-use pattern. Since about 1930 much of East Texas has undergone this conversion from cotton to commercial for-est, causing the Cotton Belt to vanish from

the area east of the Trinity River (Figure 8.20). Parts of the Piney Woods probably have more forest cover today than in the 1820s or 1830s when the first cotton planters arrived. Woodland plantation products are diverse and include lumber, pulpwood, and Christmas trees (Figure 8.21).

The development of the woodland plan-tation is closely linked to the rise of sci-entific forestry. The virgin pine forests of East Texas were largely destroyed by a wave of exploitive cutting before 1920. With the cooperation of individuals from both the public and the private sectors, and espe-cially from lumber companies, indiscrim-inate cutting was halted, the number of forest fires significantly reduced, and in-creased tree planting encouraged. As a re-sult, annual tree growth in the East Texas forest region exceeded annual harvest by

Figure 8.19. Cotton harvesting near Fort Stockton in Pecos County. (Photo: Texas Highway Depart-ment.)

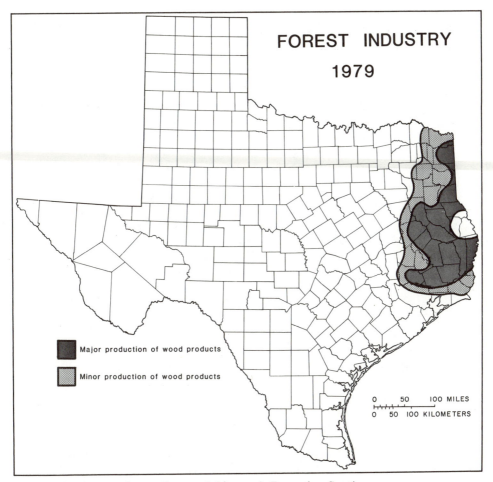

FOREST INDUSTRY 1979

■ Major production of wood products

▨ Minor production of wood products

0   50   100 MILES
0   50   100 KILOMETERS

Figure 8.20. Source: Texas Crop and Livestock Reporting Service.

more than 30 percent by the end of the 1970s.

The timber producing region of the state in the Piney Woods includes some forty-three counties of East Texas, and all of the major state and national forests of Texas are located within this region. Softwood and hardwood production from this region amounts to more than 400 million cu ft (11,320,000 cu m) annually. About 86 percent of the harvest is pine, most of which is used in the manufacture of paper products, lumber, and plywood. Some of the lumber is treated with creosote and used for utility poles, pilings, fence posts, cross ties, and construction poles. As recently as the mid-1970s, there were 112 sawmills and

9 pulp mills in East Texas. The pulp mills consume a greater annual volume of cut timber than all of the sawmills combined.

COMMERCIAL GRAIN FARMING

The commercial character of Texas agriculture, set early in the nineteenth century by livestock ranching and plantation agriculture, also extends to other types of farming. Texas grain cultivation fits the pattern of market-oriented agriculture as well.

Wheat was the first cash grain crop of major importance in the state. As early as 1860, the northern Blackland Prairie, centered on Dallas, had become the "Texas

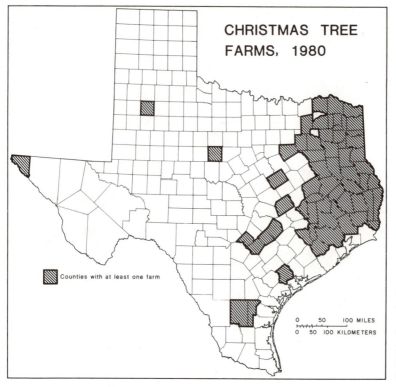

Figure 8.21. Sources: Robert A. Miller, "Texas, An Emerging State in the Development of Christmas Tree Plantations," *Program Abstracts of the Association of American Geographers, 1981* (Washington, D.C., 1981), p. 227, and Texas Christmas Tree Growers Association.

wheat region" (Figure 8.22), but as the frontier expanded westward, so did wheat. Cotton shunted much of the commercial grain farming out of the Blackland Prairie in the 1870s, and today the major wheat producing region is in the northern High Plains, where most of the wheat is dry-farmed. In the 1980 production year, wheat was harvested on 1,110,000 irrigated acres (450,000 ha) and on 4,090,000 nonirrigated acres (1,656,000 ha). Even in the High Plains, where the Ogallala formation supplies irrigation water for many products, wheat was harvested from 1,560,000 dryland acres (632,000 ha) compared with 890,000 irrigated acres (360,000 ha) (Figure 8.23). In addition to the High Plains region, significant wheat production occurs in a belt extending south from Wichita Falls across the Lower Plains and in a belt that extends across the northern portion of the Blackland Prairie (Figure 8.24). As such, the Texas wheat region forms the southernmost part of the midwestern Wheat Belt, which is centered in the Great Plains. Culturally as well as economically, the wheat growing counties of Texas display many midwestern, as opposed to southern, traits.

In 1979 wheat ranked second only to sorghum as the most important cash grain crop in Texas, but in many years during the 1970s, both corn and rice were more valuable. The erratic nature of wheat production stems from the fact that most of it is raised on dry farms in West Texas where precipitation patterns are fickle.

The other small grains—barley, oats, and rye—are produced on a very small scale in Texas. Barley is scattered in northern and western Texas, with Parmer and Deaf Smith counties being the leading producers. Oats are produced on a larger scale, scattered throughout Central and North Texas, and one-third of the rye is raised in Eastland and Comanche counties. Although Texas accounts for only about one-tenth the corn production of Illinois or Iowa, in many years the crop is more important than wheat

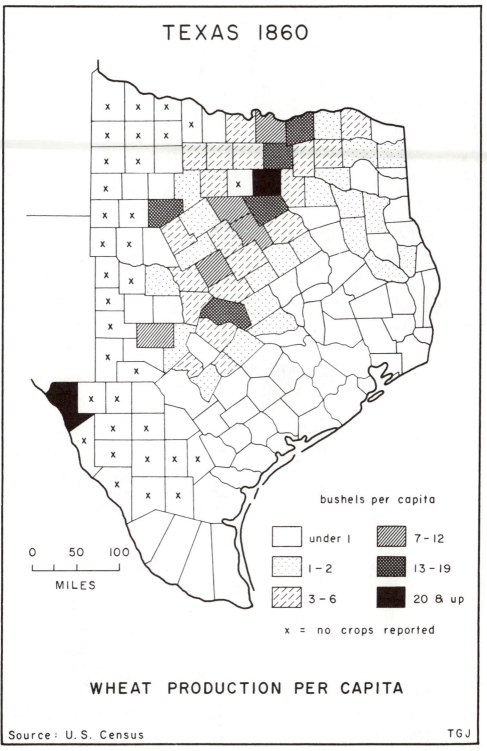

Figure 8.22. Reprinted, by permission, from Terry G. Jordan, "The Imprint of the Upper and Lower South on Mid-Nineteenth-Century Texas," *Annals of the Association of American Geographers* 57 (1967), 680.

Figure 8.23. Wheat field near Sunray in the Panhandle. (Photo: Texas Highway Department.)

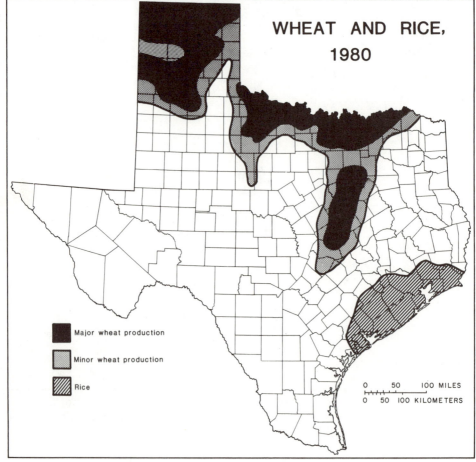

WHEAT AND RICE, 1980

Major wheat production

Minor wheat production

Rice

0   50   100 MILES

0   50   100 KILOMETERS

Figure 8.24. Source: Texas Crop and Livestock Reporting Service.

as a cash grain in the Texas economy. This situation has been especially true in recent years as corn, like grain sorghum, has gained impetus because of its cattle fattening potential (Figure 8.25). In fact, recent trends suggest that irrigated corn and grain sorghum are taking over in some of the traditional cotton producing counties of the South Plains in Northwest Texas, such as Parmer, Castro, Hale, Lamb, and Bailey (Figures 8.16 and 8.26). In 1979, 50 percent of all the corn produced in Texas was raised in those five counties. Indications are that both corn and grain sorghum will become more widely planted within the next several years. Elsewhere, corn production is widely scattered through the central and southern portions of the state, where Hidalgo and Uvalde counties are leading producers.

Rice also had a greater value than wheat during certain years of the 1970s, though production is restricted to a few counties in the eastern portion of the Coastal Prairie (Figure 8.24). Optimum environmental conditions normally prevail for rice production within that region, except for the occasional tropical storms that can occur during the harvest season. Early rice production in Texas was hardly more than an extension of the Louisiana rice region, and production was minimal until the early 1900s when several Japanese families moved into Chambers and Jefferson counties. Commercial rice production quickly became more widespread, expanding to the west along the coast. In 1979 the rice harvest was worth $238 million. Wharton County is the leading producer, but considerable rice is also raised in Matagorda, Colorado, Brazoria, Jackson, Jefferson, Chambers, and Liberty counties.

The single most important grain crop of present-day Texas is grain sorghum (Figure 8.27). In recent years this crop has experienced an exceptional spread in the state, paralleling the development of the High Plains feedlot industry. Irrigation promotes yields per acre that are consistently out-

Figure 8.25. Corn in Northwest Texas. (Photo: William M. Holmes, 1981.)

176

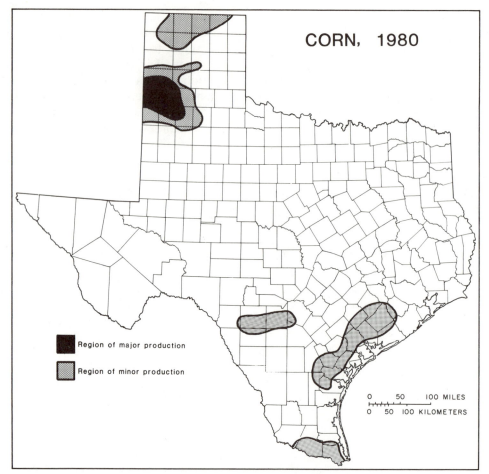

Figure 8.26. Source: Texas Crop and Livestock Reporting Service.

Figure 8.27. Grain sorghum field near Dumas in Moore County. (Photo: Texas Highway Department.)

standing. Although substantial quantities of sorghum are produced in the Blackland Prairie, the outstanding regions are the southern Coastal Plain and the Rio Grande Valley. The feedlot counties of the High Plains are also major producers of grain sorghum (Figure 8.28).

The importance of commercial grain farming to Texas is suggested by the fact that through most of the 1970s, the cumulative value of grains was about twice the value of cotton. In all of its forms, commercial grain farming represents a "midwesternization" of Texas agriculture.

MARKET GARDENING

Vegetable, fruit, flower, and nut production represents an activity traditionally con-

fined to rural garden plots and orchards, largely for household or farm family consumption. However, the growth of large urban centers created attractive markets and encouraged the development of another lucrative commercial enterprise. Farmers who presently live near large urban centers find it profitable to specialize in the land-intensive production of seasonal vegetables and fruit. Some market their produce at "farmers markets," roadside stands, or even from the backs of trucks parked along busy thoroughfares. In all, some 200 counties in Texas, involving 200,000 acres (81,000 ha), produce garden crops for both the fresh and the process markets. The statistical division of the Texas Department of Agriculture collects data on twenty-two vege-

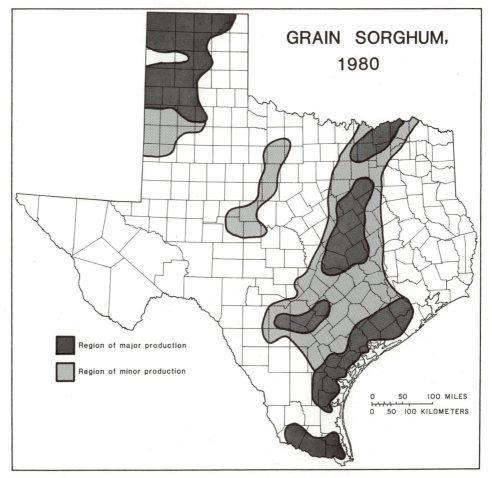

Figure 8.28. Source: Texas Crop and Livestock Reporting Service.

tables, potatoes and sweet potatoes, citrus fruit, peaches, pecans, and minor fruit crops. In most years, Texas ranks third behind California and Florida in the production of vegetables and fruit for market, but unusual weather conditions (such as frosts, floods, high winds, and drought), labor problems, transportation problems, storage problems, and insects combine to place this form of agriculture in a very vulnerable position. The leading market gardening counties are Hidalgo, Starr, and Cameron in the lower Rio Grande Valley; Frio and Uvalde in the winter-garden district of Southwest Texas; Duval in the Brush Country; and Deaf Smith on the High Plains (Figure 8.29).

The most important vegetable producing region is the winter-garden district, centered on Crystal City. San Antonio, Laredo, and Eagle Pass serve as shipping points from which winter-garden vegetables are moved to all parts of the country. The major winter crops are beets, broccoli, cabbage, carrots, cauliflower, lettuce, and spinach (Figure 8.30). Dry onions are grown for spring harvest, and marketing begins in March. Snap beans, cantaloupes, carrots, cucumbers, sweet corn, honeydew melons, bell peppers, squash, and tomatoes are shipped from April to June, and fall crops include cabbage, cucumbers, and bell peppers.

The lower Rio Grande Valley, centered in Hidalgo, Cameron, and Willacy counties,

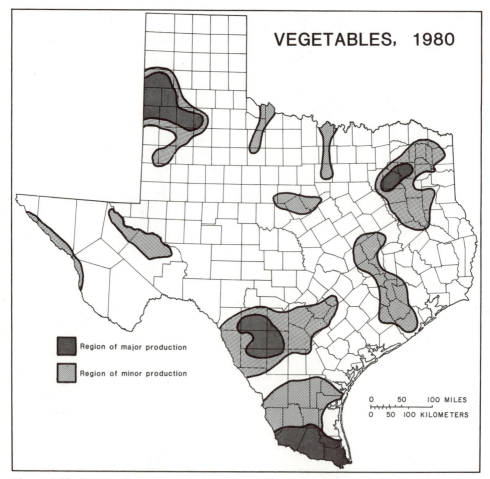

Figure 8.29. Source: Texas Crop and Livestock Reporting Service.

Figure 8.30. Lettuce field near Mission in Hidalgo County. (Photo: Texas Highway Department.)

produces many of the same market garden crops as the winter-garden district, in addition to citrus fruit. Texas grapefruit, including the famous sweet ruby red, and oranges are major products of the lower Rio Grande Valley. Valencia and navel oranges are both important, and some tangerines, lemons, and tangelos are marketed (Figure 8.31).

Other market garden clusters tend to be small and confined either to a "halo" fringe around major urban centers, particularly Houston, or to some environmentally advantageous pocket. In the latter category would be the tomato farms around Dell City in Hudspeth County and the growing of cantaloupes in the Pecos Valley, sweet potatoes and roses in the Tyler area of East Texas, peanuts in the sandy lands of Eastland and Comanche counties, and the peaches of the Pedernales Valley east of Fredericksburg in the Hill Country (Figure 8.32).

In 1979 Texas led the nation in pecan production with 80 million lbs (36,280 t).

That was a bumper year for this unreliable product and represented the largest pecan crop in Texas history. By comparison, the cumulative total for the three previous years had amounted to only 78 million lbs (35,373 t). In the 1979 season, five counties—San Saba, Hood, Guadalupe, Gonzales, and Mills—produced more than 5 million lbs (2,268 t) each. It is interesting that such urban counties as Bell, Bexar, El Paso, and Tarrant were also among the leaders in pecan production.

CAUSES OF AGRICULTURAL DIVERSITY

The geographer Derwent Whittlesey, in a classification in the 1930s, identified some thirteen types of agricultural regions in the world as a whole. It is a good measure of Texas's agricultural diversity that half of Whittlesey's types occur in the state.

180

Figure 8.31. Citrus grove in lower Rio Grande Valley. (Photo: Texas Highway Department.)

Figure 8.32. Cantaloupes produced near Pecos in Reeves County. (Photo: Texas Highway Department.)

Some of the causes of the great agricultural diversity of Texas have already been suggested. Principal among them are the physical environment, the ethnic composition of the population, and the influence of market conditions. In no small part, the agricultural variety rests upon environmental diversity. Citrus cultivation in far South Texas rests, however precariously, upon the mild winters of that region; rice farming on the Coastal Prairie was encouraged by the table-flat terrain that facilitated flood irrigation; the broken terrain and sparse vegetation of the Edwards Plateau–Hill Country gave an advantage to sheep and goats; and the native distribution of the pine forests provided a regional framework for the woodland plantation agriculture. It is not surprising, in an economic endeavor tied so closely to the land as agriculture, that the influence of the physical environment would be felt.

Important though the environment may have been in helping shape the character of Texas agriculture, the human factors must also be considered. Each rural ethnic and cultural group introduced its own distinctive farming practices and dietary preferences, with significant results for the agricultural development of the state. For example, studies in Texas have revealed that farmers of recent European heritage, such as the Czechs and Germans, tend to work the land more intensively, devote more attention to the care of their livestock, rely more on family labor, have a higher rate of landownership, invest more money in equipment and maintenance, and engage more in mutual cooperation than do Anglo or black agriculturists (Table 8.2). Similarly, German and Czech stock raisers win a disproportionately large share of the prizes at livestock shows around the state. The role of German and Japanese farmers in

Table 8.2. A Comparison of German and Anglo Farmers in South Central Texas, 1850–1880

	Germans	Anglos
Cash value of farm produce per acre, 1870	$ 5	$ 3
Value of farm implements and machinery, 1880	$118	$51
Money spent on fences, per farm, 1880	$103	$78
% of farmers owning their land, 1880	96%	75%
% of farmers owning slaves, 1860	4%	72%
% of farmers owning sheep, 1880	36%	9%
% of farmers raising tobacco, 1850	29%	1%
Weight of wool sheared per sheep, 1880	5 lbs (2.3 kg)	4 lbs (1.8 kg)
Eggs laid per unit of poultry, 1880	3.2 dozen	2.8 dozen
Cash value of farm, per acre, 1880	$ 9	$ 6

Source: Terry G. Jordan, German Seed in Texas Soil: Immigrant Farmers in Nineteenth-Century Texas (Austin: University of Texas Press, 1966).

the development of market gardening around Houston was also very great.

The Hispanic contribution to Texas agriculture has been very distinctive. Spaniards were the first livestock ranchers in the state and contributed many of the cowboy skills and paraphernalia. Civilians from the Canary Islands and Spanish mission fathers built the first irrigation systems in Texas, most notably at San Antonio and El Paso. Today, Mexicans provide most of the vital labor force for the ranches and the market gardens of South Texas.

Besides ethnicity and environment, market patterns helped shape the agricultural map of Texas. A century and a half ago, the German farmer-scholar J. H. von Thünen first recognized that commercial types of agriculture tend to be arranged in concentric zones around markets. The more-intensive types, such as market gardens and dairying, occur closest to market, both because they occupy high-priced land and because they produce perishable goods that require rapid access to consumers. Successively less-intensive types of agriculture are found at increasing distances from market in the Thünenian pattern, meaning that commercial grain farming and ranching will occur on the outer peripheries.

The concentric zone model of land use helps explain the distribution of types of agriculture in Texas. Markets on both the state and the national level are involved. Local urban markets such as Dallas–Fort Worth and Houston are ringed by dairy farms and market gardens, just as von Thünen would have predicted. On a national scale, the major market for Texas agricultural produce has traditionally been the industrial Northeast. At increasing distances from that market, progressively less-intensive agricultural types are arranged in belts or regions. The U.S. Dairy Belt, livestock fattening (the Corn Belt), commercial fiber (the Cotton Belt), commercial grain (the Wheat Belt and Rice Belt), and livestock ranching, successively less-intensive forms of land use, are arranged in roughly concentric zones at increasing distances from

the industrial Northeast. The fiber, grain, and ranching zones all cut across Texas. The recent massive relocation of people into the Sun Belt has greatly reduced the influence of the Northeast, and local markets for agricultural products have grown accordingly. As a result, the agricultural zonation within Texas is undergoing rapid change and will continue to be modified. In general, the trend will be toward ever-more-intensive forms of agriculture, a reflection of the growing market within the state. Von Thünen would not be surprised. Less-intensive forms of agriculture in Texas, particularly ranching and cash grain farming, would seem to be endangered by this trend.

*   *   *

Texas, then, is very diverse agriculturally, displaying internal contrasts caused by environment, cultural heritage, and market patterns. That rural diversity, in turn, is reflected in the cultural landscape created by Texas farmers and ranchers, which is described in the next chapter.

SOURCES AND SUGGESTED READINGS

Agricultural Bulletins: "Fruits and Pecans," "Poultry," "Dairy," "Livestock," "Field Crops," "Cotton," "Vegetables," "Small Grains," "Texas County Statistics." Austin: Texas Crop and Livestock Reporting Service, published annually.

Atkins, Irvin M. *A History of Small Grain Crops in Texas*. Bulletin B-1301. College Station: Texas Agricultural Experiment Station, 1980.

Chambers, William T. "Edwards Plateau: A Combination Ranching Region." *Economic Geography* 8 (1932), 67–80.

Clarke, Neville P. *Texas Agriculture in the 80's: The Critical Decade*. College Station: Texas Agricultural Experiment Station, 1979.

Foscue, Edwin J. "Agricultural Geography of the Lower Rio Grande Valley of Texas." Ph.D. dissertation, Department of Geography, Clark University, Worcester, Massachusetts, 1931.

Glick, Thomas F. *The Old World Background of the Irrigation System of San Antonio,*

Texas. El Paso: Texas Western Press, 1972.

Gregor, Howard F. *Geography of Agriculture: Themes in Research.* Englewood Cliffs, N.J.: Prentice-Hall, 1970.

Holmes, William M. "An Historical Geography of Dry Farming in the Northern High Plains of Texas." Ph.D. dissertation, Department of Geography, University of Texas, Austin, 1975.

Jordan, Terry G. *German Seed in Texas Soil: Immigrant Farmers in Nineteenth-Century Texas.* Austin: University of Texas Press, 1966.

————. *Trails to Texas: Southern Roots of Western Cattle Ranching.* Lincoln: University of Nebraska Press, 1981.

Lamb, Robert B. *The Mule in Southern Agriculture.* University of California Publications in Geography, vol. 15. Berkeley and Los Angeles: University of California Press, 1963.

Prunty, Merle. "The Renaissance of the Southern Plantation." *Geographical Review* 45 (1955), 459–491.

Skrabanek, Robert L. "The Influence of Cultural Backgrounds in Farming Practices in a Czech-American Rural Community." *Southwestern Social Science Quarterly* 31 (1951), 258–266.

Texas Historic Crop Statistics 1866–1975. Austin: Texas Crop and Livestock Reporting Service, 1977.

Tiller, James W., Jr. *The Texas Winter Garden: Commercial Cool-Season Vegetable Production.* Monograph no. 33. Austin: University of Texas, Bureau of Business Research, 1971.

Types of Farming in Texas. Bulletin no. 964. College Station: Texas Agricultural Experiment Station, 1960.

von Thünen, Johann Heinrich. *Von Thünen's Isolated State: An English Edition of* Der isolierte Staat. Translated by Carla M. Wartenberg. Elmsford, N.Y.: Pergamon Press, 1966.

Whittlesey, Derwent S. "Major Agricultural Regions of the Earth." *Annals of the Association of American Geographers* 26 (1936), 199–240.

Wilhelm, Gene. "Dooryard Gardens and Gardening in the Black Community of Brushy, Texas." *Geographical Review* 65 (1975), 73–92.

CHAPTER 9

RURAL SETTLEMENT GEOGRAPHY

The landscape reveals a visible, tangible aspect of culture. Members of each culture and subculture, working over decades and centuries, fashion their own distinctive landscapes from the raw materials provided by the natural environment. Geographers, working in the subdiscipline known as settlement geography, have traditionally devoted considerable attention to these landscapes, perhaps because they so accurately mirror the cultures that created and occupy them.

The content of the rural cultural landscape is both varied and complex. Most geographical studies focus on three principal aspects of the rural landscape: vernacular architecture, patterns of land division, and settlement patterns. Of these, perhaps the most readily visible in the Texas countryside is the traditional architecture. It provides clear, visible evidence of the multiple peopling of the state and remains vivid yet today, in spite of the advent of "placeless" architecture, mobile homes, and other visual joys of the machine age.

People reveal a great deal about themselves—their society, economy, and way of life—in the form of the buildings they erect. Each ethnic group that entered Texas had a distinct architectural heritage, a distinct tradition that is evident in style, floor plan, and choice of building materials. Most groups adapted to some degree to their new cultural and physical environment in Texas, sacrificing part of their traditional architectural heritage to adopt new, more-expedient forms. But much remains in the cultural landscape that serves to remind us of the varied architectural traditions.

MIDDLE ATLANTIC FOLK ARCHITECTURE

The areally prevalent Anglo-American folk architecture in Texas was derived from the Middle Atlantic subculture of the eastern United States, one of three subcultures found on the eastern seaboard (see Chapter 4). The Middle Atlantic colonies were ethnically diverse, containing a hodgepodge of English, German, Scotch-Irish, Swedish, and other European groups. The Middle Atlantic architectural tradition is a result of the blending of contributions from these various peoples. So practical and environmentally adaptive were the architectural ideas of the Middle Atlantic folk that some traits spread further south than most other facets of this subculture, making inroads in the Gulf Coastal Plain areas, which are, in other cultural respects, part of the Lower South. In Texas, a Middle Atlantic architectural influence can be detected in most parts of the state, but it appears in its purest form in the districts settled by upper southerners.

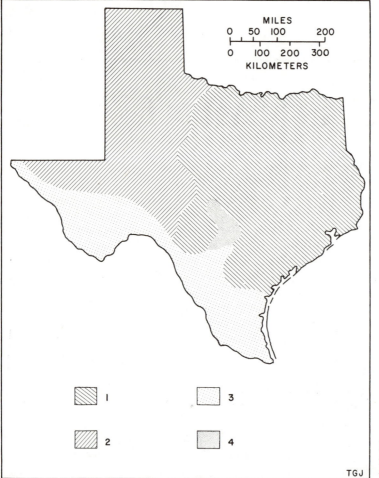

MILES
0   50   100   200

0   100   200   300
KILOMETERS

1   3

2   4

TGJ

Figure 9.1. Traditional building materials in folk architecture.

Key: 1 = log culture complex: log construction, replaced later by frame construction. 2 = western prairies: dugouts; sod houses; occasionally palisade, stone, adobe, or log houses; quickly superseded by frame construction. 3 = Spanish-Mexican: adobe and picket construction dominant, occasional stone walls, some brush shelters. 4 = German Hill Country: log construction initially, quickly replaced by half-timbering (*Fachwerk*) and stone construction.

The hallmark of Middle Atlantic folk architecture is log construction, a method introduced to the Delaware Valley in Pennsylvania, New Jersey, and Delaware in colonial times by Swedes, Finns, and Germans. Such construction, characterized by horizontal logs notched at the corners, was a very practical solution to the problem of frontier housing, and as a result, the technique spilled over onto the inner coastal plains of the Lower South. Log construction once prevailed in the eastern half of Texas (Figure 9.1).

The structural key to log construction is the corner notch, since that joint both bears the weight and prevents lateral slippage of the timbers. Four major notch types, derived from the eastern United States—and ultimately from continental Europe—occur in Texas log buildings: half-dovetail, square, V, and saddle notches, each of which has a regional concentration within Texas (Figure 9.2). Half-dovetailing was used in over a third of the surviving log houses in Texas and occurs most commonly in the post-oak belts of Central and North

Texas. A similar spatial pattern characterizes V-notching, which reached Texas by way of the Ohio Valley–Upper South and is found in about one-fifth of all Texas log structures. Square and saddle notches are primarily East Texas types and suggest ancestral ties to the coastal plain pine forests of the eastern South.

A Middle Atlantic influence is also revealed in a variety of floor plans of traditional dwellings. Of these, the most important in Texas are the single-pen, Cumberland, central hall, saddlebag, I, and Corn Belt houses (Figure 9.3). The simplest Middle Atlantic folk house in Texas is the single-pen, or one-room, plan. English in origin, the prevalent single-pen house in Texas is square or nearly so, measuring roughly 16 ft (5 m) on each side (Figure 9.4). Aligned front and rear doors facilitate ventilation, and warmth is provided by a fireplace positioned centrally in one of the gabled sidewalls. Such houses in Texas vary from one to one-and-a-half stories in height and usually have a rear shed room.

Enlargement to double-pen size in Texas was often accomplished by adding a second log pen on the gable end opposite the chimney, forming the Cumberland plan that is very common in central and western parts of the state. Also typical is the central-hall house, in which the second pen was separated from the original one by an enclosed hall, causing the house to be very wide from gable to gable. Less numerous are saddlebag houses, formed by adding the second pen on the chimney gable, with the fireplace opening into both rooms. Addition of a full second story above a double-pen house formed the tall, narrow "I" (pronounced "eye") house, the prestige dwelling of rural upper-southern Texas, particularly the Blackland Prairie (Figure 9.5). Midwesterners often enlarged their homes beyond the I-plan, producing the rambling two-story structure called the Corn Belt house (Figure 9.6). The cultural influence of midwestern settlers from Iowa, Illinois, and Kansas in rural Texas is strikingly revealed by these imposing structures.

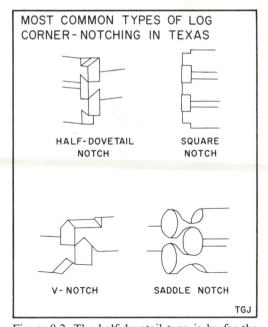

Figure 9.2. The half-dovetail type is by far the most common notch found in log houses in Texas. It is widely distributed in the eastern United States, but perhaps more common in the Upper South and Midwest. The V-notch is almost exclusively an upper-southern–midwestern type and is, predictably, found mainly in Central and North Texas. The square notch, by contrast, occurs more frequently in lower-southern states such as Alabama and Mississippi, as well as in Central and East Texas. Saddle notching is used in log houses mainly in the pine woods of the Lower South, including East Texas, but its use in barns and other log outbuildings is more widespread. (Based on Fred Kniffen, "On Corner Timbering," *Pioneer America* 1 [January 1969], 1–8.)

Many log houses were covered with protective boards on the exterior side, concealing the logs. After the frontier era had passed, the Middle Atlantic folk abandoned log construction and began building frame structures. In West Texas, where the absence of forests largely prevented log construction even in the pioneer years, frame buildings prevailed almost from the very first. Railroads imported the needed lumber.

Middle Atlantic architecture in Texas

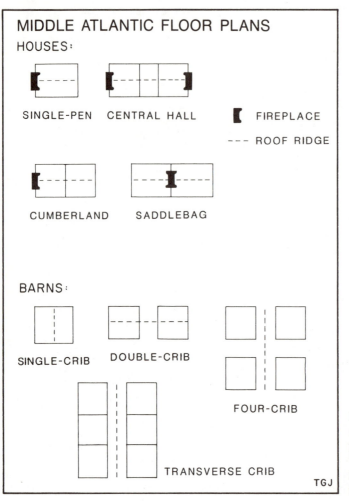

MIDDLE ATLANTIC FLOOR PLANS

HOUSES:

SINGLE-PEN   CENTRAL HALL

▐ FIREPLACE
--- ROOF RIDGE

CUMBERLAND   SADDLEBAG

BARNS:

SINGLE-CRIB   DOUBLE-CRIB   FOUR-CRIB

TRANSVERSE CRIB

TGJ

Figure 9.3. These are the most common Middle Atlantic floor plans for dwellings and barns in Texas. All occur in the Upper South, and most have prototypes in Europe.

Figure 9.4. The simplest Middle Atlantic folk house, a single-pen log dwelling in Gillespie County, Texas. (Photo: Theodore H. Albrecht, Gillespie Co. No. 20, Texas Log Cabin Register, N.T.S.U. Museum Archive, Denton.)

Figure 9.5. A central-hall I-house with rear ell, Hill County, built in the Blackland Prairie by a settler from Ohio. (Photo: 1883, Taulman Collection, University of Texas Archives.)

Figure 9.6. A Corn Belt house, built on the Grand Prairie of Denton County by midwestern settlers. (Photo: Terry G. Jordan, 1977.)

Figure 9.7. A double-crib log barn, in the Between the Creeks section of northeastern Titus County. (Photo: Terry G. Jordan, 1978.)

also includes a distinctive array of traditional barn types (Figure 9.3). The single-crib barn, the most common Texas type, consists of one log unit. A front-facing gable and sheds on one or both eave sides further characterize the single-crib barn. Some are simply corn cribs, but others are somewhat taller and contain a hay loft above the granary. The double-crib barn is formed of two log units separated by a roofed, open passage or runway (Figure 9.7). Gables face the sides, and shed roofs on the eave sides are common. Still larger are the four-crib barns, which consist of four log cribs under one roof, separated by two passageways, which form a cross. If one passageway is closed off to form two additional cribs, the result is a transverse-crib barn (Figure 9.8). All of these basic barn types were later copied in frame construction.

Occasionally, larger barns that also reveal Middle Atlantic influence can be found in Texas. An excellent example is a barn lo-cated in the rural community of Chalk Mountain, Erath County (Figures 9.9 and 9.10). Three major features of this structure resemble the famous Dutch barns of the Pennsylvania Germans, including (1) a two-level floor plan, (2) a banked ramp entrance to the upper level, and (3) a projecting forebay on the barnyard side of the structure. So closely are these three elements linked with the Keystone State that the appellation "Pennsylvania Barn" is normally used in describing structures that possess this complex of traits. Other multilevel bank barns in Texas, some with forebay, have been observed in Bell, Bandera, and Gonzales counties—all in the zone of Middle Atlantic settlement.

LOWER-SOUTHERN FOLK ARCHITECTURE

Another widespread and persistent folk architectural tradition in Texas is derived

Figure 9.8. Transverse-crib barn with stock pen enclosed by a post-and-rail fence, Dallas County. The transverse crib, particularly of frame construction, is one of the most common types in the upper-southern counties of Texas. (Photo: Terry G. Jordan, 1977.)

Figure 9.9. The Hamic barn, Erath County, with the projecting forebay on the right. (Photo: Terry G. Jordan, 1979.)

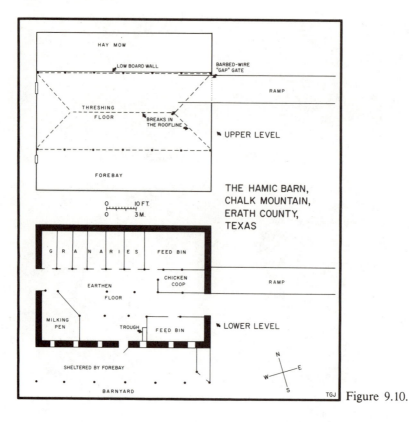

HAY MOW

LOW BOARD WALL

BARBED-WIRE "GAP" GATE

RAMP

THRESHING FLOOR

BREAKS IN THE ROOFLINE

▲ UPPER LEVEL

FOREBAY

0   10 FT.
0   3 M.

THE HAMIC BARN,
CHALK MOUNTAIN,
ERATH COUNTY,
TEXAS

G R A N A R I E S   FEED BIN

CHICKEN COOP

RAMP

EARTHEN
FLOOR

MILKING PEN

TROUGH   FEED BIN

▲ LOWER LEVEL

SHELTERED BY FOREBAY

BARNYARD

Figure 9.10.

from the lower-southern subculture, based in the Tidewater and on the Gulf and Atlantic coastal plains. Its roots lie in and around Williamsburg, Charleston, and New Orleans among a creolized people of British, French, Spanish, and African heritage.

Log construction was not part of this lower-southern tradition during its formative years and was not used in the Tidewater coastal fringe. In the inner coastal plain, Middle Atlantic log carpentry penetrated the lower-southern culture realm, where it was adopted as an expedient method of construction. Generally, however, the lower-southern tradition favored frame construction and, particularly in French Louisiana, half-timbering, in which a framework of squared beams is erected as the weight-bearing skeleton of the structure and the interstices are filled with brick or wattle and daub (Figure 9.11).

Lower-southern-dwelling floor plans are, in some instances, similar to those of the Middle Atlantic, since the British influenced both traditions. The single-pen, or one-room English plan—roughly 16 ft (5 m) on each side, with aligned doors, side-facing gables, and an exterior chimney at one gable—is more common in the Lower South than the Middle Atlantic, but the two-room type, or Cumberland plan, in the Middle Atlantic tradition is also a typical lowland type. Too, the creole house of French Louisiana, typically formed of two main rooms flanking a huge central chimney, is similar to the saddlebag house of the Middle Atlantic culture, and the British I-house occurs in both subcultures as well (Figure 9.12).

Other floor plans and floor-plan features, however, are distinctively lower southern. One of the hallmarks of the region is the dogtrot house, which consists of two main rooms separated by a roofed, open-air passageway. This type is so common in the zone of lower-southern settlement as to be

Figure 9.11. The Smith house, Shelby County. Its dogtrot has been enclosed to become a hallway, but other typically lower-southern traits—such as the brick piers, porch, and frame construction—remain intact. (Photo: H. L. Starnes, Library of Congress, 1936.)

Figure 9.12. A frame I-house, with dogtrot on the first floor and semidetached kitchen, San Augustine County, East Texas. In typically lower-southern fashion, the house is raised on brick piers. Similar houses can be seen in the Virginia and North Carolina Tidewater districts. (Photo: H. L. Starnes, Library of Congress, 1936.)

called the East Texas house (Figure 9.13). Splendid examples of dogtrots built using the typical lower-southern frame construction are abundant east of the Trinity River, and there are also many log dogtrots, representing the blending of a lower-southern floor plan with the Middle Atlantic construction technique. The open breezeway of the dogtrot house makes good sense in the humid, subtropical climate of the Gulf Coastal Plain.

Another very common lower-southern house type is the shotgun house, a deep, narrow dwelling only one room wide and two to six rooms in depth. The roof ridge is at right angles to the front, and there is no fireplace (Figure 9.14). The shotgun, closely associated with the black population, is believed to be an African type, introduced from the slave coast to Haiti in colonial times and brought to French Louisiana in the late 1700s. It has since spread from New Orleans to much of the United States. In both urban and rural areas of Texas, the shotgun house is associated with blacks. A notable rural concentration of shotguns can be seen in the old bottomland plantation district between the Brazos and Little Brazos rivers in Robertson County.

By placing two shotguns side by side and covering them with a single roof to form one house, the bungalow, or double-shotgun, type is created. Though indirectly of African origin, these front-gabled bungalows have been widely adopted by rural and urban whites throughout most of Texas.

Other distinctively lower-southern floor-plan features include the freestanding or semidetached kitchen and the elaborate development of porches. The problem of heat retention in the summer, coupled with the fire danger inherent in cooking, led to the custom of the cook house or freestanding kitchen. In time, most of these kitchens were attached to the house, at least by a roofed passageway, and many examples can still be seen in the rural landscape (Figure 9.12). The porch may be of West Indian or African origin, and most lower-southern dwellings exhibit multiple porches, often enclosed with screen wire.

Adding to the distinctiveness of lower-southern folk architecture are tall foun-

Figure 9.13. Dogtrot house in Newton County, East Texas. (Photo: Terry G. Jordan, 1978.)

Figure 9.14. Shotgun house in New Orleans, the original U.S. area for this African type of house. (Photo: Terry G. Jordan, 1979.)

dation piers of brick or wood that elevate the house above the ground to facilitate ventilation and escape flood damage (Figure 9.11 and 9.12). If the piers are unusually high and built of bricks, the result is the tidewater raised cottage.

Lower-southern roofs are also distinctive. Perhaps most common is the Louisiana roof, a side-gabled type consisting of two unbroken pitches, with an attic extending out over the front porch and rear shed rooms. Even more common are fully hipped and pyramidal roofs, which seem to be derived from African types. Dormer windows are often cut into the roof.

HISPANIC FOLK ARCHITECTURE

Forming a highly distinctive contrast to the Middle Atlantic and lower-southern architectural styles in Texas are the traditional buildings of Mexican-Americans. Along most of the Rio Grande border and

as far to the interior as San Antonio, a variety of Hispanic structures are in evidence (Figure 9.1).

Three principal construction materials are typical of Hispanic folk architecture in Texas. In the drier western part of the borderland, from the Pecos River west to El Paso, adobe brick is the preferred building material among both Mexicans and Hispanicized Indians (Figure 9.15). South Texas, by contrast, contains more picket (*palisado*) construction, with walls formed of poles inserted vertically in the ground or in a horizontal sill. Picket houses are often daubed with clay, plastered, and whitewashed. The crudest huts constructed in this manner are called *jacales*, but more-substantial dwellings are also built of pickets. Some notable examples survive in the La Villita section of San Antonio. Anglos adopted picket construction from the Mexicans and carried it through much of West Texas, where trees were not large enough to permit notched log construction. In the

Figure 9.15. Flat-roofed, adobe Mexican house in El Paso County. Note the typical Spanish doors. (Photo: Marvin Eichenroth, Library of Congress, 1936.)

Hill Country, Anglo double-crib barns are sometimes of picket construction, without daubing or plastering.

Mortared stone construction is also common in the Hispanic borderland, particularly South Texas (Figure 9.16). Numerous noble ranchsteads along the Rio Grande, some dating from colonial times, are built of rock. The higher the socioeconomic class of the owner, the more likely that stone was used as the building material. If stone was not locally abundant, as in parts of the Rio Grande plain, sawed blocks of caliche were sometimes substituted. Regardless of the material used in the wall construction, plaster and paint are usually applied to both the exterior and the interior. Pastel pinks, greens, and blues are often preferred to whitewash on the outside of the house.

Floor plans vary little and normally consist of simple one- and two-room types. Only a relatively few people, the wealthy, lived in traditional Iberian patio or courtyard houses, in which the rooms formed a hollow square. The Governor's Palace in San Antonio is one of the few surviving examples of this plan. After Texas independence in 1836, Mexicans increasingly adopted southern-Anglo floor plans while retaining traditional adobe and *palisado* construction. This blending of architectural traditions can be widely seen in San Antonio and the lower Rio Grande Valley.

Roof form varies in the borderland, closely paralleling the adobe/*palisado* division. From Del Rio to El Paso, in the western part of the borderland, the typical Mexican roof is flat and consists of poles and brush covered with clay and plaster (Figure 9.15). The aridity of the region makes flat roofs practical. Although the flat roof is not lacking in South Texas, the prevalent type there is gabled and closely resembles southern-Anglo roof types. In the lower Rio Grande Valley and adjacent northeastern Mexico, a distinctive parapet gable, possibly of Irish origin, prevails (Figure 9.16). Thatching originally covered these gabled Mexican roofs, but no known surviving examples exist in Texas.

Other features of Mexican domestic ar-

Figure 9.16. Mexican ranchstead, Zapata County, South Texas. The structures are built of stone. Some display the typical Hispanic flat roof; others have the parapet gables commonly found in South Texas. (Photo: A. W. Stewart, Library of Congress, 1936.)

chitecture in Texas include the distinctive Spanish door, which opens in two vertically divided halves, and the small size and number of windows (Figure 9.15). In upper-class homes, grillwork and tiles are common.

In the recent northward spread of Mexican-Americans in Texas, many migrants have moved into dwellings built by Anglos. When such replacement occurs, the presence of the Hispanic culture is often revealed by a variety of superficial architectural and landscaping changes. The dwelling acquires a pastel color to replace the unrelenting white traditionally preferred by Anglos, some windows are boarded up or equipped with baffles, a fence is erected around the front yard, and flower beds replace the lawn.

TEXAS-GERMAN FOLK ARCHITECTURE

Several of the diverse European immigrant groups that settled in Texas left their mark on the domestic architecture of the state. This is true in particular of the immigrants who entered Texas in large numbers before the Civil War, most notably Germans, Poles, and Catholic Irish (Figure 9.17). Because they came in larger numbers than any other European ethnic group, the Germans made the greatest architectural contribution to the state, particularly in South Central Texas.

A prime example of the architectural influence of the Germans in that area is the widespread use of *Fachwerk*, or half-timbered construction, in which a framework of wooden studs is erected and filled in with stone or brick (Figure 9.18). In Texas, the filler is usually native limestone or sandstone and occasionally kiln-fired or adobe brick; in Germany, wattle and daub or brick is most often used. The plastering and whitewashing of the walls of the houses, both inside and out, represents another example of German influence. Many times the plastering conceals the half-timbered construction. The common use of stone as a filler has allowed the German folk houses to survive for over a century. This striving

Figure 9.17. Polish folk house of the Pawelek family in Cestohowa, Karnes County. Built of rock and covered with plaster and whitewash, this structure dates to the nineteenth century. (Photo: A. W. Stewart, Library of Congress, 1936.)

Figure 9.18. A half-timbered (*Fachwerk*) German house in Comfort, Kendall County. The profile and floor plan of the house are typically southern, but the construction method is German. Limestone blocks fill the interstices between the timbering. (Photo: Terry G. Jordan, 1978.)

Figure 9.19. German stone house in Fredericksburg, Gillespie County. The floor plan is typically Anglo-American, but the German desire for permanence caused the builder to use stone rather than log or frame construction. (Photo: Terry G. Jordan, 1961.)

for permanence is a well-known German characteristic, easily observable in the European homeland, and is in sharp contrast to the temporary nature of the early Anglo-American frontier homes. Another German influence can be seen in the widespread use of casement windows and shutters. After a decade or two of building half-timbered dwellings, the Texas Germans, particularly in the Hill Country, shifted to pure stone construction, another type known in their European homeland (Figure 9.19).

The Germans were quick to realize that the houses they had occupied in Europe were in many ways not practical in the warmer Texas climate, in which average monthly and average annual temperatures are 15° F (8° C) or more higher than those in Germany. The German settlers learned to copy the native Anglo-American architectural styles and floor plans they observed in the surrounding counties and towns. To these southern-Anglo styles they applied their own German building methods. The house types they occupied were radically different from those in Germany—as is

evident in the lower angles of the roof slope; the open, covered porches; the outside stairways; the separation of kitchen and barn from the house; and the typical single- and double-pen plans of the Upper South and the dogtrot of the Lower South. Overall, the Texas-German houses were much smaller than the ones the settlers had known in Germany. Between about 1880 and 1900, the Texas Germans built many larger rock houses, often two full stories in height. Close inspection reveals these to be typical Anglo I-houses rather than distinctive German plans.

The best surviving clusters of Texas-German folk architecture can be found in and around the Hill Country towns of Fredericksburg and Comfort, with a significant outlier to the south in the Alsatian community of Castroville. Many of the old houses are being preserved and remodeled, but scores of others have been destroyed in recent decades.

In some of the small German ethnic islands elsewhere in Texas, rather different Old World architectural traits were implanted. A good example is provided by the Russian-German colonies of northern Texas, where German-speaking immigrants from the steppes of Russia and the Ukraine introduced a distinctive building style that is very different from that seen in the German area of South Central Texas. Representative of Russian-German house architecture is the Moser home in the settlement of Hurnville, Clay County (Figure 9.20). Perhaps most striking are its partially hipped gambrel roof with dormer windows and the absence of a front door. The Moser house has stone walls 2 ft (0.6 m) thick, covered with milled wooden siding. These and several other features cause it to resemble Russian-German houses in Kansas and on the eastern European steppes.

SURVEY AND CADASTRAL PATTERNS

Few decisions have a more lasting influence on the rural cultural landscape than those concerning land survey. Once made, such decisions, which involve division of the land, tend to be durable. In some instances, their influence on the countryside persists for thousands of years, shaping not only the configuration of property ownership, but also the road network and economic organization of space. Different cultural and subcultural groups generally possess their own distinctive forms of cadastral land survey, which allows them to place a unique and persistent mark on the landscape.

Figure 9.20. A Russian-German dwelling in Clay County, Texas. (Photo: Terry G. Jordan, 1975; see also Terry G. Jordan, "A Russian-German Folk House in North Texas," in Francis E. Abernethy, ed., *Built in Texas* [Waco, Tex.: E-Heart Press, 1979], p. 136.)

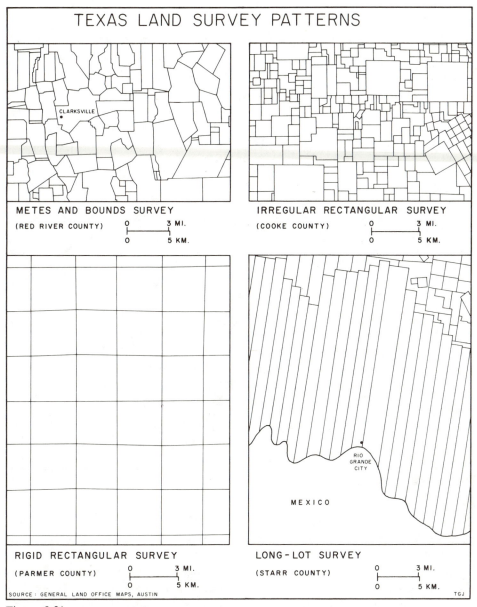

Figure 9.21.

To a considerable degree, the survey patterns visible in the rural Texas landscape can be linked to different cultural and ethnic groups. At least four distinct survey types can be discerned in the state (Figure 9.21). The first of these is the metes-and-bounds survey, characterized by very irregular geometric shapes. No two parcels of land have

the identical shape, and considerable use is made of natural features of the landscape as borders. Creeks, rivers, or large trees are frequently used to mark boundaries or points where the survey line changes direction. In general, this highly irregular pattern occurred when individual immigrants were given a headright grant entitling

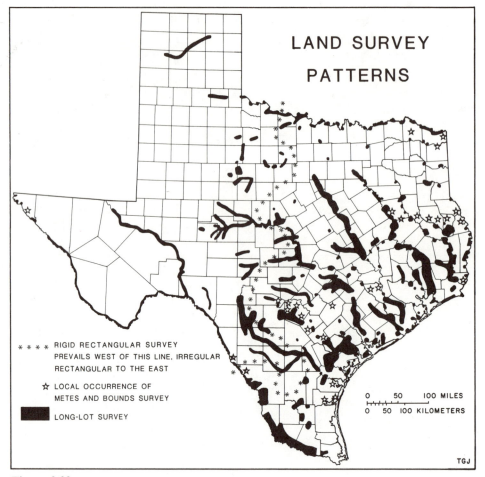

Figure 9.22.

them to a certain amount of land. With certain minor restrictions, that land could be laid out according to the wishes of the grantee on a first-come, first-served basis. In Texas, only small areas of the irregular metes-and-bounds survey can be found, and they are scattered widely throughout the eastern and southern parts of the state (Figure 9.22). It is nowhere the dominant form, but its widespread occurrence suggests that it was important in the heritage of one or more of the ethnic groups that settled Texas.

In sharp contrast to the irregular metes-and-bounds system is rigid-rectangular survey. In this system the survey lines are nearly always oriented to the cardinal directions, and each unit surveyed is roughly square and the same size as all others in the grid. The result is a quite striking checkerboard pattern, totally divorced from the nature of the local terrain, hydrogeography, and vegetation. In Texas the rigid-rectangular system is highly localized, dominating most of western and northwestern Texas but largely absent elsewhere.

The third land survey system is perhaps best described as irregular-rectangular survey. The individual holdings are rectangular or square, as in the rigid-rectangular system, but they vary greatly in size and lack an orderly grid pattern. The lines often do not adhere to the cardinal directions. Even so, the pattern displays more regularity than is found in the chaotic metes-and-bounds system. Irregular-rectangular survey is the most common type in Texas and is found widely through the eastern central, northern, and southern parts of the state.

A fourth land survey system found in Texas is the long-lot type. In this system the parcels are long and narrow, with the depth exceeding the width of the parcel by four times or more. Long-lot surveys line most of the major rivers of Texas, with the narrow side of the individual parcels fronting the stream. No sizable areas of Texas lack concentrations of long-lots, and such surveys exist in a great variety of sizes and degrees of elongation.

Complicating this multiple pattern of survey systems is the fact that there are many fragmented landholdings. In all four of the survey types, the land granted to any one person was often divided into two or more separate parcels, rather than remaining as a unit block. Typically, the grantee settler sold all but one of the parcels, so that fragmented landholdings did not actually result. In some other cases, the fragmentation involved a town lot and outlying farmland so that a farmer could live in town.

The explanation for the multiplicity of survey and cadastral patterns in Texas lies in the state's varied political experience. Both the government of Spain, which ruled Texas until 1821, and the government of Mexico, which held sovereignty from 1821 to 1836, allowed local and provincial officials considerable freedom in choosing survey patterns. Few decisions were dictated from the national level. Texas was a self-governing republic from 1836 to 1845 and thus held the decision-making power concerning land surveys during that period. Upon joining the United States in 1845, the state of Texas retained ownership of its unsurveyed public lands, rather than ceding them to the government of the United States. Therefore, the Texas public lands did not become subject to any survey laws of the United States. All of the survey systems of Texas, then, were shaped by choices and decisions made within the state, not dictated by outside governments.

The metes-and-bounds survey system seems to have had a dual origin. Perhaps the more important of these was the survey tradition of the southern Anglo-American, the cultural group that came to dominate Texas. Many Anglo-Texans derived from Tennessee, Kentucky, Virginia, the Carolinas, and eastern Georgia, where the metes-and-bounds type of survey had been dominant since the early colonial period. Indeed, the southerners had known no other survey system prior to about 1800. It is not surprising that they sought to implant this system in Texas.

At the same time, the irregular metes-and-bounds survey was also used in Mexico. According to Spanish records in the General Land Office of Texas, many grants surveyed for Spanish-speaking settlers in Texas during the periods of rule by Spain and Mexico were laid out in the metes-and-bounds fashion. Many of these surveys occurred long before the southern Anglo-Americans entered Texas; hence the metes-and-bounds system has a Hispanic as well as an Anglo-American background.

The rigid-rectangular survey system, adopted about the middle of the nineteenth century by the government of Texas, was derived directly from the United States. In the 1780s, the federal government of the newly independent thirteen states adopted the rigid-rectangular system. It was first employed in eastern Ohio and subsequently used to parcel out federal lands throughout most of the United States. The basic unit of the system was a square 640-acre (260-ha) section of land, measuring exactly 1 mi (1.6 km) on a side. A block of thirty-six sections, 6 mi (9.7 km) on each side, was called a township, a term derived from the New England area. There is evidence that Thomas Jefferson, one of the originators of the rigid-rectangular type of survey, was influenced by an ancient Roman survey system called *centuratio*. Large areas of the American South were surveyed under the rigid-rectangular system, including most of Georgia, Alabama, Mississippi, Arkansas, and Missouri as well as the western third of Tennessee. Many Anglo-Texans were derived from these areas, and there can be little question that the rigid-rectangular survey system was part of their cultural heritage. The similarity between the Texas and U.S. systems of rigid-rectangular survey is quite striking. In some districts of West Texas, the term *township* was even applied. The government of Texas adopted the rigid-rectangular survey as a conscious effort to bring the state's method of transfer of public domain into harmony with the federal system. However, many or most of the Texas surveys departed from the square-mile size that was universal in the United States.

The irregular-rectangular survey pattern can best be understood as a merger of the rigid-rectangular and the metes-and-bounds systems. Such a mixture is not surprising, since many Anglo-Texans had experienced both of these systems in the American South. They retained the terminology of metes and bounds, together with the tradition of blazing trees to mark survey corners, but also accepted the principle that landholdings should be square or rectangular. But the designers of the irregular-rectangular system resisted the total rigidity of the Jeffersonian system.

The riverine long-lot survey was characteristic of seventeenth- and eighteenth-century French colonies in North America. The ultimate origins of this system probably lie in Central Europe, and from there long-lots spread to northern France and then to North America. The French colonies in the Mississippi Valley provided the example from which Texas's long-lots originated. The long-lot survey system was first used in Texas in 1731, and one century later, a state law made this pattern of survey mandatory for lands lying adjacent to major streams.

The tradition of farm villages with outlying farms was introduced to Texas by the Spaniards in the early 1700s, reinforcing a pattern used by the farming Indian tribes of East Texas. Subsequently, in the 1840s, German immigrants in Central Texas also founded some farm villages. Farmsteads were located on lots in towns or villages, rather than being situated out in the country. Each farmer also owned land outside the village where he grew crops and herded animals. Often this outlying farmland was in two or more separate parcels, adding still more fragmentation to the landownership pattern. The Spanish civilian settlement founded by people from the Canary Islands at San Antonio in 1731 employed this farm-village pattern, as did the initial German settlers at New Braunfels and Fredericksburg. In time, however, the southern Anglo-American system of dispersed farmsteads and unit-block landholdings overwhelmed the Hispanic-German tradition, and the farm villages largely vanished.

The rural landscape of Texas, then, bears the imprint of diverse survey and cadastral systems, each of which has a different areal distribution and cultural heritage. These patterns reveal the multiethnic character of the Texas population. In particular, the Texas systems of land division can be traced to Anglo-American, Franco-American, and Hispanic influences.

TRADITIONAL FENCING

Heightening the visibility of the survey and cadastral patterns are a variety of fence types. In the era before machine-produced barbed wire became available, each major culture and subculture within the state created distinctive types of fences, and many of these traditional enclosures survive and help to reveal cultural regionalization.

Southerners built two typical kinds of folk fence. To enclose their fields and gardens, southern Anglos and blacks erected Virginia worm fences, consisting of split rails stacked in a zigzag or snake configuration so that posts were unnecessary (Figure 9.23). If these were braced at the joints by angular stakes, the result was a stake-and-rider fence. Livestock pens required stronger enclosures, and for that purpose the southerners built the post-and-

Figure 9.23. Stake-and-rider Virginia worm fence bordering a Travis County cornfield. The worm fence is the traditional southern type used to enclose gardens and fields. (Photo: Terry G. Jordan, 1968.)

rail or pole fence, in which units of two adjacent posts about 4 inches (10 cm) apart were placed about every 6 ft (1.83 m) (Figure 9.8). Split rails or poles were then stacked between the posts, producing a rather substantial pen.

Mexican fences are very different from those of the Anglos and blacks. Around their corrals, the Mexicans erected palisades or pickets of cedar poles inserted in the ground and bound together with strips of leather, essentially the same *palisado* technique used to build the walls of houses in South Texas (Figure 9.24). Mexican picket corrals were adopted by Anglos in Southwest Texas and are still being built today, though wire has replaced leather as the binder. Mexican gardens and yards were traditionally enclosed with brush or cactus fences, and a few of these survive in the predominantly Hispanic counties along the Rio Grande in far South Texas.

German farmers and ranchers in the Texas Hill Country contributed to their distinctive landscape by building dry rock fences to enclose pens, fields, and even pastures (Figure 9.25). Hundreds of miles of such fences can still be seen in Gillespie, Mason, Kendall, Comal, and adjacent counties, though few have been built since the advent of barbed wire a century ago. Norwegian farmers in Bosque County built similar rock fences.

*   *   *

The rural cultural landscapes of Texas, then, are diverse and generally reflective of the major cultures and subcultures that were brought into the state. Beneath the layer of broad, predictable regional differences that reveal Middle Atlantic, lower-southern, Mexican, and German implantations is an array of apparent landscape anomalies that both warn against overgeneralization and underline the remarkable degree of cultural/ethnic diversity in the state. Much of Texas is properly regarded as a cultural shatter belt, and its rural landscapes provide abundant evidence to support that view.

Figure 9.24. A Mexican picket, or *palisado,* corral fence, Mason County. The cedar poles are inserted in the ground and bound together with wire. (Photo: Gilbert J. Jordan, 1975.)

Figure 9.25. A rock fence enclosing a pasture in a German-settled portion of Kendall County. (Photo: Terry G. Jordan, 1978.)

Most Texans, however, no longer reside in the countryside. Today they are preponderantly an urban people. Our revelation of internal geographical contrasts turns, therefore, to the city, and the next chapter deals with the urban geography of the state.

SOURCES AND SUGGESTED READINGS

Abernethy, Francis E., ed. *Built in Texas.* Waco, Tex.: E-Heart Press, 1979.

Evans, Elliot A. P. "The East Texas House." *Journal of the Society of Architectural Historians* 11 (December 1952), 1–7.

Grider, Sylvia Ann. "The Shotgun House in Oil Boomtowns of the Texas Panhandle." *Pioneer America* 7 (July 1975), 47–55.

Jordan, Terry G. "Antecedents of the Long-Lot in Texas." *Annals of the Association of American Geographers* 64 (1974), 70–86.

————. "A Forebay Bank Barn in Texas." *Pennsylvania Folklife* 30 (Winter 1980–81), 72–77.

————. "German Folk Houses in the Texas Hill Country." In Glen Lich and Dona B. Reeves, eds., *German Culture in Texas: A Free Earth*, pp. 103–120. Boston: Twayne Publishers, 1980.

————. "German Houses in Texas." *Landscape* 14 (Autumn 1964), 24–26.

————. "Land Survey Patterns in Texas." In Robert C. Eidt, Kashi N. Singh, and Rana P. B. Singh, eds., *Man, Culture, and Settlement: Festschrift to Prof. R. L. Singh*, pp. 141–146. National Geographical Society of India, Research Publication no. 17. New Delhi and Ludhiana: Kalyani Publishers, 1977.

————. *Texas Log Buildings: A Folk Architecture.* Austin: University of Texas Press, 1978.

Kniffen, Fred B. "Folk Housing: Key to Diffusion." *Annals of the Association of American Geographers* 55 (1965), 549–577.

Newton, Ada L. K. "The Anglo-Irish House of the Rio Grande." *Pioneer America* 5 (January 1973), 33–38.

Robinson, Willard B. "Colonial Ranch Architecture in the Spanish-Mexican Tradition." *Southwestern Historical Quarterly* 83 (1979), 123–150.

Vlach, John M. "The Shotgun House: An African Architectural Legacy." *Pioneer America* 8 (1976), 47–70.

Wilhelm, Hubert G. H. "German Settlement and Folk Building Practices in the Hill Country of Texas." *Pioneer America* 3 (July 1971), 15–24.

CHAPTER 10

URBAN GEOGRAPHY

Texas is a dominantly urban state. Its popular image as a sparsely settled land of ranches, farms, and oil fields is more than a half century behind reality. Over four-fifths of its population resides in cities and towns, and 79 percent of all Texans are concentrated in twenty-five Standard Metropolitan Statistical Areas (SMSAs), the major centers of population and industrial activity (Figure 10.1 and Table 10.1). In spite of statewide similarities in the age of the material structures, the role of the automobile, attitudes toward growth and urban planning, certain land-use patterns, and some demographic features, the overall diversity of Texas is abundantly revealed in its urban geography. Texas cities are not identical. The state's urban centers vary greatly in population size, ethnic makeup, economic function, degree of suburbanization, and several other characteristics. In addition, some parts of Texas have a relatively dense pattern of urban places, both large and small, and other regions contain only a few, relatively small towns that serve a still dominantly rural economy.

Many factors interacted to yield the current urban pattern. The imprint of a much earlier settlement pattern remains evident in some areas, although recent, very rapid urban growth has obliterated traces of the past in many other areas. The development and expansion of a modern rail network initiated the changes, which were soon intensified by a rapid surge of economic activity accompanying the discovery and exploitation of vast mineral deposits. The transition to an industrial economy (Chapter 11) furthered the metamorphosis from a rural to an urban society. More recent factors include a shift to technologically intensive forms of manufacturing; the increasing importance of the service sector of the economy; and the Sun Belt location of Texas, which contributed strongly to the immigration of more than 1.5 million people from other parts of the nation between 1970 and 1980.

URBAN EVOLUTION IN TEXAS

The early American and European immigration to Texas was largely in response to the available soil and vegetative resources, and the immigrants were mainly agriculturists, not town or city dwellers. This pattern continued largely unchanged throughout most of the nineteenth century. As late as 1870, only the cities of Galveston (13,818) and San Antonio (12,256) contained more than 10,000 residents (Table 10.2). Houston, now the most populous city between the Mississippi River and the West Coast of the United States, contained only 9,382 people in 1870. Although many towns appear on maps of Texas for this period, only thirteen had a population of 2,000 or more, and these early settlements were concentrated in the eastern and south-central parts of the state (Figure 10.2). With the exception of Laredo on the Mexican border, there were no settlements with as many as 500 residents located west of San Antonio. Few people lived west of a Laredo–San Antonio–Austin-Waco-Dallas line.

Several factors fostered both population growth and urban development during the later decades of the nineteenth century. Major factors contributing to population growth included the arrival of large numbers of dispossessed and displaced southerners fleeing the economic ravages of the Civil War and the entry of substantial numbers of immigrants from northern and north-central parts of Europe. The expansion of a rail network throughout much of the eastern third of the state greatly increased the rate of urban development. The coming of the railroad meant that farmers and ranchers, who then composed an overwhelming majority of the state's population, no longer had to produce so much of their needed equipment, tools, clothing, and other necessities. Their products could now be shipped to distant markets and the income used to purchase goods produced in the more industrially developed parts of the nation. The rapid expansion of commerce stimulated the growth of new trade centers and promoted the growth of fortuitously located existing towns.

The state's population nearly quadrupled during the last three decades of the nineteenth century (Table 3.1), and the number of cities with more than 10,000 residents

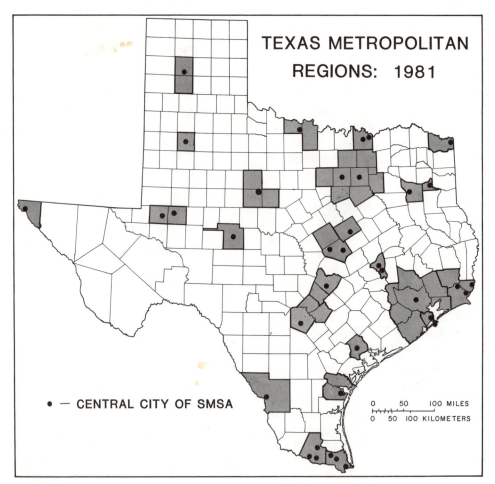

Figure 10.1.

Table 10.1. Population of Standard Metropolitan Statistical Areas, 1980

SMSA	Population	% of Texas Population	Change, 1970–1980[a]
Abilene	139,085	1.50%	22.0%
Amarillo	173,550	1.22	20.2
Austin	456,298	3.21	41.2
Beaumont—Port Arthur—Orange	372,374	2.62	7.6
Brownsville-Harlingen—San Benito	208,125	1.46	48.3
Bryan—College Station	93,487	.66	61.2
Corpus Christi	324,213	2.28	13.8
Dallas—Fort Worth	2,961,225	20.81	27.7
El Paso	478,834	3.37	33.3
Galveston—Texas City	194,091	1.36	14.3
Houston	2,886,962	20.29	44.4
Killeen-Temple	214,005	1.50	33.9
Laredo	99,027	.70	35.9
Longview	150,099	1.05	24.3
Lubbock	211,846	1.49	18.2
McAllen-Pharr-Edinburg	279,187	1.96	53.8
Midland	82,311	.58	20.5
Odessa	115,204	.81	20.3
San Angelo	84,215	.59	18.5
San Antonio	1,065,441	7.49	20.0
Sherman-Denison	89,199	.63	7.2
Texarkana (Texas portion)	74,928	.53	10.5
Tyler	127,178	.89	30.9
Waco	170,590	1.20	15.6
Wichita Falls	129,908	.91	0.0
TOTAL	11,181,382	79.11%	29.8%

[a]Change in population between 1970 and 1980 calculated using 1980 boundaries for both years.

Table 10.2. Number of Cities by Size and Share of State Population, 1870–1980

Year	>10,000 N	>10,000 %	>50,000 N	>50,000 %	>100,000 N	>100,000 %	>250,000 N	>250,000 %	>500,000 N	>500,000 %	>750,000 N	>750,000 %
1870	2	3.19										
1880	5	5.07										
1890	10	9.71										
1900	10	9.35	1	1.75								
1910	19	15.55	4	8.75								
1920	30	23.90	5	13.78	4	12.12						
1930	36	30.89	10	22.62	5	18.03	2	9.49				
1940	44	34.00	11	24.64	4	17.32	3	14.55				
1950	71	47.78	15	34.11	7	27.04	4	22.23	1	7.71		
1960	102	62.16	21	45.58	11	38.42	5	29.63	3	23.02	1	9.79
1970	126	66.20	27	49.50	10	38.36	6	33.04	3	24.39	2	18.55
1980	147	65.67	33	50.54	15	41.35	6	32.26	3	24.18	3	24.18

Source: U.S. Census.

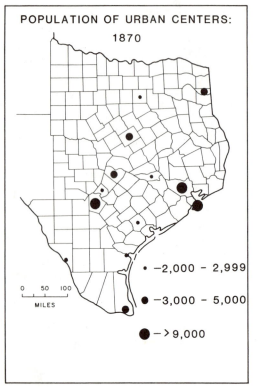

POPULATION OF URBAN CENTERS: 1870

• −2,000 – 2,999

● −3,000 – 5,000

● −>9,000

0   50   100
MILES

Figure 10.2.

increased to eleven. Several of these cities were relatively large for their early stage of commercial development. By 1900, San Antonio, with 53,321 residents, was the most populous city, closely followed by Houston, Dallas, and Galveston. Urban development continued to be concentrated in the regions of early Anglo-American settlement in the eastern and south-central areas (Figure 10.3), although the impact of the relatively dense railroad network in the northeastern quadrant is reflected in the number of small cities that developed there.

The greatest single impetus to economic growth and urban development in Texas was the discovery of the Spindletop oil field near the small lumber milling and port city of Beaumont on January 10, 1901. Spindletop, the world's first major crude-petroleum discovery near ocean shipping facilities, immediately attracted thousands of fortune seekers from other parts of the

nation, and by July 1901 the population of Beaumont had increased from less than 10,000 to more than 50,000. The discovery of vast quantities of easily extractable crude petroleum at Spindletop caused a boom in drilling activity along the upper Texas coast. Many of these efforts were successful, especially in the vicinity of Beaumont and Houston, as were subsequent efforts in many other parts of Texas. The need to provision work crews in the oil fields and the subsequent development of petroleum refineries and oil-field-equipment manufacturers rapidly changed the basic economic structure of the state (see Chapter 11).

These activities also provided a new basis for urban expansion. The rapid influx of newcomers stimulated the demand for agricultural and forest products, thus promoting the growth of agriculturally oriented trade centers in nonpetroleum producing parts of the state. At the same time, many farm workers migrated to the oil fields and new industrial centers. These changes were accompanied by the rapid growth of many existing cities located near the oil fields and by the creation of new cities where none had existed previously. The population of Texas increased by nearly 850,000 during the first decade of the petroleum era and by more than 3 million between 1900 and 1940. But as the state's total population more than doubled, the rural population grew by less than 40 percent. Increasingly, the population was becoming concentrated in the urban centers.

Both the number and the size of cities increased considerably during the first few decades of the twentieth century. By 1930 both Houston and Dallas contained more than 250,000 residents, and San Antonio and Fort Worth were not far behind. Nearly one-third of the state's population was in the thirty-six cities that had a population of more than 10,000, and more than one-fifth was in cities with more than 50,000 residents. Significant urban centers began to appear outside the eastern and south-central areas. The east-west, urban-rural dichotomy—previously so pronounced—

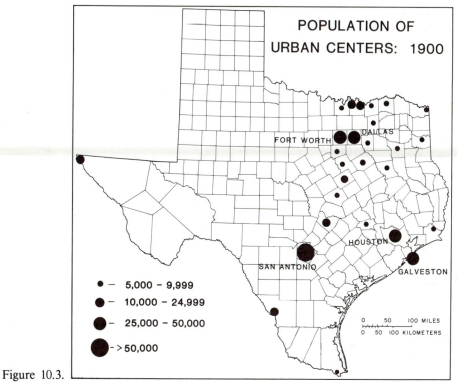

Figure 10.3.

was dissipating, a trend that has continued to the present.

The economic turmoil of the 1930s affected Texas less severely than most other areas of the United States. The minerals industries continued to grow, but the agricultural base weakened, and the forest industries declined markedly. The rate of urban expansion slowed only slightly, and by 1940 over one-third of the state's population lived in cities of more than 10,000, and nearly one-half was concentrated in urban places. San Antonio joined Houston and Dallas in the over-250,000 class, and Fort Worth neared 200,000. Seven other cities had more than 50,000 residents. Texas was no longer dominantly rural; the urban population was about to surpass the rural.

The surge in economic activity that accompanied World War II, and the changes in the structure of industrial activity in subsequent decades, have been major factors in the further acceleration of urban growth. The entire 1940–1970 period wit-

nessed a continuing decrease in the size of the rural population (Table 3.1), a rapid increase in the size of the urban population, and a pronounced growth in the number of medium and large cities (Table 10.2). These trends have resulted in the emergence of Texas as the third most populous state and one of the most highly urbanized in the Union.

In 1980 most Texas cities with a population of 25,000 or more were in metropolitan regions; only five were in nonmetropolitan regions. One-fourth of the cities of that size were suburbs within the Dallas–Fort Worth SMSA (Figure 10.4). Currently more than four-fifths of the population resides in urban places, and nearly one-half lives in cities with populations of more than 50,000. The three most populous cities are Houston (1,594,086), Dallas (904,078), and San Antonio (785,410), each of which is among the largest in the United States; respectively ranking fifth, seventh, and eleventh in the nation. Collectively these three cities contain more than one-fifth of the total state population, and their SMSAs contain nearly 50 percent of the state's residents (Table 10.1). Several relatively large cities dominate other parts of the state. Three—El Paso (425,259), Fort Worth (385,141), and Austin (345,496)—exceed 300,000 population, and another nine cities exceed 100,000. However, the most rapid urban growth is not occurring in the central cities of the metropolitan regions, but in their suburbs—especially around Houston and in the Dallas–Fort Worth metroplex.

Urban growth has not been restricted to the metropolitan regions, however. Most cities that had more than 10,000 residents in 1970 registered growth during the next ten years. The pattern is more varied for the smaller cities, especially in the less-urbanized parts of the state (Figure 10.5), and even though many of the smaller cities are growing rapidly, a substantial number continue to decline in population. The in-creasing concentration of major industrial activity in the metropolitan regions and in the larger nonmetropolitan cities offers better economic opportunities and attracts population from the smaller cities (Figure 10.6). Another major contributor to urban growth during the last decade has been immigration from other states. This Sun Belt migration is largely attributable to a perception of lower costs of living, better economic opportunities in an expanding economy, spaciousness, physical environmental amenities, and easy access to other regions through excellent air transportation services.

TOWN PLANS

Each region of Texas has a distinct urban personality and individuality. In part this diversity rests in the morphology, the physical structure and layout of urban places, and the town plan is one basic aspect of morphology.

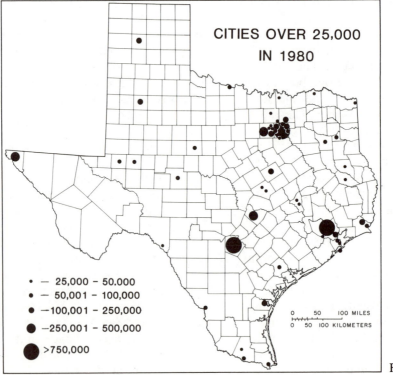

Figure 10.4.

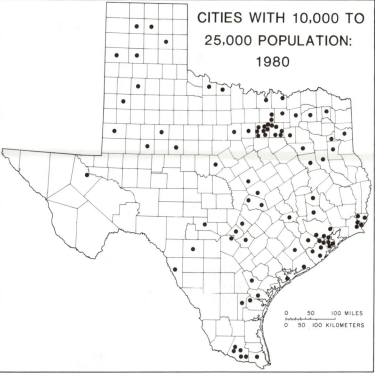

CITIES WITH 10,000 TO 25,000 POPULATION: 1980

Figure 10.5. More than three-fifths of the cities with 10,000 to 25,000 population are in metropolitan regions. Very large concentrations are in the Dallas–Fort Worth and Houston SMSAs. Cities of this size are absent from the metropolitan regions in the western part of Texas where large-scale suburbanization has not occurred.

Some of the contrasts in town layout are traceable to the very founding of the urban places by different cultural-heritage groups. Spaniards, Anglos, and Europeans all placed their distinctive mark on the state's urban morphology. The form of the Spanish-Mexican town reflected careful planning and was centered upon an open main square, or *plaza mayor*. Normally somewhat elongated and often tilted off the cardinal directions, the *plaza mayor* was traditionally an open, dusty expanse. In the 1860s, Empress Carlota in Mexico initiated a beautification campaign that resulted in the planting of trees, flowers, and grass, together with the building of fountains and bandstands, in the main plaza, a campaign that spread across the international border into South Texas. Fronting the *plaza mayor*, typically, are a Catholic cathedral or church on one side, a city hall or other government building on another, and homes of the wealthiest citizens. Good surviving examples of the Spanish-Mexican *plaza mayor*

arrangement include San Antonio, where the San Fernando Cathedral and Bexar County courthouse face the landscaped main plaza; San Diego in Duval County; Castroville west of San Antonio; and San Elizario near El Paso. Beyond the *plaza mayor* in the Spanish-Mexican town, a grid pattern of narrow streets is encountered. Outlying, additional plazas are typical, as is a roofed public market, usually located several blocks from the *plaza mayor*. Again, San Antonio provides good examples of such features.

Southern Anglo-Americans, or more exactly, upper southerners bearing the cultural heritage of southeastern Pennsylvania, introduced a rather different town plan into Texas. Its distinguishing trait was the county seat with a central courthouse square. A grid pattern of streets, usually oriented to the cardinal directions, was made to accommodate a spacious square, in the middle of which was erected the county courthouse, which served as the principal symbol of civic pride. Around the perimeter of the

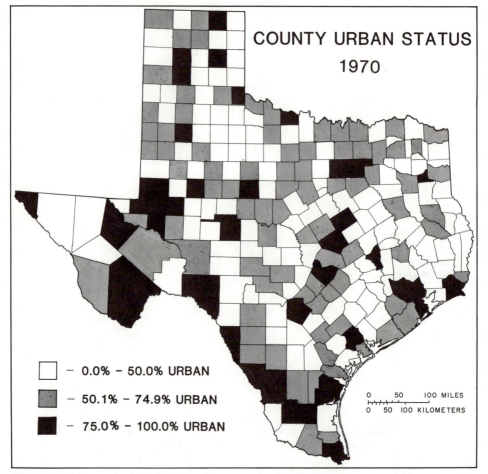

Figure 10.6. Several of the highly urban counties in the western parts of Texas actually contain only one small town and a few rural residents. Most of the more populous eastern and central counties contain much larger numbers of urban residents, although they have a smaller proportion of their total population in urban places.

square, facing the courthouse, the principal shops and stores of the town were situated, which added a mercantile function to the governmental role of the courthouse (Figure 10.7). Residences and churches did not find a place on this focal square and were instead located on access avenues and back streets. A variety of courthouse-square types occur in Texas, but the most common is the so-called Shelbyville plan, named for a town in the south-central part of Tennessee from which the plan seems to have spread (Figure 10.8). The oldest plan is the type labeled Lancaster, introduced into early colonial Pennsylvania from northern Ireland along

with the county form of government. This ancestral Scotch-Irish town plan underwent modification in the United States to produce the Shelbyville and other variant forms. The central courthouse square still remains a viable and highly visible aspect of urban morphology in many Texas counties today.

European town builders introduced a third tradition into Texas. The focus was a central marketplace, in the middle of which a church was often built. Fredericksburg, a German town in Gillespie County, and Panna Maria, the earliest Polish settlement in Texas, are examples of this tradition. In other cases, a decorative

Figure 10.7. Courthouse square in the Hill County seat of Hillsboro. The Hillsboro plan is of the type called the Shelbyville square. (Photo: John L. Bean, 1981.)

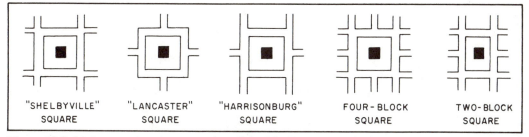

Figure 10.8. Major courthouse-square plans found in Texas. Terminology is derived from Ed Price, "The Central Courthouse Square in the American County Seat," *Geographical Review* 58 (1968), 29–60.

Figure 10.9. European-style fountain in the market square in the center of New Braunfels. (Photo: Terry G. Jordan, 1962.)

fountain was made the focal point of the market square, as in the German town of New Braunfels (Figure 10.9).

OPENNESS

Developments in the twentieth century have generally acted to diminish the traditional regional contrasts in Texas's urban morphology. One of the form elements that most Texas cities seem to have in common is openness. The impression of openness—or compactness—that an individual forms about a city is really a simple visual measure of population density, or number of people per unit area. The cities of Texas, both large and small, generally are lower in population density than are cities in the Northeast and Midwest. In many parts of the United States, and elsewhere around the world, population densities on the order of 5,000 to 8,000 persons per sq mi (2,000 to 3,000 per sq km) are not uncommon, and much higher densities are found in many of the very largest cities. Most Texas cities have densities below $3,500/\text{mi}^2$ ($1,350/\text{km}^2$), and the highest density for a major Texas city is that of San Antonio at slightly more than $4,000/\text{mi}^2$ ($1,544/\text{km}^2$) in 1980. Nationally, the density of cities tends to increase with increasing population size, and this relationship is generally characteristic of the cities of Texas (Table 10.3). Many of the smaller urban centers have densities below $1,500/\text{mi}^2$ ($579/\text{km}^2$), lower than those of rural regions of intensive subsistence agriculture in parts of Asia and the Middle East.

The most significant factors affecting urban population density are those that influence the value of land. These include the total quantity of usable land in relation to the different types of demand, the transportation network for both people and goods, and the cost of compensating for undesirable physical environmental conditions. An additional factor of considerable importance is the attitude of residents regarding space in their living environment, an attitude that is largely conditioned by cultural heritage. Although Texas is very diverse in many respects, there is little difference in these factors from one part of the state to another. Urban land costs, although increasing rapidly, remain lower than in many other urban regions of the United States. Highway and internal thoroughfare construction are the responsibility of the state government, and the effort to provide a dense network of quality facilities has been statewide. Further, the construction of a system of modern highways and internal thoroughfares began before the most rapid phase of population growth in many cities and has generally either led or kept pace with the rate of population increase. Few cities in Texas face significant restric-

Table 10.3.   Selected Characteristics of Cities with Population Over 25,000 (1970)

City	Pop. per mi²	Median Age of Residents	% of Single Family Houses	City	Pop. per mi²	Median Age of Residents	% of Single Family Houses
Abilene	1,197	25.2	83.9	Killeen	1,366	21.9	55.2
Amarillo	2,092	28.0	82.8	Kingsville	2,677	21.9	77.3
Arlington	1,471	24.2	66.0	Laredo	3,367	21.8	85.5
Austin	3,492	23.9	66.7	Longview	2,015	29.0	84.8
Baytown	1,731	28.2	84.0	Lubbock	1,970	23.3	77.8
Beaumont	1,642	27.9	81.9	McAllen	2,788	23.1	84.0
Big Spring	2,245	26.4	80.7	Mesquite	2,137	22.7	90.5
Brownsville	3,455	20.8	85.6	Midland	2,036	26.8	86.7
Bryan	2,007	25.0	82.3	Odessa	4,260	25.6	87.2
Corpus Christi	2,033	24.4	80.0	Pasadena	2,522	24.4	70.4
Dallas	3,179	27.5	62.4	Port Arthur	1,190	30.6	85.9
Denton	1,445	22.3	68.4	Richardson	1,735	24.9	82.8
El Paso	2,724	22.8	70.9	San Angelo	1,896	26.9	85.7
Farmers Branch	2,272	25.0	86.2	San Antonio	3,555	24.8	77.2
Fort Worth	1,919	28.1	75.7	Sherman	1,522	29.2	81.1
Galveston	2,943	31.1	62.8	Temple	1,479	31.8	82.3
Garland	1,885	24.0	84.8	Texarkana	1,883	32.4	81.6
Grand Prairie	576	24.4	84.8	Texas City	580	26.2	84.4
Haltom City	1,480	27.7	87.0	Tyler	2,501	29.6	87.2
Harlingen	1,489	24.1	84.4	Victoria	2,491	24.8	85.6
Houston	2,841	26.1	67.3	Waco	1,624	30.7	78.8
Hurst	2,474	24.6	77.1	Wichita Falls	2,281	26.0	79.8
Irving	2,413	24.3	69.7	State as a whole	43	26.6	80.6

Source: U.S. Census, 1970.

tions on land availability or usefulness because of the physical environment. The major exception is probably Galveston, where the quantity of land is limited because of the island location and where a substantial proportion of the total land area is not suitable for dense urban development. Finally, even the cultural factor of attitude toward spaciousness is generally similar throughout the state. Until the recent migration of large numbers of people from the Northeast and Midwest, most of the newcomers to Texas cities were from rural areas, where openness was common and accepted as the natural order of things. There is, however, a fairly consistent pattern of higher-than-average population densities in cities where the per capita income is low or blacks or Hispanics constitute a relatively large proportion of the population.

The pattern of population densities within individual cities is considerably more varied and complex than the pattern of general urban densities. The highest residential densities generally are found in the inner core with increasingly lower densities toward the outer, more recently developed, and more prosperous parts of the city. Secondary concentrations of high density frequently occur near major employment centers, such as major industrial complexes and universities, and in areas inhabited largely by low-income or minority populations. Internal density patterns are further complicated by the existence of sizable tracts of undeveloped land in Texas cities of all sizes. Open tracts of land as large as 5 acres (2 ha) on the periphery of the downtown business centers are not uncommon in even the largest cities in the state and similar tracts of 100 acres (40 ha) or more occur in the outer parts of many cities. Such undeveloped areas frequently amount to 1 mi² (2.5 km²) or more in areas of "leapfrog" suburban development in the major metropolitan regions.

TYPES OF HOUSING

The dominance of the single-family home in Texas is most pronounced in the small cities of less than 10,000 population, where more than 90 percent of the households are of this type. In many of these small urban centers, the proportion approaches 100 percent. The proportion in the larger nonmetropolitan cities, and in many of the older metropolitan suburbs, is only slightly lower than in the small cities (Table 10.3). Apartments are much more common in the central cities of the larger metropolitan regions. These relationships are not absolute, however, as unique conditions bring major deviations from the norm. The situations in the cities of Killeen and Denton provide good examples. Killeen, with a 1980 population of 46,146, is one of the two primary cities in a small metropolitan region and is adjacent to a very large military base. Because many military personnel and their families reside in Killeen, the city has almost as many apartment units as single-family homes. Denton, the location of two state universities, is at the northern edge of suburban development associated with Dallas. More than one-third of the households in Denton live in multiunit facilities, a rapidly increasing proportion of which consists of apartment complexes serving both the university population and people who are employed either locally, in Dallas, or in other northern suburbs of that city.

Other exceptions to the normal pattern occur in several fast-growing suburbs within the larger metropolitan regions, most notably around Dallas–Fort Worth, Houston, San Antonio, and Austin. A combination of factors contributes to the increasing importance of multiunit structures in these areas. Two interrelated factors are rapid growth and soaring construction costs, which cause the prices of single-family homes to exceed the financial reach of an increasing number of residents. Also of major importance are the effects of changing life-styles and the relatively large proportion of newcomers who recently migrated from urban regions where apartment living has been more prevalent than in urban Texas. Twenty years ago, more than nine out of ten urban households in Texas resided in single-family homes; today only about three-quarters do. This change has not occurred uniformly throughout all Texas cities and metropolitan regions. Instead, significant variations exist in the housing mixture between cities of different sizes and between the central cities of the metropolitan regions and their suburbs.

Architecturally, multifamily housing in the state's urban regions consists almost entirely of low-rise structures. Only in the principal cities of the larger metropolitan regions are high-rise residential structures found, and then infrequently.

THE ROLE OF THE AUTOMOBILE

The automobile has been as significant in forging the internal form and structure of modern Texas cities as the railroads and the early exploitations of minerals were in determining which of the small urban centers of the late nineteenth century would emerge as centers of commerce and industry. Economic development and population growth followed the construction of highways and arterial streets; areas bypassed by these facilities faced obstacles to both economic expansion and population growth. The importance of the motor vehicle is reflected also in general land-use patterns; more land is devoted to streets and parking than to any other nonresidential use in most cities. The dominant role of the automobile as a mechanism for shaping Texas cities is easily understandable when it is recognized that the people in more than 90 percent of the metropolitan households own an automobile, and it is quite common to find ownership rates approaching one per adult in many neighborhoods. The ratio of motor vehicles to population does not vary very much between different parts of the state. Only in a few of the smaller urban centers and in the cities where Hispanos are a major element in the population is the ownership ratio markedly lower.

As a result, Texas cities are spatially expansive. That is, they utilize much more land area to support a given population and level of economic activity than is typical for the nation as a whole. They are characterized by large residential homesites, numerous vacant tracts scattered through built-up areas, and horizontal development of both commercial and industrial areas. Multilane freeways, crossing and encircling the urbanized areas, have been constructed to improve access to distant parts of the metropolitan regions (Figure 10.10). Even many of the smaller cities contain such systems. The freeways have stimulated a "leapfrog" development of both residential neighborhoods and commercial-industrial complexes on the outskirts of all but the smallest urban centers. This pattern of linear expansion along the freeways and major arterials is not restricted to those cities and metropolitan regions that have undergone rapid growth during the automobile era, but is also present in many of the older cities. As a result, many downtown centers are deteriorating as businesses move to the outer fringes of cities.

Cities that have experienced significant growth during the past few decades generally have a two-phase arrangement of

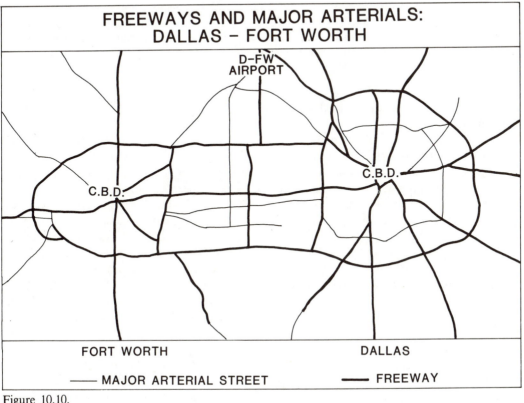

Figure 10.10.

Figure 10.11. Suburban development north of Dallas. Plano is a fast-growing suburb; its population increased from 17,872 in 1970 to 71,956 in 1980. The street pattern in the residential neighborhoods shields the ground observer from the large undeveloped spaces and the commercial developments scattered through the area. (Photo: John L. Bean, 1981.)

nonarterial streets. The streets in the older residential neighborhoods and the original commercial-industrial core typically form a rectangular grid, and the more recently developed areas tend to be characterized by irregular street patterns, which make movement through the area difficult (Figure 10.11). Arterial streets frequently slice angularly through the basic pattern, masking its nature from the casual observer. Further, the imposition of arterials subsequent to the development of the basic street pattern has often involved the absorption of the front parts of residential lots or even the demolition of existing structures. As a result, large areas of many cities have been altered as different, and frequently incompatible, types of land use move into the disrupted arterial frontages.

ETHNIC MAKEUP

"What is a city, but the people?" queried Shakespeare (*Coriolanus*, 3.1.198). The typical urban center in Texas today is ethnically diverse, perpetuating a very old tradition. Even in Spanish colonial times, San Antonio, then the only substantial urban place in Texas, consisted of clearly defined ethnic quarters. Pureblood Spaniards, mainly of Canary Islands ancestry, lived in the *villa* on the right bank of the San Antonio River, and persons of mixed blood and Christianized Indians were obliged to live in *la villita* (the "little town"), a slum on the left bank.

By the time of the federal census in 1850, the ethnic diversity of Texas towns had become even more complex, and a

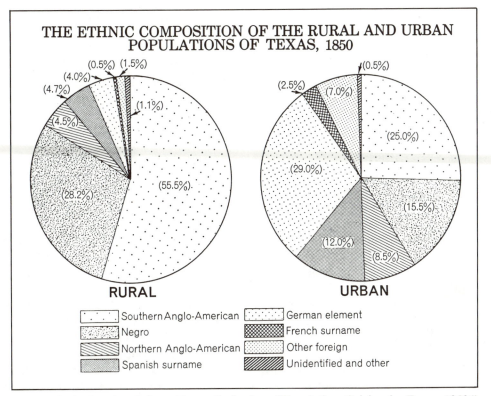

THE ETHNIC COMPOSITION OF THE RURAL AND URBAN
POPULATIONS OF TEXAS, 1850

RURAL

URBAN

Southern Anglo-American   German element
Negro   French surname
Northern Anglo-American   Other foreign
Spanish surname   Unidentified and other

Figure 10.12. Reprinted from Terry G. Jordan, "Population Origins in Texas, 1850," *Geographical Review* 59 (1969), 100, with the permission of the American Geographical Society.

major urban-rural contrast was evident (Figure 10.12). Ethnic and racial minorities formed a much larger proportion of the urban population than of the rural areas, with the exception of blacks. San Antonio was partitioned into Anglo, Hispanic, and German quarters, and other urban places such as Houston and Galveston also had ethnic neighborhoods. Each town had its own distinctive mixture of ethnic groups (Table 10.4).

Today the same basic pattern prevails, though no noteworthy European ethnic neighborhoods survive. Hispanos and blacks are the only major urban ethnic and racial groups in Texas. Fewer than one-sixth of the blacks remained in rural areas by 1970; nearly two-thirds resided in the central cities of metropolitan regions, and most of the others lived in urban centers outside the metropolitan regions. Very few resided

in suburban cities, a pattern that remains to the present. The flow of blacks into the cities continued during the 1970s, and by 1980 nearly 90 percent resided in the urban centers of the state. Today blacks compose over one-fourth of the populations of Dallas, Houston, and Beaumont—among the cities of over 100,000 inhabitants (Table 10.5)—and have achieved or are approaching majority status in numerous medium-sized and small cities. Just as blacks were originally concentrated in the rural areas of East Texas, they are now clustered in the cities of the eastern half of the state. Most urban centers in the western part contain relatively few blacks.

Until the late 1960s, legal restrictions and informal agreements severely limited the parts of Texas cities in which blacks could reside. Although the legal impediments have now disappeared, strongly held

Table 10.4. Ethnic Makeup of Urban Places of Over 1,000 Inhabitants, 1850

Urban Place	Population	% Southern Anglo	% Yankee	% Black	% Spanish Surname	% German Element	% French Surname	% Other Foreign
Galveston	4,177	24	13	17	.5	33	3	9
San Antonio	3,488	18	7	7	42	17	3	6
Houston	2,396	38	9	22	.3	22	3	5
Marshall	1,189	57	4	35	0	1	1	2
New Braunfels	1,298	5	1	5	.2	88	0	.3

Source: Hand count of the manuscript population schedules, U.S. Census.

attitudes continue to limit their residential choice in many cities. In the larger urban centers, blacks are slowly emerging from congested ghetto neighborhoods and moving into the general residential areas, but few have moved into the more affluent and prestigious neighborhoods of the central cities, and very few reside in the fastest-growing large suburbs. Tarrant County, the location of Fort Worth, presents a typical example of the spatial concentration of blacks in major Texas cities. Blacks composed more than 11 percent of Tarrant County's 716,317 residents in 1970, but 92 percent were concentrated in only 26 of the more than 150 census tracts in the county, and one-sixth of the census tracts contained no blacks (Figure 10.13). Most of the remaining census tracts contained fewer than ten blacks each.

Hispanos are more widely dispersed, but they had become the most numerous ethnic minority in Texas by 1970. Although members of this group constituted a significant proportion of the rural and urban populations of South Texas and of cities in the border region even before the Texas Revolution, it is only in the past few decades that they have moved in significant numbers into cities in other parts of Texas. They now compose a majority of the population of most cities, both large and small, in the

Table 10.5. Ethnic Makeup of Selected Cities of Over 100,000 Population, 1980

City	Population	% Black	% Hispanic	% Black & Hispanic
Amarillo	149,230	5.5	9.2	14.7
Arlington	160,123	2.9	4.0	6.9
Austin	345,496	12.2	18.7	30.9
Beaumont	118,102	36.7	3.5	40.2
Corpus Christi	231,999	5.1	46.6	51.7
Dallas	904,078	29.4	12.3	41.7
El Paso	425,259	3.2	62.5	65.7
Fort Worth	385,141	22.8	12.6	35.4
Houston	1,594,086	27.6	17.6	45.2
Lubbock	173,979	8.2	18.8	27.0
San Antonio	785,410	7.3	53.7	61.0
Waco	101,261	21.8	11.1	32.9

Source: U.S. Census, 1980, advance counts.

225

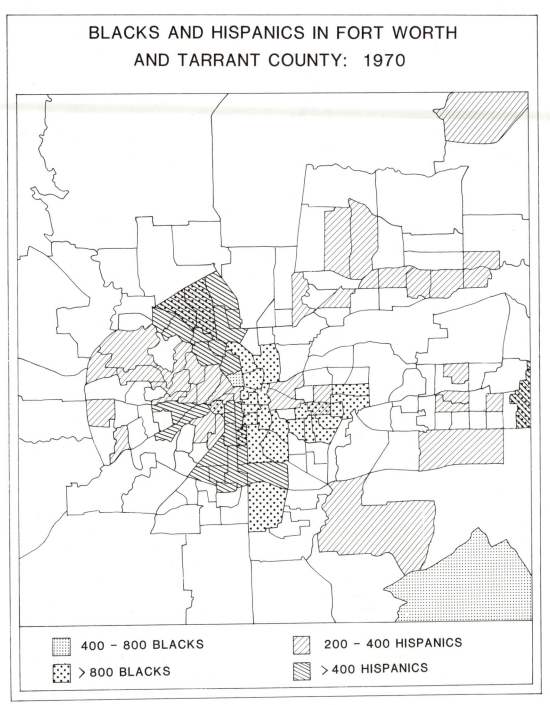

Figure 10.13.

lower Rio Grande Valley and are also the majority in several of the larger cities elsewhere in the state, including San Antonio and El Paso (Table 10.5). Although they remain relatively few in number in the smaller cities of East Texas, their numbers are increasing there and over most of the rest of the state as well.

Hispanos, like the blacks, were restricted to residence in designated areas of many Texas cities until quite recently, but they have been more successful than the blacks in diffusing into the general residential areas, particularly when they achieve middle-class status. Although easily identifiable Hispanic neighborhoods are found in most cities where large numbers of Mexican-Americans are present, many people of this ethnic group have moved from these neighborhoods into other parts of the central cities and into the suburbs. For example, the modest-sized Hispanic population of the middle-class Dallas suburb of Irving is dispersed through the city, and there is no suggestion of an ethnic neighborhood. Their relative success in dispersing can also be seen in Tarrant County and Fort Worth, where blacks remain segregated. Although relatively few Hispanos resided in Tarrant County in 1970, they were more diffused spatially than the blacks. Approximately 55 percent were concentrated in 25 census tracts; the remainder was spread among more than 100 census tracts. Only 11 tracts were devoid of Hispanos, and several of those were located within totally black neighborhoods. Indeed, the most pronounced residential segregation found in Texas urban areas exists between Hispanos and blacks. Both of these minorities mix with Anglos more than they mix with each other.

Few other identifiable ethnic groups are found in significant numbers in Texas urban areas. Three American Indian neighborhoods, largely Choctaw, have developed in Dallas, and Cajun French are numerous in the smaller industrial satellites around Beaumont in Southeast Texas. Individual streets and cul-de-sacs in the middle-class

and upper-middle-class neighborhoods of Dallas, Fort Worth, and some other cities are dominated by Jews, Italians, or Greeks. In Dallas, a large northern section, extending into the suburb of Richardson, approaches the status of an affluent Jewish "ghetto." All in all, though, the northerner visiting Texas cities will be struck by the absence of European ethnic neighborhoods, and this absence is one of the major differences between southern and northern cities.

AGE STRUCTURE

The cities of Texas vary markedly in several other demographic and socioeconomic characteristics that are useful in defining a city's image. A good example is the comparative age structure of the population. The median age of the population of Texas was 26.6 years in 1970 (Table 10.3), a slight decline from previous periods, and all available evidence indicates that the decline is continuing; this trend contrasts with the national pattern in which the median age of the population is increasing. The ongoing decline in the median age of Texas residents reflects the impact of large-scale immigration from other regions of the United States and from Mexico. Most of the newcomers, both the refugees from the Frost Belt of the Northeast and Midwest and from Mexico, are younger and settle in the metropolitan centers. As a result the populations of both the central cities and their suburbs are increasingly younger than the populations of the smaller cities, whose age patterns are skewed toward older age groups (Figure 10.14).

Not all of the metropolitan regions share equally in the influx of people from other areas; the larger central cities absorb a disproportionately large share of the Hispanos, and many of the Sun Belt seekers settle in the suburban cities of the metropolitan regions. The results of these locational choices are reflected in variations in the urban age structure. Thus, cities in which Hispanos compose a large proportion

227

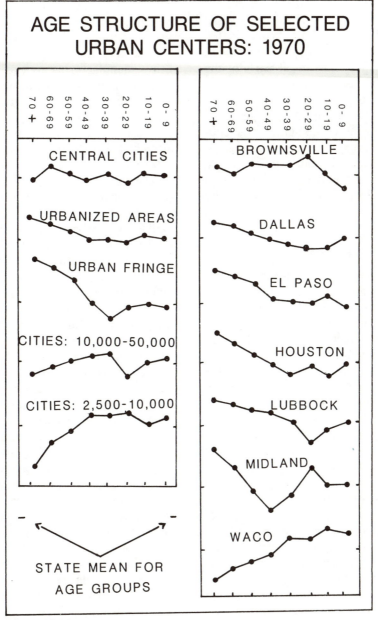

Figure 10.14.

of the population generally have large numbers of people in the younger age groups. Examples include Laredo, Brownsville, El Paso, and most of the other cities along the Rio Grande. Cities with high median-age populations include the older, stable, medium-sized centers such as Texarkana, Galveston, Waco, and Port Arthur in the eastern third of the state. Also included are many smaller cities in all parts of the state except the Rio Grande Valley. With the exception of El Paso, the population age structures of the largest cities generally parallel that of the entire state. Large suburbs within the major metropolitan regions are typically relatively young, reflecting the large numbers of young families migrating from other industrial regions of the United States.

SUBURBAN DEVELOPMENT

Suburbanization, the concentration of a significant proportion of the urban population into smaller cities around the peripheries of larger cities, was late in coming to the Texas urban scene. Less than 10 percent of the metropolitan population lived in suburban cities in 1950. One of the reasons was the relatively broad annexation powers possessed by large cities until the early 1960s. Changes in the state's annexation laws at that time provided additional protection to small towns adjacent to large urban centers; and the suburbs have subsequently increased in population at a much greater rate than the central cities. By 1970 the suburbs contained nearly one-quarter of the metropolitan population, and the trend continues. The larger central cities now contain only about two-thirds of the population in metropolitan regions.

The intensity of suburban development and growth varies widely among the metropolitan regions. With the exception of the San Antonio area, a very high proportion of the populations of these largest metropolitan regions is concentrated in the suburbs. The ratio of suburban to central-city population is about fifty-fifty in the Dallas–Fort Worth region, and it is only slightly lower in the Houston region. However, many of the smaller, more widely separated metropolitan regions have relatively little suburban development. Amarillo, Laredo, Lubbock, Midland, Odessa, San Angelo, Sherman-Denison, and Tyler fit this pattern. The smaller metropolitan regions that have large concentrations of heavy manufacturing are exceptions, as exemplified by the Beaumont–Port Arthur–Orange and Galveston–Texas City areas. Each contains several smaller cities possessing certain characteristics of both an industrial satellite and a residential suburb.

The most complex pattern of suburban development, and the largest concentration of suburban population, is found in the Dallas–Fort Worth region (Figure 10.15). Dallas is almost completely bounded by suburban municipalities; Fort Worth is bounded on the east and northeast but defensively annexed a narrow strip around its southern and western suburbs. More than four-fifths of the region's population is concentrated in Dallas and Tarrant counties, where these two cities are located. These two counties also contain nearly fifty suburban municipalities, each with more than 2,500 residents, and several other suburban cities in adjacent counties are contiguous to the suburbs in Dallas and Tarrant counties. Many of the suburban cities are relatively large: three contain more than 100,000 residents, three others are above 50,000, and another sixteen have populations exceeding 10,000. Although most are bedroom communities, serving primarily as a labor source for Fort Worth and Dallas, several are also centers of commercial, service, and manufacturing activities. Because Dallas is surrounded by contiguous suburban development and Fort Worth can expand territorially only in directions away from the most dynamic areas of economic expansion, future population growth is expected to occur principally in the suburbs.

Houston has been quite aggressive in annexing undeveloped territory and in in-

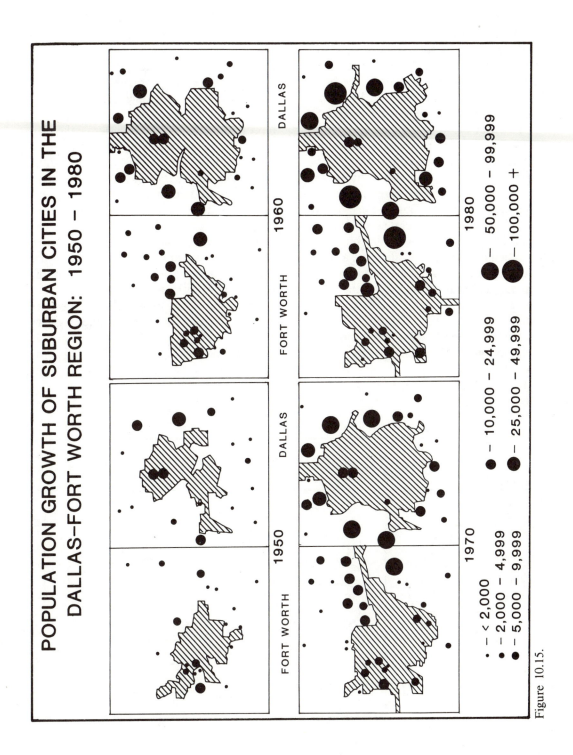

Figure 10.15.

corporating adjacent small towns into its fold, but it has expanded to the point that it is bounded by suburban cities around much of its perimeter. Because of its aggressive annexation policy, however, Houston has more internal space available for future population growth than do the other large cities of the state. Most of Houston's western suburbs are largely residential in character, but those to the east and southeast of Houston are more nearly industrial satellites than bedroom communities. The pattern of suburban development in the other metropolitan regions is relatively simple compared to the Dallas–Fort Worth and Houston regions. Several suburban municipalities adjoin San Antonio, but none are particularly large, and all serve a dominantly residential function. Suburban development is less pronounced in other metropolitan regions, which contain very few suburban communities. Essentially all of those that do exist serve as residential havens for workers in the primary cities of the regions.

ZONES, SECTORS, AND NUCLEI

The spatial patterning of commercial centers, industry, residential density, housing quality, and ethnicity exhibits a considerable degree of symmetry in most urban areas. Three general models have been identified in the geographical literature as best representing these general patterns: the concentric-zone, sector, and multiple-nuclei models (Figure 10.16). The concentric-zone model depicts a series of generally circular zones arranged around the central business district (CBD). No Texas city provides a satisfactory example of this pattern. The sector model, by contrast, suggests a pattern in which the various categories of land use emanate as wedge-shaped areas from the CBD. The multiple-nuclei model is characterized by a dominant CBD, the presence of one or more secondary and tertiary commercial-industrial nodes, and relatively complex patterns of sectors or land-use zones focusing on those nodes.

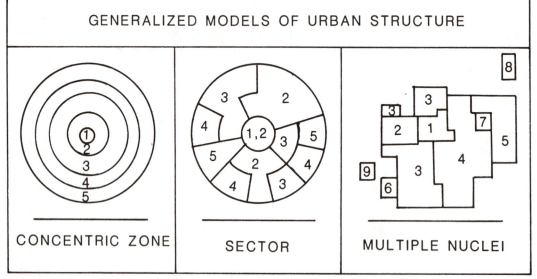

Figure 10.16.
Key: 1 = central business district; 2 = light manufacturing and wholesaling; 3 = low-income residential; 4 = medium-income residential; 5 = high-income residential; 6 = heavy manufacturing; 7 = secondary business district; 8 = residential suburb; 9 = industrial satellite.

The sector model dominated the internal spatial arrangement of nearly all Texas cities and urban complexes until about twenty-five years ago. Today, however, most of the larger cities and many of the medium-sized and small cities present an altered pattern that reflects the increased importance of commercial-industrial nodes in outlying parts of the city. Generally only those cities that have experienced growth patterns considerably below the state's urban norm still exhibit a clearly dominant sectoral pattern; two of the best remaining examples are Beaumont and Fort Worth. Significant variations from a simple sector pattern are visible even in these cities, however. Most of the smaller urban places, particularly those with populations under 20,000, continue to exhibit a pattern that is closer to the sector arrangement than to the other general models.

The purest examples of the multiple-nuclei arrangement of land use are found in small to medium-sized urban centers, particularly in the lower Rio Grande Valley, where most urbanization has occurred during the past two to three decades. Nearly all of the dynamic, large urban complexes, as well as the largest cities, have patterns that reflect a combination of the sector arrangement in the older parts of the city and the multiple-nuclei arrangement in the more recently developed outlying zones. Critical elements in this marriage of spatial patterns have been the advent of the modern suburban shopping center–business complex, the shift of manufacturing to locations on the urban periphery, and the concomitant building of urban freeway systems. A major contributor to alterations in the residential density and housing quality patterns has been the process of filtering, in which a family moving to the suburbs is replaced in the inner city by a larger, and poorer, family.

A few municipalities have land-use patterns that bear no visible resemblance to any of the three basic models. Most of them are residential, or bedroom, suburbs. Very few are true cities, and their irregular patterns are the result of special conditions, such as dominance by one major employer or physical environmental restrictions. Galveston provides an excellent example of the latter situation.

Commercial and industrial activities are quite diffused in most Texas cities and metropolitan regions (Figure 10.17). The principal city of each metropolitan region, and many of the smaller nonmetropolitan cities, contain an easily recognizable CBD, the skyline of which may be relatively impressive when viewed from ground level at some distance. However, such a perspective often obscures the linear, open configuration of many CBDs and the large amount of space devoted to streets and parking. The CBDs of most Texas cities are much smaller geographically than might be expected for a given population and level of economic activity. For example, the Houston CBD, which serves as the central hub of a city of more than 1,500,000 and which is the dominant commercial center for the southern part of the state, encompasses fewer than 5 sq mi (12.5 sq km), and more than one-third of its surface is devoted to the automobile (Figure 10.18). Both Dallas (Figure 10.19) and Fort Worth (Figure 10.20) present very similar patterns. The CBDs of many of the smaller cities are unimpressive, frequently consisting largely of older, low-rise structures. The CBDs of most of the smallest urban places are visible only from ground level after the observer has arrived in their midst.

The diffusion of commercial activities into peripheral parts of the city is nearly universal in the more-dynamic metropolitan regions, but it is more apparent visually in some of the largest cities, where both isolated skyscrapers and clusters of tall buildings dot the skyline. Houston and Dallas–Fort Worth are both examples of this diffusion as there are few locations in the newer parts of either region in which such structures or complexes are not visible. Several of the clusters in Houston and Dallas are comparable in size and diversity to the CBDs of only slightly smaller met-

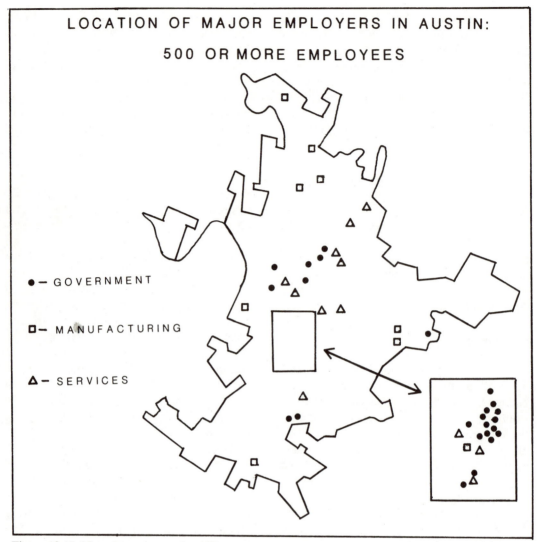

Figure 10.17. Note the segmentation of large commercial and manufacturing employers into different parts of the city. The large number of public service facilities reflects the presence of the center of state government.

ropolitan centers. The complexes along South Main Street and the Galeria in Houston are outstanding examples. Although not so visually apparent, the scattering of commercial activities into peripheral parts of the city is also occurring in many small cities, even though the physical structures are generally much smaller and the degree of spatial diffusion is greater. Overall, the fragmentation of the CBD is most pronounced in those cities and urban regions

that have experienced the greatest population growth and economic expansion during the last two decades. Relatively stable urban centers contain less evidence of such scattering.

The most significant factors contributing to the diffusion of commercial activities are generally similar for all Texas urban centers. Low population densities and the absence of good public transportation systems make travel to and from the central

Figure 10.18. Aerial view from the east of the Houston CBD and part of its freeway loop. (Photo: John L. Bean, 1981.)

core difficult, even with nearly universal automobile ownership and modern freeway systems. Employers of large numbers of workers can combine information on their labor force profile with projections of the city's direction of residential growth to secure an advantage in recruiting new employees. This is particularly advantageous for firms that employ large numbers of professionals and other white-collar workers who are increasingly becoming concentrated in the newer suburbs. The outward movement of retail stores into suburban shopping centers is part of an established national trend; the primary goals are to ease access for customers and to provide adequate parking space (Figure 10.21). Efforts to reverse or retard the diffusion of

commerce from the CBDs have included the physical rejuvenation of parts of the downtown centers of several cities. The architectural and aesthetic results have been outstanding in a few cities—such as San Antonio and Dallas—but universally unsuccessful in stemming the outward migration of commercial activity.

Manufacturing is nearly as scattered spatially in the metropolitan regions and cities of Texas as are other types of commercial activity. Manufacturing plants increasingly are being relocated into planned industrial parks in the outlying parts of the cities where land is much cheaper than in the inner core, where highway and rail access are less affected by traffic congestion, and where skilled workers can live in newer

Figure 10.19. Aerial view from the south of the Dallas CBD. Secondary commercial developments and a few high-rise apartment buildings appear in the background. Some of the undeveloped tracts are as large as 50 acres (20 ha). Dense urban development extends for more than 10 mi (16 km) beyond this view. (Photo: John L. Bean, 1981.)

residential neighborhoods. The structures within these industrial parks usually are only one or two stories in height but spread horizontally to provide large amounts of floor space. Landscaping of both the building sites and the large parking areas is common. The design of the structures, combined with the landscaping, frequently makes it feasible to locate moderately large, light manufacturing, wholesaling, and other commercial facilities adjacent to new suburban developments without substantial opposition from the residents.

Only two types of manufacturing activity remain largely immune to this outward migration. Manufacturers that require access to water transportation—such as the large, export-oriented petroleum refineries and petrochemical plants in the southeastern part of the state—are still drawn to sites that are adjacent to the major waterways. These plants are clustered in the few locations where the critical transportation facilities are available. The other

exception involves manufacturing plants that utilize large numbers of unskilled and semi-skilled workers. Such firms frequently find it advantageous to retain locations in or very near the core area of a city in order to be near their less-mobile labor supply.

Relatively little difference exists among the metropolitan regions and other urban centers of the state in the degree of scattering of commercial and industrial activities away from the central core. Certainly there is little contrast among the various parts of the state. The only real basis for such differentiation, and it is weak, relates to the size and growth rates of the cities.

The locational distribution of multiunit housing varies within cities principally according to population growth trends. Cities in particular regions of the state present disparate patterns, and the variations from one part of the state to another are not consistent. The central cities of the larger metropolitan regions are relatively comparable, largely because their population growth trends have been somewhat similar. The older, pre–World War II residential neighborhoods near the inner cores of such cities contain many former single-family homes that have been converted into small apartments. Residential neighborhoods somewhat farther out and some of the older suburbs (ca 1955–1970) contain numerous duplexes and other small multiunit structures. A scattering of medium-sized apartment complexes, most containing fewer than fifty units, characterize these areas. The pattern for the newer, rapidly growing suburbs is more complex. Many of these suburbs impose legal restrictions that prohibit large, multiunit housing developments. Other suburbs, especially those containing large employment clusters, welcome, or at least tolerate, apartment complexes. Clusters of large apartment buildings are increasingly common in some suburbs, as well as in the fastest-growing parts of the

central cities, particularly in the major metropolitan regions such as Dallas–Fort Worth, Houston, and Austin.

Multiunit housing is both less important and less predictable in its location in the smaller metropolitan regions. The two outstanding characteristics of these smaller centers are a dominance by single-family homes and a prevalence of duplexes and other relatively small structures among the multiunit structures. Apartment complexes are typically smaller than in the larger metropolitan regions and frequently contain fewer than forty units each. Only in some of the more dynamic cities—such as Odessa, Wichita Falls, and Amarillo—are notable exceptions to the size and cluster norms found. Further, the suburbs of most of these smaller metropolitan regions consist almost entirely of single-family homes. The spatial mixture of housing types varies markedly in these centers. Single-family

Figure 10.20. Aerial view from the south of the inner city of Fort Worth. The CBD in the center is surrounded by a complex mixture of manufacturing, trade, services, and residential land uses. Open, undeveloped land is present along the Trinity River floodplain and as open spaces within areas of urban development. (Photo: John L. Bean, 1981.)

Figure 10.21. A new shopping center at the extreme edge of residential development in southwest Fort Worth. The land beyond, to the south and southwest, is all ranchland. (Photo: John L. Bean, 1981.)

homes that have been converted into apartments occur thoughout the central cities, as do small apartment structures that contain from ten to twenty units. Larger apartment complexes, generally with fewer than fifty units, are also scattered in seemingly random fashion.

The most important derivative of the mixture of housing types is the impact of neighborhood residential density on such factors as automotive traffic and the cost of essential public services. Neighborhoods that consist largely of single-family homes obviously tend to have lower internal traffic densities and higher costs per housing unit for municipal and other public services. For example, one of the reasons that good public transportation systems are lacking in most Texas urban regions is the low potential load factor per route mile. The residential density in the older neighborhoods typically is in the range of six or seven homes per acre (fifteen to seventeen per ha). Densities drop to about half this level in the newer parts of most cities and

are even lower in the fringe areas. Such low housing densities, coupled with the wide scattering of commercial-industrial activity, contribute to the relatively high levels of automotive traffic on major arterial streets. Too, the marked directional bias in the location of newer housing developments contributes to severe rush-hour congestion on freeways and other major arterials leading to the suburbs. North Dallas and southwest Houston are excellent examples of this phenomenon, but similar patterns are to be found in many of the smaller metropolitan regions as well.

*   *   *

The differences among Texas cities are of a lower order of magnitude than the differences encountered in landforms, climate, rural settlement patterns, agriculture, and industrial activity. City differences appear to relate more to size and economic function than to regional location, or even to metropolitan or nonmetropolitan status. The almost universally dominant development creeds of Bigger is Better and New and Bigger is Best are major contributors to the pattern of general similarity. The quest for continual growth, whatever the cost, and for replacement of usable, but older, structures is apparent in the material newness of Texas cities. This "dynamic" might have yielded a set of cities nearly identical in appearance and nature, but only if some master plan were being followed. Instead, the fierce independence of the people, expressed in their antagonism toward uniformity and planning, has assured a moderate degree of urban diversity. For example, Houston has no zoning laws, and the results are readily apparent to the first-time visitor. Too, the diverse cultural beginnings of urban development in Texas played a role in assuring a modest degree of urban diversity.

Rapid industrialization has been the major contributor to the growth of urban population and to the growth and broadening of economic activity in both the urban and rural regions of Texas. The next chapter focuses on industrial activity, with particular emphasis on manufacturing.

SOURCES AND SUGGESTED READINGS

Bean, John L. "Central City Annexation Policy and Suburban Municipal Growth: Dallas and Fort Worth as Examples." *Municipal Matrix* (North Texas State University for Community Studies) 9 (June 1977), 14.

Conway, Dennis, et al. "The Dallas–Fort Worth Region." In *Contemporary Urban America, Twentieth Century Cities*, ed. John S. Adams, vol. 1, part 4, pp. 1–39. Association of American Geographers Comparative Metropolitan Analysis Project. Cambridge, Mass.: Ballinger Publishing Co., 1976.

Davidson, Claud M. "Population and Urban Growth on the Texas South Plains." *Ecumene* 11 (1979), 12–27.

————. *A Spatial Analysis of Submetropolis Small-Town Growth*. Research Monograph no. 35. Austin: University of Texas, Bureau of Business Research, 1972.

DeAre, Diana, and Poston, Dudley L., Jr. "Texas Population in 1970: 5. Trends and Variations in the Populations of Nonmetropolitan Towns, 1950–1970." *Texas Business Review* 47 (1973), 11–16.

Harris, Joe B., et al. *Urban Texas: Past—Present—Future*. Austin: Texas Urban Development Commission, 1971.

Holz, Robert K. "Texas Population in 1970: 7. Patterns of Population Distribution." *Texas Business Review* 47 (1973), 125–129.

Larsen, Lawrence H. *The Urban West at the End of the Frontier*. Lawrence: Regents Press of Kansas, 1978.

Nelson, Howard J. "Townscapes of Mexico: An Example of the Regional Variation of Townscapes." *Economic Geography* 39 (1963), 74–83.

Palmer, Martha E., and Rush, Marjorie N. "Houston." In *Contemporary Urban America, Twentieth Century Cities*, ed. John S. Adams, vol. 1, part 4, pp. 107–149. Association of American Geographers Comparative Metropolitan Analysis Project. Cambridge, Mass.: Ballinger Publishing Co., 1976.

Price, Ed. "The Central Courthouse Square in the American County Seat." *Geographical Review* 58 (1968), 29–60.

Reed, S. G. *A History of the Texas Railroads*. Houston: St. Clair Publishing Company, 1941.

Rodriguez, Louis J., ed. *Dynamics of Growth: An Economic Profile of Texas*. Austin: Madrona Press, 1978.

Smith, Lamar. "Texas in the Seventies: 8. The Urbanization of Texas." *Texas Business Review* 44 (1970), 228–233.

Zlatkovich, Charles P., et al. *Texas Metropolitan Area Profiles*. Austin: University of Texas, Bureau of Business Research, 1979.

CHAPTER 11

INDUSTRIAL GEOGRAPHY

The transition of the society of Texas from being overwhelmingly rural to dominantly urban occurred during a relatively brief span during the first half of the twentieth century. This metamorphosis accompanied significant changes in the state's basic economic structure. Although the acquisition of raw materials from the land—crops, minerals, and timber—remains critically important even today, the economy of Texas is increasingly focused on processing, distribution, and service activities. The primary instrument of this change was the development of a large industrial base.

LOCATIONAL FACTORS

Industrial development is not automatic, and very rapid development of large-scale industrial activity is relatively rare. A myriad of factors interact to foster the growth of industrial activity and to influence its locational pattern. Most of these industrial location factors may be grouped into three general categories: production inputs, market, and transportation. Production inputs are those elements that are required for the operation of a manufacturing plant. They include land, capital, raw materials, labor, and energy. The market consists of the eventual consumers of the products and services of industry and includes individuals, businesses, and other manufacturers.

Thus the size of the market is affected by the size of the population, the level of commercial activity, the amount of other industrial activity present, and the wealth of the market members. The transportation element is particularly important because it is essential for the assembling of production inputs and for moving products to market. The transportation facilities in modern industrial regions include much more than highways, railroads, and waterways; electric power transmission systems, pipelines, and airports are also essential. Several major industrial location factors—such as locational amenities, public policy, the personal preferences of founders or current management, and geographic inertia—do not fit well into these three general categories.

The different locational factors vary considerably in the spatial scale at which they operate and in the way they influence specific Texas industries. Some factors are nearly ubiquitous over relatively large regions. Capital, energy, land, taxes, public policy, and some amenities are examples. Generally, these factors are most useful in helping us understand why certain industries have, or have not, developed on a large scale in a particular region of Texas; they are infrequently useful in explaining the precise location of individual activities within a region. Certain other industrial location factors tend to be more spatially restrictive. Labor-intensive industries are attracted to large urban centers, where the labor supply is larger and more varied than in small towns and rural areas. The market for consumer goods, and also for most industrial goods, is generally stronger in urban regions than in rural regions, and the opposite is true for such products as farm supplies and equipment. Transport facilities vary markedly in quality and availability, even within individual major urban centers. Access to highways and electric power networks may be almost universal in such centers, but good access to a railroad, waterway, or pipeline system is generally very limited. Finally, many raw materials are highly localized and thereby exert a strong locational attraction to user industries.

Specific industries are affected in quite different ways by individual location factors. For example, refineries using large quantities of imported crude petroleum require good port facilities. However, such facilities are usually of minimal importance to industries such as food processing, printing and publishing, apparel, and precision instruments. Nevertheless, a few broad generalizations can be made regarding the role of individual factors:

1. Industries that employ large numbers of workers are attracted to areas of major population concentrations. Quite clearly, the available labor supply in sparsely settled rural regions and small towns is generally inadequate to meet either the quantitative or the qualitative requirements of firms employing many hundreds, or thousands, of workers. Thus in Texas, as elsewhere, most large industrial facilities, whether relocating or newly developing, are sited in the larger metropolitan centers.

2. Industries employing largely unskilled or semiskilled workers are attracted toward low-wage regions, or at least toward the lowest-wage area within a region. Thus, food processing and the mass manufacture of wearing apparel tend to be located in the smaller cities and within the inner cities of major metropolitan regions. This bias is well illustrated, on both the intraregional and the interregional scales, in the patterns of food processing and wearing apparel manufacturing in Abilene, Brownsville, El Paso, McAllen, and San Antonio.

3. Industries are attracted toward the source of necessary raw materials if a significant decrease in weight, bulk, or perishability occurs during processing. The lumber and paper industries of East Texas are good examples.

4. Industries are attracted toward their market centers if a significant increase in weight, bulk, or perishability occurs during processing. The strong concentration of bottling plants and bakeries in the metropolitan centers illustrates this factor.

5. Industries that require frequent personal contact with their customers are attracted toward the location of those customers. The overwhelming concentration of financial and business services in the Houston and Dallas areas provides good examples. Other illustrations include the concentration of designer fashions in Dallas and suppliers of high technology components for the aerospace industry in both Dallas and Fort Worth.

6. Industries that rely on specific forms of transportation or communication facilities are strongly attracted to the locations where such facilities are well developed and easily accessible. The prime example of this relationship in the southwestern United States is the association of petroleum refining and petrochemicals production with the port facilities of the upper Texas Gulf Coast.

7. Industries that rely on a highly skilled or specialized labor force are attracted toward high-amenity locations. Dallas–Fort Worth, Houston, and many other Sun Belt metropolitan centers are frequently perceived as offering "a higher quality of living potential" than many of the older, established industrial centers of the Northeast and Midwest. These high-amenity cities are experiencing rapid economic growth and are widely thought of as centers of oppor-

tunity by skilled workers from other parts of the nation. This is a major element in the attractiveness of the Sun Belt for high technology industries.

8. Industries with a large fixed investment in plants and facilities, or which previously have attracted substantial affiliated industries, may remain in a location long after changes in fundamental location factors would make it difficult for the successful development of the industry if it were just commencing to operate in the location. Much of the industrial development in Texas is too new for this factor to be significant; only the continuing concentration of producers of oil field equipment in the Beaumont and Houston areas long after the center of exploration and development has shifted to distant locations provides a good example.

MEASURING INDUSTRIAL ACTIVITY

One of the problems in describing and analyzing a broad range of industrial activities is the selection of an appropriate method to measure the levels of activity. Each industry is different and is best viewed through indicators that measure its unique characteristics. For example, capital and the value of loans outstanding are good criteria of the level of banking activity. The dollar value of sales is appropriate for retail trade, wholesale trade, and perhaps the service industries. The quantity of cargo carried might be used for transportation. Manufacturing activity can be revealed by a wide assortment of measures such as number of plants, number of employees, value of payroll, and value added by manufacturing (VABM). Although no single measure is ideal for all industries, the best compromise is probably the number of employees. Detailed employment data, broken down into relatively small geographic units such as counties and cities, are readily available for all major industrial sectors. One disadvantage of this index is the likelihood of reducing the apparent importance

of highly automated, technologically advanced industries, but if we remain aware of this potential problem and do not accept employment as an absolute measure of the importance of an activity, an acceptable degree of accuracy and understanding can be achieved. In the following discussion of industrial activity in Texas, the number of employees will be utilized as the primary criterion of measurement. Additional criteria will be used, as appropriate, in describing the various industrial sectors.

TYPES OF INDUSTRIAL ACTIVITY

Industrial activity is frequently divided into nine major categories: (1) contract construction; (2) finance, insurance, and real estate; (3) federal, state, and local government; (4) manufacturing; (5) mining; (6) retail trade; (7) services; (8) transportation, communication, and utilities; and (9) wholesale trade. More than 70 percent of Texas's industrial employment is nearly equally divided among four of those categories: manufacturing, government, retail trade, and services (Figure 11.1). Contract construction, wholesale trade, the transportation-communication-utility sector, and the finance-insurance–real estate group are roughly comparable to one another in employment. Mining, which was a critical element in opening the way for change in the Texas economy, has become the lowest-ranking employment sector.

The immense changes that began to alter the economic structure of Texas after the turn of the century apparently have not yet run their course, although their pace and intensity have been greatly reduced. The most pronounced and significant change of the last two decades has been the increased importance of the service sector (Figure 11.2). This change is not unusual, as it is typical of a maturing industrial economy. It derives from the increased importance of hotels and motels, repair services, entertainment and recreation businesses, health care, social services, and the like.

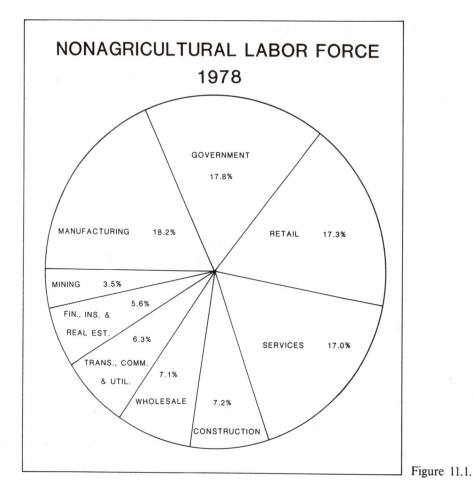

NONAGRICULTURAL LABOR FORCE
1978

GOVERNMENT

17.8%

MANUFACTURING   18.2%

RETAIL   17.3%

MINING   3.5%

5.6%

FIN., INS. &

REAL EST.

6.3%

SERVICES   17.0%

TRANS., COMM.

& UTIL.   7.1%

WHOLESALE   7.2%

CONSTRUCTION

Figure 11.1.

A second notable change has been the decreased proportion of the state's industrial employees in the transportation-communication-utilities sector. This change is relatively complex, reflecting a very slow growth in transportation employment resulting from changes in the relative importance of railroads, ships and barges, and trucking. At the same time, employment in both the communications and the utility sectors have increased quite rapidly. A somewhat similar circumstance is reflected in the finance-insurance–real estate group, which, as a whole, has remained relatively steady. Recent growth has been entirely within the banking and real estate sectors while employment in the insurance sector has declined by nearly one-third during the past two decades. The decrease in the rel-

ative importance of retail trade is probably attributable largely to the replacement of many small retailers by a much smaller number of chain store operations. The emergence of a large manufacturing industry was the catalyst for much of the economic change in Texas.

MANUFACTURING RESOURCE BASE

The development of a resource base capable of supporting a high level of manufacturing activity commenced on a large scale well after the beginning of the twentieth century. Although the pace of urban development had quickened with the provision of a railroad network during the last two decades of the nineteenth century, the

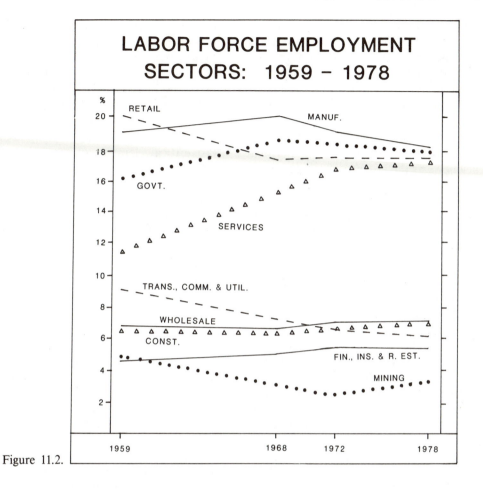

Figure 11.2.

state's economy initially had retained its agrarian orientation. As late as 1900, the basic processing of meat, grains, timber, and cottonseed accounted for more than 40 percent of total manufacturing employment. The same activities generated more than one-half the total value of all manufacturing products. These manufacturers were largely export oriented, and their products were shipped to other parts of the United States and to Europe. All except meat packing were concentrated in the smaller urban centers in the areas that produced the raw materials. The pattern included lumbering in Southeast Texas, grain milling and cottonseed processing in the central region, and meat packing in the larger cities. Industries that focused on supplying the needs of the rapidly growing

population operated on a considerably smaller scale. They included other types of food processing, railroad equipment, printing, apparel, and metals fabrication. The primary centers of industrial activity at the turn of the century were the cities of Houston, Dallas, and San Antonio, but every town and city had its own bakery, foundry, ice plant, print shop, and in South Central Texas, brewery. Major regions of specialized industrial activity had not yet developed, and Texas was not a major center of industrial activity. There was not yet a sufficient industrial resource base.

The construction of the railroad network and the resultant growth in population had begun to supply the two essential elements of an industrial resource base The development of deep-water ports and ship channels to the Gulf of Mexico at Houston and Beaumont added to the transport base. A small base of capital was developing from the profits of the expanding cotton, commercial grains, ranching, and lumbering activities. But the relative isolation of Texas, in culture as well as distance, from the more industrially developed parts of the nation remained a problem. Another critical deficiency was the absence of a large energy source. The beginning of the solution to both of these deficiencies came in January 1901 with the discovery of the Spindletop oil field. It was just south of Beaumont and adjacent to the deep-water ship channel then being constructed along the lower Neches River and lay less than 25 mi (40 km) from the Gulf of Mexico. Spindletop was not the first oil field in Texas. Earlier oil discoveries had occurred in Nacogdoches County in East Texas (1866) and in Navarro County on the Blackland Prairie (1895), but those small fields were incapable of providing a base for significant industrial development. Spindletop was different. For a short time, daily production from Spindletop exceeded the combined production of the rest of the world's oil fields, and Texas became more important to the nation and the world. Within three months, the first tanker load of Texas crude was outbound from Beaumont for Europe. Further, the discovery of Spindletop stimulated exploration, and discovery, in other parts of the state. In addition to many smaller fields in Southeast Texas, major discoveries were made in Wichita County (1911), Eastland County (1917), and Limestone County (1920). The largest discovery, made in 1930, marked the beginning of the famous East Texas oil field.

Suddenly Texas possessed what appeared to be a limitless source of industrial energy and a raw material that could provide the basis for a major processing industry. Images were altered. Texas was no longer perceived as a backward, southern agricultural state, but instead as a southwestern, dynamic one. Thousands of people flocked to Texas in search of their fortunes. Many of these newcomers were skilled in business practices and were soon to provide the management skills needed by the state's growing industrial firms. But more than people were attracted to Texas by the discovery of oil. Capital flowed into the state to finance exploration for new oil fields and to support industrial development. The last critical elements of the industrial resource base were becoming available.

Texas rapidly evolved into a major mineral-producing state, largely because of its increasing crude-petroleum production, which reached nearly 100,000,000 barrels per year by 1920 (Figure 11.3). Although much of the production was exported to other places, enough remained to support a new, large, high-wage, and very profitable petroleum refining industry. Production grew rapidly, doubling every ten years through 1950.

Crude petroleum and natural gas have dominated the Texas minerals industry since the beginning of the twentieth century, but other minerals are also important to the state's economy. Texas currently ranks first in the United States in the production of crude petroleum, natural gas liquids, natural graphite, magnesium metal, helium, and recovered sulphur. It ranks second to Louisiana in the production of natural gas. Other important minerals include lignite coal, salt, lime (cement), and construction materials such as sand, gravel, and shell. These minerals are more restricted spatially in occurrence than oil and natural gas are and have been chiefly important in the development of more-localized industries.

Although Texas is a significant supplier of numerous minerals to other regions of the United States, most of the state's production is either processed or consumed directly within the state. This pattern has been particularly pronounced for petroleum and several of the lower-value minerals such as sand, lignite, gravel, stone, and shell. This feature of the consumption pattern has been of critical importance in the transformation of the state's economic structure. If most of the petroleum, a critical

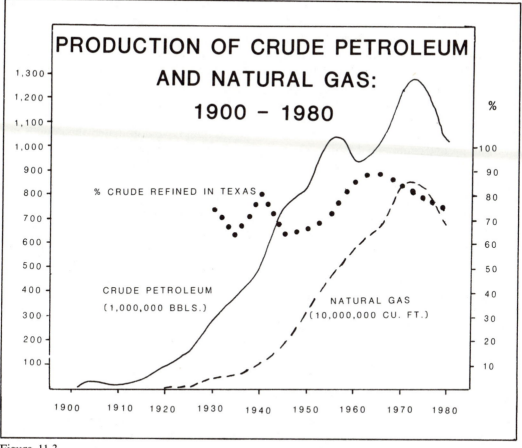

Figure 11.3.

industrial raw material, had been exported to other regions, there would have been a much weaker industrial resource base. This is a problem that has long plagued many of the major mineral-producing countries of the developing world.

The raw materials base for Texas industry is not limited to minerals. The products of the agricultural sector constitute the major resource in several parts of the state (see Chapter 8), and the size of the labor forces for and the value of the products from the agricultural and timber industries continue to increase. That growth reflects increased levels of raw materials production of many of those items, as well as the increased importance of processed foodstuffs in our diet and the shift from a simple conversion of timber into lumber

to the production of plywood, paper, and furniture.

MANUFACTURING STRUCTURE

Manufacturers have the common trait of processing a raw material into a more usable or useful form, but they often differ substantially in other respects. One relatively simple means of differentiating between types of manufacturing is based on the nature of the raw material input. This approach can be quite useful in describing the evolution of industrial activity within a general region. Another method of differentiation is by product category, an approach appropriate in examining the locational pattern of industrial activity within a large complex region.

Industries utilizing previously unprocessed raw materials are called primary manufacturers. This group includes most food processing plants, textile mills, lumber mills, paper mills, many chemical plants, petroleum refineries, tanneries, and primary metal smelters. Each uses as its basic raw material a product of the extractive activities, which include agriculture, forestry, mining, and commercial fishing. These primary manufacturers tend to have several other common traits. Most are considered aesthetically undesirable and are often visually displeasing and noisy. Several of the industries require relatively large amounts of land for a plant, and an orientation to rail and/or water transport facilities is common. This group of manufacturers is strongly attracted to the source regions of their basic raw materials.

The initial manufacturing development of a region frequently is concentrated in one or more of these primary industries. In early Texas the processing of food and other agricultural products and lumber milling provided the primary industrial base. The second stage of Texas industrial development, from the early years of the twentieth century to about the middle 1950s, also emphasized the primary industries, including petroleum refining, petrochemical production, and the continued expansion of the previously developed industries. Primary manufacturers remain very important in the state's overall industrial scene, but they no longer form the central focus of industrial growth.

Many types of industry use practically no unprocessed raw materials. These types include the manufacturing of apparel, furniture, some chemicals, leather goods, fabricated metals, machinery, electrical and electronic equipment, transportation equipment, and instruments as well as printing and publishing. There appears to be less commonality among the characteristics of this group of manufacturers than for the primary processors. Apparel plants and leather goods producers are attracted toward lower-wage areas, but wage rates tend to be high in chemicals, machinery, and transportation equipment production. Some of these industries, such as printing, may be visually and aurally unobtrusive, whereas fabricated metals plants are frequently considered to be aesthetically offensive. These technologically advanced manufacturers, who use the output of the primary manufacturers, have dominated the growth picture of Texas's industrial activity during the past few decades (Figure 11.4). For example, the growth patterns of aircraft assembly and the production of electrical and electronic equipment have been particularly dynamic. Such activities also stimulate the growth of the primary manufacturers who supply the processed raw materials.

GENERAL LOCATION OF MANUFACTURING

The metamorphosis of Texas industry in the twentieth century took place in three distinct periods. The first covers the time from the discovery of the Spindletop oil field in 1901 to the end of the Great Depression of the 1930s; the second period, the 1940s and most of the 1950s; and the third, the next two decades.

Manufacturing employment in Texas grew nearly continuously during the first third of the twentieth century. But even though the number of manufacturing employees more than quadrupled between 1900 and 1939, the proportion of the state's population employed in manufacturing remained in the general vicinity of 2 percent (Figure 11.5). Most manufacturing involved the processing of basic raw materials and was therefore locationally oriented toward the source region of the raw materials. It was concentrated spatially almost exclusively in the eastern and east-central parts of Texas. Local processing of agricultural products in the western regions was poorly developed. Even as late as 1940 the only notable concentrations of manufacturing activity were in the Dallas–Fort Worth,

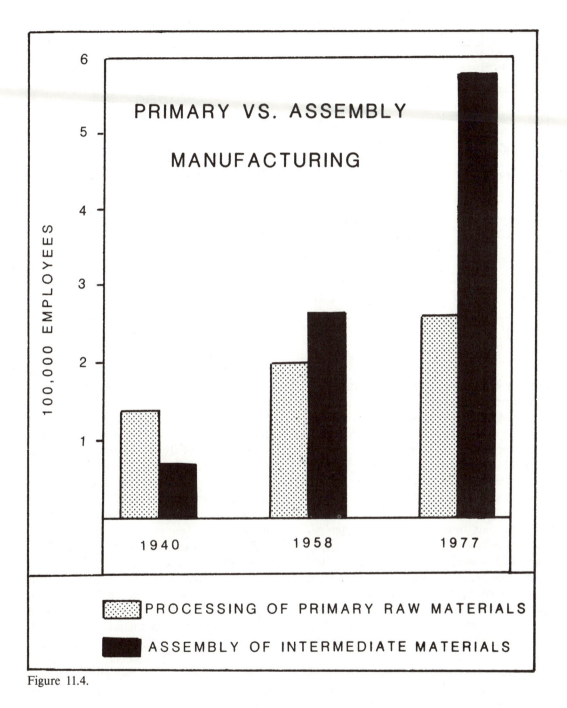

Figure 11.4.

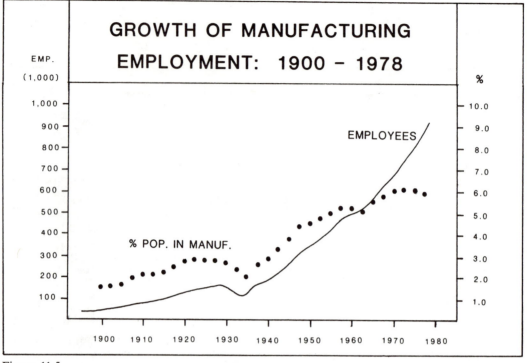

Figure 11.5.

Houston-Galveston, and Beaumont–Port Arthur areas.

Manufacturing employment grew rapidly in Texas during the 1940s and 1950s. Initially the spur was the defense-oriented production of petroleum products, lumber, and processed foods accompanying the U.S. involvement in World War II. The continued emphasis on the processing of basic raw materials into gasoline and other petroleum-related products, building materials, and processed foods put the state's manufacturers in a position to benefit from the national economic boom of the immediate postwar period. Even the recessionary period of the middle 1950s had little noticeable negative impact. But the growth in the level of manufacturing activity was accompanied by marked changes in the locational pattern of manufacturing, which became increasingly concentrated in the largest metropolitan centers. A few of the medium-sized urban centers also improved their relative status, but most small

towns and cities beyond the immediate influence of the larger urban centers saw their manufacturing employment either hold steady or decline. The eastern and east-central parts of Texas continued to dominate the manufacturing picture, although the beginnings of future manufacturing concentrations were becoming evident in a few of the larger cities in the western half of the state.

By 1960 Texas had become one of the major manufacturing states in the United States. It ranked ninth in number of manufacturing employees, tenth in value of payroll, tenth in VABM, and ninth in new capital investment in manufacturing facilities. The rapid growth of the state's manufacturing industries has been accompanied by major changes in the structure and orientation of manufacturing, and the processing of intermediate materials had finally surpassed the processing of basic raw materials (Figure 11.4). The subsequent two decades brought additional changes. Employment in manufacturing increased by more than 80 percent between 1960 and 1980, and during the same period, the dominance of intermediate-materials processing continued to increase. It now accounts for more than two-thirds of all manufacturing acitivity in Texas. Locationally the Houston and Dallas regions continue to dominate in number of employees—each county contains about 20 percent of the state's total manufacturing employment. However, an increasing number of other counties have significant concentrations of manufacturing employees, and more than one-fifth of the state's 254 counties have at least 2,000 manufacturing employees. Another 27 counties contain at least 1,000 employees. Overall, counties with 1,000 or more manufacturing employees account for more than 95 percent of the state's total. The rapid proliferation of minor concentrations of manufacturing across the state has resulted in a broader spatial distri-

bution of such activity than at any time since the beginning of World War II (Figures 11.6 and 11.7).

LEADING MANUFACTURES

The diversity of products manufactured in Texas is enormous. A system of classification by type of product is essential to any effort to differentiate manufactures by relative importance. The U.S. Department of Commerce uses the Standard Industrial Classification (SIC) system to classify manufacturing activities according to their principal products. The simplest form of the SIC system divides manufacturing activity into twenty general classes (Table 11.1) Each of the twenty major product categories is further divided according to the nature of the specific product. For example, transportation equipment (SIC 37) is a major product category. It is subdivided into motor vehicles and equipment, aircraft and

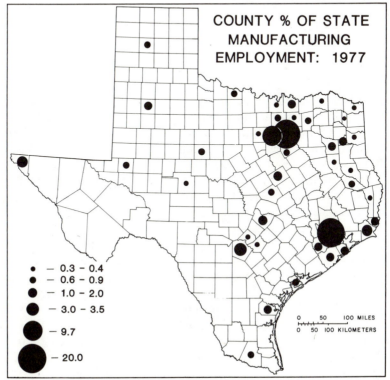

Figure 11.6.

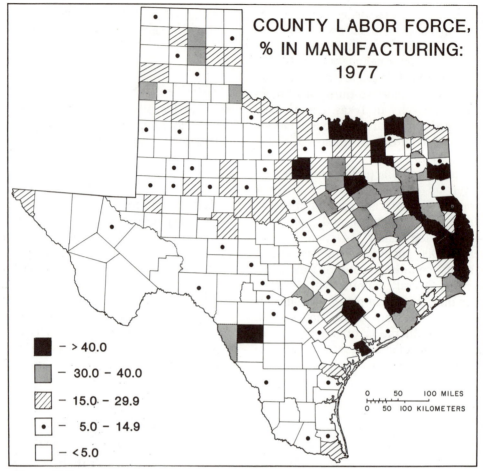

Figure 11.7.

parts, ship and boat building, railroad equipment, guided missiles and space vehicles, and miscellaneous transportation equipment. These subcategories can be further subdivided to yield a five-digit system that is largely product specific. The SIC system, on even the two-digit level, provides an excellent mechanism for differentiating between major types of manufacturing. It will be used as the basis for the following description of the relative importance and locational patterns of manufacturing in present-day Texas.

Detailed data on the amount of activity present are not available by type of manufacturing for most counties and cities. Generally, the smallest geographic area for which adequate data can be obtained are

the Standard Metropolitan Statistical Areas (SMSAs). Consequently, descriptions of the locational pattern of specific types of activity focus principally on the twenty-five SMSAs in Texas.

All except one of the twenty major classes of manufacturing are present in Texas; the sole exception is tobacco products. A few classes dominate the scene, and only six account for 55 percent of total manufacturing employment. These are machinery, food products, fabricated metals, apparel, electric and electronic equipment, and chemicals (Figure 11.8). Petroleum refining, which was so critical in the earlier stages of manufacturing growth in Texas, has slipped to eleventh position in product employment.

Table 11.1. Structural Characteristics of Manufacturing, 1977

SIC #	Product Group	Employees (000)	Payroll ($000,000)	VABM ($000,000)	New Capital Investment ($000,000)
20	Food	84.8	961.2	3,040.7	251.9
22	Textiles	7.1	60.7	140.0	22.2
23	Apparel	73.4	481.2	985.7	34.1
24	Lumber, wood	33.1	302.9	706.3	49.3
25	Furniture	17.4	148.1	305.5	13.8
26	Paper	19.8	272.0	663.0	178.2
27	Printing	47.4	525.6	1,159.9	61.6
28	Chemicals	67.7	1,264.2	7,310.0	2,269.2
29	Petroleum refining	35.3	692.3	4,184.0	1,031.7
30	Rubber	25.5	288.2	736.1	58.8
31	Leather	6.6	44.1	95.4	2.7
32	Stone, clay, glass	35.6	417.2	1,157.4	158.4
33	Primary metals	38.6	594.9	1,715.4	288.2
34	Fabricated metals	78.3	988.4	2,234.9	159.1
35	Machinery, excluding electrical	115.4	1,587.4	3,862.1	331.8
36	Electric and electronic equipment	67.8	891.9	2,061.0	185.1
37	Transportation equipment	61.1	947.0	2,023.6	62.8
38	Instruments	14.1	151.6	435.7	24.7
39	Miscellaneous	12.5	117.0	264.2	11.1
	Administrative, auxiliary	44.9	917.2	—	—
	TOTAL	886.4	11,653.1	33,080.9	5,194.7

Source: U.S. Census of Manufacturing.

Manufacturing employment is highly concentrated in the metropolitan regions (Table 11.2). Texas's SMSAs contained over three-quarters of the state's population in 1980, but they accounted for more than 85 percent of employment in manufacturing. Further, their dominance of manufacturing as measured by the number of plants with more than twenty employees, payroll, VABM, and new capital investment is of comparable strength. A strong positive correlation exists between the population size and the amount of manufacturing in each; the only major exceptions to this pattern are San Antonio, El Paso, and Beaumont–Port Arthur–Orange. Both San Antonio and El Paso have considerably less manufacturing activity than their size would indicate, and a much higher concentration of manufacturing exists in Beaumont–Port Arthur–Orange than would be expected in light of its population.

The two most populous counties in Texas are Harris and Dallas. Combined they con-

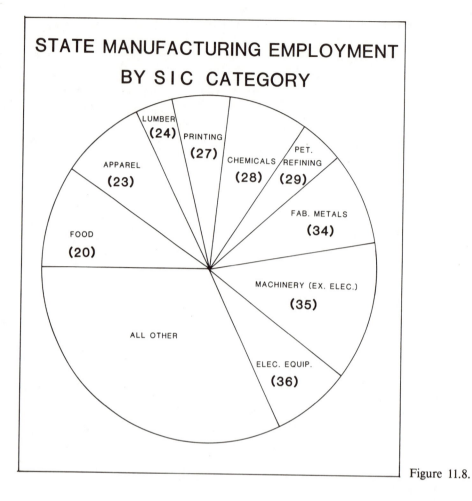

STATE MANUFACTURING EMPLOYMENT BY SIC CATEGORY

LUMBER (24)

PRINTING (27)

CHEMICALS (28)

PET. REFINING (29)

APPAREL (23)

FAB. METALS (34)

FOOD (20)

MACHINERY (EX. ELEC.) (35)

ALL OTHER

ELEC. EQUIP. (36)

Figure 11.8.

tain slightly more than one-quarter of the state's population, and they account for approximately 40 percent of manufacturing in the state. In 1977 Harris County alone provided about one-fourth of the state's manufacturing payroll and VABM and more than one-third of the new capital investment in plants and equipment.

A strong correlation exists between the location of manufacturing and the major population centers of Texas, but manufacturing is of critical importance locally in many areas that are relatively insignificant in terms of the amount of activity present. It is more important in the local industrial structure in many counties than is typical for the state as a whole. A simple method of identifying such counties is to compare their share of the total state manufacturing employment with their proportion of the total state population. The resulting ratio provides an index of per capita manufacturing employment.

This per capita index of manufacturing activity offers a particular perspective as it is an indicator of the importance of manufacturing to a local economy. Regions that dominate the state scene in amount of manufacturing activity seldom achieve a high index, but high values are not unusual among counties in which the amount of activity is relatively low (compare Figures 11.6 and 11.7). For example, Angelina, Calhoun, Carson, and Morris counties have indexes greater than 2.00; none of the four contains as much as 1 percent of the state's manufacturing employment. Similarly, more than three-quarters of the counties with a

Table 11.2. Manufacturing activity by SMSA, 1977

SMSA	Employees (000s)	Payroll ($000,000)	VABM ($000,000)	New Investment ($000,000)
Abilene	5.9	51.4	106.9	8.1
Amarillo	7.7	94.0	474.8	16.1
Austin	20.7	259.0	553.6	75.5
Beaumont–Port Arthur–Orange	38.3	683.3	2,626.3	556.0
Brownsville–Harlingen–San Benito	9.0	74.3	201.3	19.2
Bryan–College Station	2.1	22.2	55.5	4.9
Corpus Christi	12.1	178.6	734.7	398.1
Dallas–Fort Worth	269.9	3,508.9	7,869.1	500.8
El Paso	29.1	251.5	771.7	65.6
Galveston–Texas City	11.3	206.1	1,460.7	125.2
Houston	210.1	3,362.7	9,844.4	2,451.5
Killeen–Temple	5.8	55.3	159.6	n/a
Laredo	5.5	11.9	26.8	0.9
Longview	15.9	206.3	641.2	52.4
Lubbock	12.9	137.8	349.1	37.5
McAllen-Pharr-Edinburg	5.5	41.1	115.2	9.9
Midland	2.0	23.4	53.8	7.6
Odessa	5.9	86.7	232.9	n/a
San Angelo	4.8	42.6	126.3	6.2
San Antonio	40.1	399.2	905.3	92.5
Sherman–Denison	10.5	120.1	307.0	33.2
Texarkana (Texas portion)	3.6	37.0	85.1	2.7
Tyler	12.1	144.6	379.7	18.2
Waco	14.8	154.7	392.6	39.1
Wichita Falls	7.9	84.5	213.2	38.8
TOTAL	763.5	10,237.2	28,686.8	4,560.0+
SMSA % of state total	86.1%	87.8%	86.7%	87.8%

Source: U.S. Census of Manufacturing.

moderate or high index are situated in nonmetropolitan regions. Among the major SMSAs only the central counties of the Dallas–Fort Worth and the Beaumont–Port Arthur–Orange regions have indexes that are significantly above the state mean.

By comparison, the map of manufacturing employment indicates a strong concentration in the eastern half of the state (Figure 11.7). Eighty-five percent of the counties with 3,000 or more manufacturing employees are on or east of a line connecting Wichita Falls, San Antonio, and McAllen. West of this line only the primary county of each SMSA has significant manufacturing employment, whereas numerous SMSA suburban counties in East and Central Texas, as well as several nonmetropolitan counties, have more than 3,000 persons working in manufacturing plants. In addition, many other eastern and central counties have only a slightly smaller amount of manufacturing employment, but not many counties in the western areas have more than a few hundred such employees. Two belts of manufacturing activity are quite evident. The largest extends north and south along the Blackland Prairie from the

Dallas–Fort Worth SMSA, reaching to San Antonio on the south and the Oklahoma border on the north. The most important types of manufacturing in this belt include food processing, transportation equipment, fabricated metals, apparel, and electric and electronic equipment. The second belt extends along the Gulf Coast from Corpus Christi on the west, through Houston and Galveston, to the Louisiana border on the east. The leading manufactures in the belt include chemicals, machinery, petroleum refining, and fabricated metals. None of the manufacturing centers in Texas, large or small, can be accurately described as truly diversified. Most SMSAs are characterized by the presence of one or more types of activity that are of considerable importance (Table 11.3).

DISTRIBUTION BY TYPE

Each of the leading manufactures exhibits a distinctive locational pattern. The diversity of these patterns is quite apparent in an examination of these industries: machinery, food processing, fabricated metals, apparel, chemicals, electric and electronic equipment, transportation equipment, and petroleum refining.

More workers are employed in manufacturing machinery than in producing any other product in Texas, and this type of industry accounts for nearly one-seventh of

Table 11.3. Leading Manufactures by SMSA, 1977

SMSA	Leading Local Manufactures
Abilene	Food, Apparel
Amarillo	Varied, no dominant manufactures
Austin	Electric and electronic equipment, Printing
Beaumont–Port Arthur–Orange	Petroleum refining, Chemicals, Transporation equipment, Fabricated metals
Brownsville-Harlingen–San Benito	Apparel, Food
Bryan–College Station	Printing
Corpus Christi	Chemicals, Food, Petroleum refining
Dallas–Fort Worth	Electric and electronic equipment, Transportation equipment, Machinery
El Paso	Apparel, Food
Galveston–Texas City	Petroleum refining, Transportation equipment
Houston	Machinery, Fabricated metals, Chemicals, Petroleum refining, Administrative
Killeen-Temple	Furniture
Laredo	Apparel
Longview	Fabricated metals, Machinery
Lubbock	Machinery, Food
McAllen-Pharr-Edinburg	Food; Apparel; Stone, clay, glass
Midland	Machinery, Printing, Administrative
Odessa	Machinery, Chemicals
San Angelo	Food, Machinery, Fabricated metals
San Antonio	Food, Apparel, Machinery, Fabricated metals
Sherman-Denison	Food
Texarkana (Texas portion)	Lumber and wood
Tyler	Varied, no dominant manufactures
Waco	Food; Lumber and wood; Stone, clay, glass
Wichita Falls	Machinery

Source: U.S. Census of Manufacturing.

the total manufacturing employment. Almost two-thirds of such employment is concentrated in the Houston and Dallas metropolitan areas, and most is located in the central SMSA counties. More than 40 percent of the employment is engaged in producing construction equipment, of which more than one-half is located in the Houston SMSA. The emphasis in Dallas is split among construction equipment, office machines, and refrigeration equipment. Although there is some manufacturing of machinery in each of the state's other metropolitan regions and in many of the nonmetropolitan counties, only four other SMSAs—Lubbock, San Antonio, Longview, and Odessa—have more than 2,000 employees engaged in this type of manufacturing activity.

Food processing ranks second in employment among the state's manufacturing activities and generally reflects two primary location factors. The production of canned and frozen foods and the processing of grains are typically located in the raw materials source regions, and fresh foods, such as bakery goods and fluid dairy products, are generally market oriented to reduce the time between production and delivery to the consumer. Thus, although the larger metropolitan regions dominate the food processing employment picture, their shares of that type of employment are generally lower than their share of the state's total manufacturing employment; San Antonio is a notable exception. Many of the smaller SMSAs and a large number of nonmetropolitan counties have a relatively large proportion of their manufacturing employment concentrated in food processing. The most outstanding are the Abilene, Brownsville, Sherman-Denison, San Angelo, Lubbock, and Waco SMSAs. Market-oriented food processing, then, is concentrated in the eastern part of Texas, mirroring the pattern of population. Preserved foods, milled grains, edible oils, and the like are produced in agricultural areas such as the lower Rio Grande Valley and the High Plains.

Nationally, fabricated metals manufac-

turing is one of the more spatially ubiquitous types of manufacturing. In Texas, however, more than 60 percent of the employment in this activity is concentrated in the Houston and Dallas regions. This is probably an example of the clustering of an activity because of specialized market conditions. For example, the Houston and Dallas regions are major consumers of such products as structural metal products for the construction industry and forgings and stampings for the manufacturing of machinery and transportation equipment. Three other metropolitan centers—the San Antonio, Longview, and Beaumont regions—are notable in their level of this type of employment, and each has several thousand workers engaged in metals fabrication. The remaining quarter of the state's employment in metals fabrication is nearly equally divided between the other metropolitan regions and the nonmetropolitan counties. Most, however, is concentrated in the eastern and central parts of Texas.

Large-scale development of apparel and other textile manufacturing is generally associated with one, or both, of two factors—an abundance of low-wage workers and a well-established wholesale marketing facility in a major population center. Dallas County offers both and contains about one-quarter of the apparel manufacturing employment in Texas. El Paso has an abundance of low-wage labor and accounts for one-fifth of the state's activity. San Antonio, also possessing an abundance of labor available at low wages, ranks third and has shown significant growth in apparel manufacturing in recent years. Another area of recent growth, although accounting for only about 3 percent of the total employment at present, is along the border with Mexico. The remainder of the apparel manufacturing is scattered widely over the eastern and east-central parts of Texas. A relatively large proportion is located in small cities in nonmetropolitan counties.

The chemical industry ranks only fifth in employment among Texas manufacturers, but it is second in value of payroll

Figure 11.9. Aerial view of a large petroleum refinery on the west side of the Sabine-Neches ship channel below Beaumont. The ship channel connects Beaumont, Port Arthur, and Orange with the Gulf of Mexico. It is more than 40 ft (12 m) deep and accommodates ships more than 500 ft (152 m) long. Extensive marshes and the absence of highway and rail facilities have severely restricted development on the east side of the waterway, but the west bank is lined with refineries and petrochemical plants for more than 15 mi (24 km) between Beaumont and Port Arthur. (Photo: John L. Bean, 1981.)

and first in both VABM and new capital investment. The relative importance of this high-wage, export-oriented industry has increased very rapidly over the past few decades, and much of the growth has been concentrated in the upper Gulf Coast area around Houston, Galveston, and Beaumont (Figures 11.9 and 11.10). This region currently contains more than 50 percent of chemicals employment and an even higher proportion of chemicals payroll, VABM, and new capital investment. Most of the production in this area is derived from petroleum and natural gas, and a considerable portion is actually produced in petroleum refineries and natural-gas processing plants or their affiliates. Because a large proportion of the production is exported abroad, a location that is accessible to major port facilities is very beneficial (Figure 11.9). The Dallas–Fort Worth SMSA is also an important center of the chemical industry, with a concentration on the production of such inorganic chemicals as cleaning products, pharmaceuticals, and industrial chemicals. The remainder of the state's chemicals production is split between two types of location. Producers of consumer and industrial chemicals are concentrated in the cities of the other metropolitan regions, and the manufacturers of agricultural chemicals are concentrated in the Central Texas and Panhandle agricultural regions. Most of these plants are relatively small and serve small local markets.

Figure 11.10. A portion of one of the largest oil refineries in the world. This is part of the massive petroleum refining and chemicals complex located in eastern Galveston County along the west side of Galveston Bay. Much of the west side of the bay and the Houston ship channel, which connects Houston with the Gulf of Mexico through Galveston Bay, is lined with such plants. (Photo: John L. Bean, 1981.)

The electric and electronics products industry in Texas has grown very rapidly during the past few decades. Although the repair and limited manufacturing of simple electrical equipment began in Texas in the early part of the twentieth century, the industry has been significant in the state for fewer than three decades. This recent growth has been largely concentrated in two types of products and has been spatially focused on only a few areas. Nearly 80 percent is evenly split between the production of communications equipment and the production of electronic components. Spatially, the Dallas–Fort Worth region is dominant with nearly 60 percent of the total employment. Dallas County alone accounts for nearly 50 percent of the total employment, especially in the production of communications equipment. The second-ranking region is the Houston SMSA with about one-sixth of the activity. The only other significant concentration is in Jefferson County in the far southeastern corner of the state. Nearly all of the remainder is widely scattered among the cities in the other SMSAs, but very little is present in the nonmetropolitan counties.

The manufacturing of transportation equipment is both strongly differentiated structurally and spatially concentrated in Texas. More than half of the total employment is engaged in the production of aircraft and aircraft parts, and the Dallas–Fort Worth region accounts for nearly 90 percent. Fort Worth and several of its suburbs strongly dominate the industry with several very large plants that produce fighter aircraft as well as military and commercial helicopters (Figure 11.11). Most of the remaining activity in the manufacturing of transportation equipment is about equally divided between shipbuilding and the assembly of motor vehicles and automobile parts production. Fort Worth and its suburbs dominate the automotive component, and shipbuilding is concentrated in the Beaumont–Port Aurthur–Orange region, with secondary concentrations in Galveston, Houston, and Corpus Christi.

Petroleum refining was the first Texas manufacturing activity to gain outside attention. The modern industry began in Beaumont soon after the Spindletop discovery, and other refining operations developed near several of the early major fields along the coast and in the interior, but activity has continued to be concentrated along the upper coast. Beaumont, Port Arthur, Houston, Galveston, and the suburbs of these four cities contain more

than three-quarters of the state's petroleum refining employment and constitute the largest single concentration of the industry in the nation. Most of the refineries in this area are large, high-capacity plants, and many export a large part of their production to other parts of the nation. The individual refineries scattered in parts of interior Texas are generally much smaller and oriented to more local markets.

The Texas petroleum refining industry is a good example of the importance of industrial geographic inertia. The early refineries were sited at or near the location of the early oil fields. Subsequent large capital investment, coupled with the development of excellent water transportation facilities and the emergence of by-product industries such as petrochemicals, resulted in continued growth even as petroleum refining became largely oriented to markets

Figure 11.11. The largest transportation equipment manufacturing plant in Texas, located in the western part of Fort Worth. The main building, more than .5 mi (.8 km) long, looks small compared to the 12,000-ft (3,658-m) long runway on the adjacent U.S. Air Force base. (Photo: John L. Bean, 1981.)

in other parts of the nation and world. A significant portion of the machinery and shipbuilding activity along the coast is also directly related to the continued vitality of petroleum refining and associated manufactures.

THE SERVICES SECTOR

Manufacturing was the key to the industrial evolution of Texas, and although it remains the leading employment sector in the state's industrial structure, it is now being challenged for supremacy by other types of economic activity such as services. The services sector has been particularly dynamic in recent decades. Its relative proportion of Texas's nonagricultural employment has increased by more than 50 percent in the past twenty years, and it is likely to assume first position within another decade. Services are particularly sensitive to changes in the level of economic activity in a region. This characteristic is a reflection of the diversity of activities included within the sector; in some respects this sector is almost as complex structurally as manufacturing. For example, components such as automobile repair, motion pictures, professional sports, health services, social services, and museums tend to be spatially concentrated in the major population centers, and their rate of growth generally exceeds that of the population in a dynamic region such as Texas. Activities such as hotels and motels, amusement and recreation facilities, and personal services also show a locational bias toward the major concentrations of population. However, they also frequently develop on a significant scale in aesthetically desirable locations, especially around major lakes and on the coast. Business services and legal services have a strong locational bias toward the major centers of business and manufacturing.

More than 50 percent of all service employment in Texas is concentrated in the central counties of the Dallas–Fort Worth and Houston metropolitan regions.

In addition, each of the central counties of the state's other SMSAs has a significant concentration of service employment (Figure 11.12). Slightly smaller concentrations are characteristic of the most affluent suburban counties in the two largest metropolitan regions and of counties that have significant concentrations of manufacturing activity.

Earlier we found that examining manufacturing activity in terms of the per capita level of activity resulted in a different impression than if only the number of employees were considered. The same approach is valid for any type of economic activity, including the service sector. The image obtained from mapping per capita indexes of service employment is strikingly different from that of the map of number of employees (Figure 11.13). For example, no SMSA central county ranks in either of the two highest categories, and only three—Dallas, Harris, and Potter (Amarillo)—rank in the third level. Fewer than one-third of the remaining central counties of the state's metropolitan regions exceed the state mean of 1.00, and only two—Taylor and Travis— exceed it sufficiently to be included in the lowest category indicated on the map. Most of the counties in which the service sector is of particularly strong importance in the local economic picture are located outside the metropolitan regions. The importance of services in the economy of certain small cities in the Panhandle and the High Plains is clearly indicated.

THE RETAIL AND WHOLESALE SECTORS

Retailing is another strong element in the Texas economy. However, it is only one of two closely intertwined stages of an exchange process, the other being the wholesale trade. Retail trade is the most ubiquitous of all economic activities, for only the smallest hamlets are without some type of retail business. The customers of retail trade firms are mostly individuals and families. Thus the spatial distribution of retail

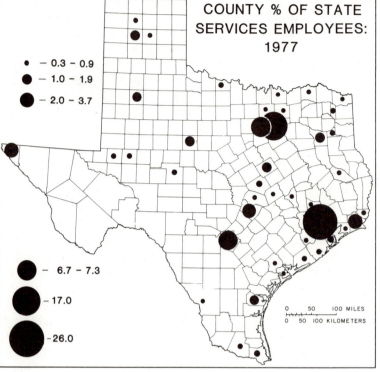

Figure 11.12.

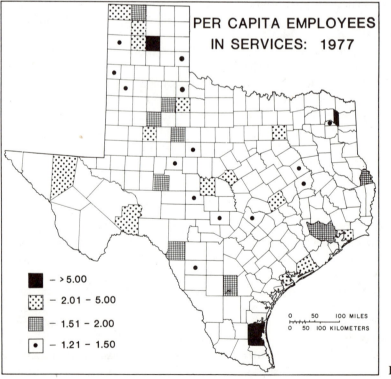

Figure 11.13.

trade largely reflects the general distribution of the population. Other businesses, including retailers, are the customers of the wholesale trade. Consequently, that activity is spatially oriented toward very large population centers, where most other businesses are located. Occasionally, however, special conditions result in the development of significant wholesale activity outside the major population centers, most often in major centers of export-oriented agricultural activity and in smaller manufacturing centers.

Wholesale trade activity is concentrated in a relatively few centers in Texas. Nearly two-thirds of its employees work in only four counties—Harris, Dallas, Tarrant, and Bexar (Figure 11.14). A relatively few other small centers of wholesale trade activity are widely distributed about the state. This open pattern reflects the need for relatively central locations within the trade territories.

The distribution of employment in the retail trade is, as suggested, much more diffuse than in the wholesale trade and the major population centers are not so dominant (Figure 11.15). For example, the central counties of the state's three most populous metropolitan regions contain only slightly more than one-half of all trade employment and a smaller proportion of the retail trade employees. The San Antonio (Bexar County) retail market area, for example, encompasses much of the southwestern part of the state even though every county in the area also has retail trade employment within the county (Figure 11.16). In addition, there are significantly more retail trade centers than wholesale centers in Texas. Also, cities in suburban counties within the metropolitan regions and nonmetropolitan cities are much more likely to develop into retail trade centers than to become centers of wholesale trade.

Only twenty-two Texas counties have a per capita concentration of trade sector employment above the state mean of 1.00,

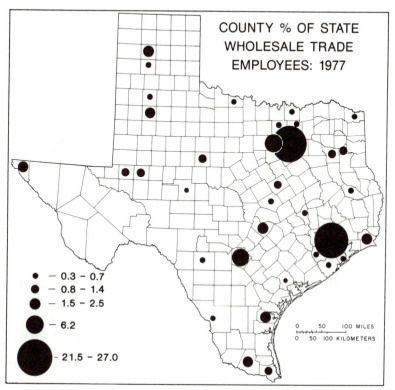

COUNTY % OF STATE
WHOLESALE TRADE
EMPLOYEES: 1977

- 0.3 - 0.7
- 0.8 - 1.4
- 1.5 - 2.5
- 6.2
- 21.5 - 27.0

0   50   100 MILES
0   50   100 KILOMETERS

Figure 11.14.

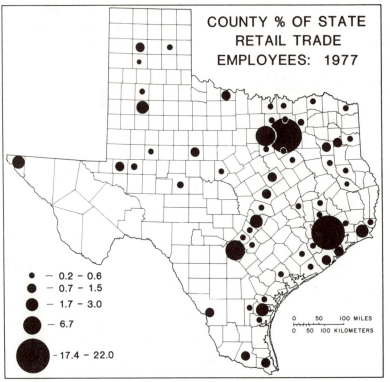

Figure 11.15.

fewer than for any other major industrial sector (Figure 11.17). The scarcity of centers where trade is a dominant element in the local industrial employment picture is largely attributable to the high degree of spatial concentration of wholesale sector employment and the high correlation of retail sector employment with population size. With the exception of Dallam County in the northwest Panhandle, every county with an index above 1.10 is the central county of an SMSA and is either a major regional wholesale trade center or a specialized wholesale center. However, most of the state's metropolitan counties, including many that contain a significant number of trade sector employees, have a low per capita ratio. Five nonmetropolitan counties have a per capita concentration slightly above the state mean, and each reflects the influence of special circumstances such as high concentrations of agribusiness or tourism or a high per capita ratio of manufacturing.

THE GOVERNMENT SECTOR

The government sector, consisting of people working for the federal, state, or local agencies, is the last of the four leading industrial components of the Texas economy. Local government employment is highly correlated with population, but employment in federal and state agencies is less directly related to community population size.

The locational characteristics of federal and state government activities differ in two important respects in Texas. First, employment in state agencies is more widespread than federal employment (Figures 11.18 and 11.19), and second, a majority of the federal employees work in the three most populous metropolitan regions, but less than one-third of state employment is concentrated in those population centers. However, the two types of employment are both focused toward the eastern and central parts of the state.

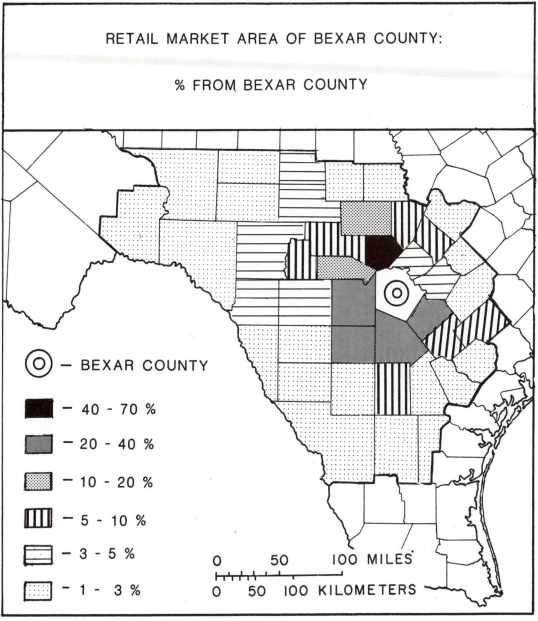

Figure 11.16.

264

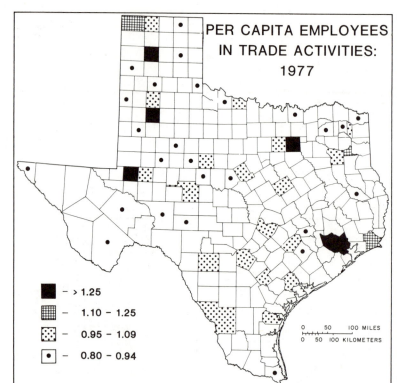

Figure 11.17.

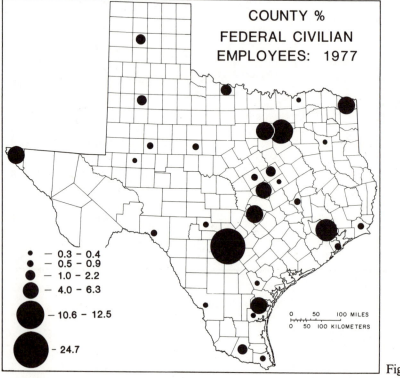

Figure 11.18.

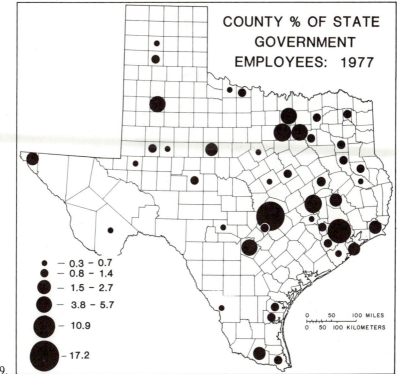

COUNTY % OF STATE
GOVERNMENT
EMPLOYEES: 1977

- 0.3 – 0.7
- 0.8 – 1.4
- 1.5 – 2.7
- 3.8 – 5.7
- 10.9
- 17.2

0   50   100 MILES
0   50   100 KILOMETERS

Figure 11.19.

Most federal civilian employees in Texas are engaged in one of three types of activity: general administrative duties in regional headquarters offices, civilian employment with the military, and nonmilitary public safety activities. These activities have relatively distinct distributional patterns. The major concentration of civilian employees of the military is in San Antonio, which is also the largest center of all federal civilian employment in Texas. Secondary centers of military employment are in the El Paso, Killeen-Temple, Dallas–Fort Worth, and Austin SMSAs. The border with Mexico and the port cities along the Gulf of Mexico are the focal points for various types of public safety employment. Regional headquarters that oversee federal activities in the southwestern United States are concentrated largely in the Dallas–Fort Worth and Houston SMSAs. Several of the smaller centers of federal employment reflect the presence of highly specialized activities, including federally owned and operated

manufacturing facilities, agricultural research stations, and health care facilities.

Nearly all employees of the state of Texas fit into one of five categories. These include employment in the executive and administrative departments and agencies, the judiciary, public health activities, public safety activities, and postsecondary education. There is not a large similarity in the distributional patterns of the various types of employees. Employment in the administrative and executive departments and agencies is largely concentrated in Austin, the capital of Texas; judicial system employment closely parallels the pattern of population distribution. Employees who are not located in the Austin area are scattered among the larger metropolitan regions, with the number of employees in each being approximately proportional to the population of the region. Many of the public health and public safety facilities, especially the eleemosynary and correctional institutions, are located in rural parts of the

266

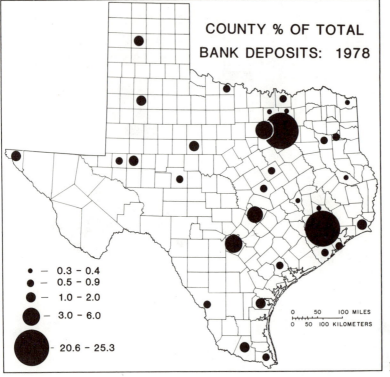

Figure 11.20.

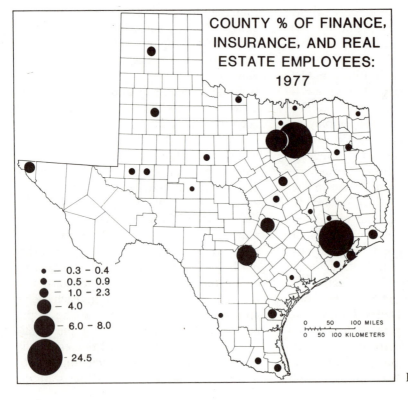

Figure 11.21.

state. The personnel of state-operated colleges, universities, and trade schools are classified as state employees. Historically, most of these institutions were located in small towns in the rural areas of Texas, with the major exception of the state university in Austin, but, within the last several decades, many of these small towns have become metropolitan centers or have been encroached upon by metropolitan regions. In addition, state universities have been established in all of the larger metropolitan centers. As a result, educational employees constitute a large proportion of the state employees in the major metropolitan regions, and they also constitute a very large majority of the state employees in many of the nonmetropolitan regions of Texas. A large majority of state government employees work in the eastern and central regions, but there is a considerably higher level of state employment in the western half of the state than is true of other major industries.

THE FINANCIAL SECTOR

There is wealth in Texas, and its derivative is a large supply of financial capital, which is generously applied to promote industrial growth and development. Texas is a relatively high-ranking resource region for financial capital, with a per capita mean of approximately $10,500. Most of the capital has been gathered into a very few centers, and Harris, Dallas, and Tarrant counties contain the nine largest banks in the state and account for more than half of the total bank assets and employment in the financial sector (Figures 11.20 and 11.21). Activity in other metropolitan centers is generally quite low, the only significant exception being San Antonio. The concentration of most of the available financial capital into a few centers significantly influences the location of economic growth. Financial capital is very mobile for large developments by established firms, but new small operators are more likely to be successful in attracting needed financial

backing if they are near the potential source. A very large proportion of the industrial growth in Texas has resulted from the establishment and growth of small plants and businesses, not the more heavily publicized very large operations employing thousands of workers.

Industrial development, then, is concentrated mainly in the eastern half of Texas and particularly in two major districts. In the following, final chapter, we will attempt to pull together the environmental, cultural, and economic multiplicities of Texas into a regional framework.

SOURCES AND SUGGESTED READINGS

Alexandersson, Gunnar. *Geography of Manufacturing.* Englewood Cliffs, N.J.: Prentice-Hall, 1967.

Beutel, A. P. "The Industrialization of the South." *Texas Business Review* 35 (1961), 5–7.

Clark, James A., and Halbouty, Michel T. *Spindletop.* New York: Random House, 1952.

Escott, Florence. *Why 122 Manufacturers Located Plants in Texas.* Austin: University of Texas, Bureau of Business Research, 1954.

Grubb, Herbert W. *The Structure of the Texas Economy.* Austin: Office of the Governor, Office of Information Services, 1973.

Hawkins, Charles F. *An Input-Output Model of the Southeast Region of Texas.* Austin: Office of the Governor, Division of Planning Coordination, 1972.

Johnson, Elmer H. *The Industrial Potential of Texas.* Austin: University of Texas, Bureau of Business Research, 1959.

————. "A Sketch of the Historical Development and Outlook of Manufacturing in Texas." *Texas Business Review* 12 (1938), 5–9.

McDonald, Stephen L. "Recent Economic Development and Change in the Structure of Manufacturing Employment in the Southwestern States." *Texas Business Review* 40:4 (1966), 1–5.

McKnight, Tom L. "The Distribution of Manufacturing in Texas." *Annals of the Association of American Geographers* 47 (1957), 370–378.

Rodriquez, Louis J., ed. *Dynamics of Growth: An Economic Profile of Texas.* Austin: Madrona Press, 1978.

Ryan, Robert H., and Adams, Charles W. *Corpus Christi: Economic Impact of the Port.* Austin: University of Texas, Bureau of Business Research, 1973.

Smith, David M. *Industrial Location: An Economic Geographical Analysis.* New York: John Wiley, 1971.

CHAPTER 12

CONCLUSION: PERCEPTUAL REGIONS

Texas is not merely a borderland, but a shatter belt, both culturally and environmentally. It not only lies astride the boundaries between Anglo-America and Latin America and between the humid subtropics and desert, but it also reveals a myriad of internal divisions. Empire it may be, but if so, more nearly like the Austro-Hungarian or Russian empires than any model suggesting internal homogeneity.

How are we to provide structure to the diversity revealed in the previous chapters? One time-honored way would be to resort to the geographer's traditional penchant for creating and mapping regions (Figure 12.1). In this manner, we could try to draw together the various environmental and cultural phenomena into a comprehensive spatial classification, an intellectual task that is both demanding and, inevitably, subjective. We rejected this approach as impractical and arbitrary. Instead, we chose to seek a vernacular or popular regionalization, one springing from the collective perceptions of the people of Texas.

Popular regions may be defined as regions that are perceived to exist by their inhabitants, and they are aspects of the popular culture at large. Rather than being the intellectual creations of professional geographers, popular perceptual regions are the products of the spatial outlook of the ordinary citizenry. Rather than being based on carefully chosen, quantifiable criteria, they are composites of people's mental maps.

To this end, we gathered data by means of a questionnaire administered under controlled conditions at thirty colleges and universities to nearly 4,000 Texans in the spring of 1977 (Figure 12.2). One question was designed to obtain special regional names or nicknames. The question read:

> Most parts of Texas have a special regional name, or popular name. Examples of such popular names from other states are 'Black Belt' (in Alabama), 'North Woods' (in Wisconsin), 'Tidewater' (in Virginia), and 'Little Dixie' (in Oklahoma). What popular name is used to describe the area containing your home county in Texas?

THE POPULAR REGIONS

Twenty-nine popular regions are mentioned consistently enough by respondents to warrant inclusion on a perceptual region map (Figure 12.3 and Table 12.1). To be included, a perceptual term had to be (1) the most commonly used name in at least

269

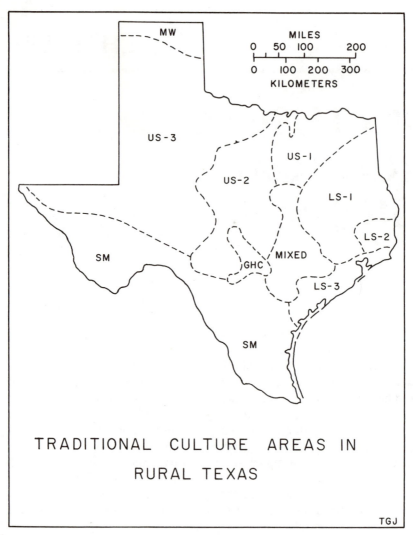

TRADITIONAL CULTURE AREAS IN
RURAL TEXAS

Figure 12.1.

LS = Lower-Southern Subculture

    1 = Plantation aristocracy: population derived from slave-cotton areas of Alabama, Georgia, and Mississippi; large rural black population

    2 = Big Thicket "poor whites": population derived from pine barrens of Gulf Coast; few blacks present

    3 = Gulf Coast: original plantation aristocracy, mainly from Louisiana, later submerged by large-scale influx of Europeans and midwesterners; recent dominance by urban-industrial complex

US = Upper-Southern Subculture

    1 = Middle-class blackland farmers: derived from Tennessee, Missouri, Kentucky, Arkansas, and southern Illinois

    2 = Hill Country "poor whites": derived from Ozarks and Appalachia

    3 = West Texas ranchers and farmers: derived from zones US-1 and US-2

  MW = Midwestern Subculture: population derived from lower Midwest

  SM = Spanish-Mexican Subculture: with overlay of Anglo-American traits

GHC = German Hill Country: zone of purest German subculture

MIXED = Mixture of LS-1, US-1, SM, and various continental European groups (especially Germans, Czechs, Scandinavians, Wends, and Poles)

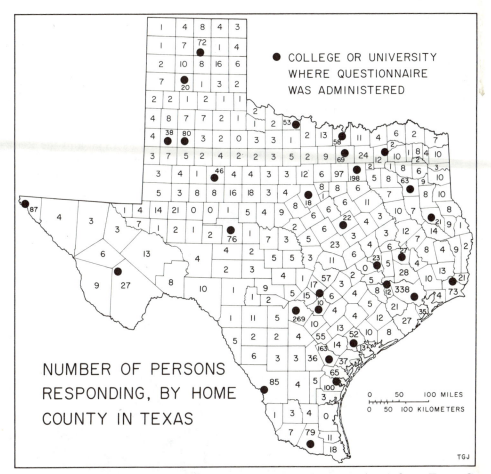

Figure 12.2. Responses to popular regions questionnaire. (Reprinted from Terry G. Jordan, "Perceptual Regions in Texas," *Geographical Review* 68 [1978], 294, with the permission of the American Geographical Society.)

one county, (2) used by at least 10 percent of the respondents in counties wholly or largely within the regions, and (3) mentioned by at least five respondents. Wherever practical and appropriate, counties were split among more than one perceptual region according to the number of responses for each term.

Regions of varying size, type, and degree of recognition were detected. Nineteen, or two-thirds, of the regions bear names based on the physical environment. As a rule, these environmental terms are old, in most cases dating back to the nineteenth century. Cross Timbers, for example, was in use at least by the 1840s, even before permanent

white colonization of that oak forest area began. Curiously, some of the environmental names are quite misleading and do not describe the actual physical character of the land. The Valley or Rio Grande Valley is not a valley at all, as it is situated on the table-flat plain of South Texas. Nor is the Permian Basin a topographic basin; rather, the reference is to the buried geological structure bearing the petroleum deposits that provide the economic base for this West Texas plains area. Similarly, one has to search long and hard to find the few small, scattered remnants of thicket vegetation that are the basis of the Big Thicket region, which in the popular mind covers part of eleven counties in south-eastern Texas. This region is presently expanding at the expense of the Piney Woods region, because of the publicity surrounding the creation of the Big Thicket National Preserve.

Many of the environmental terms seem to be fading in the popular mind, retreating before other types of vernacular regions. In the 1830–1850 period, virtually all of the Texas regions bore environmental names, many of which have been nearly or completely forgotten. Vanished altogether are the Level and Undulating regions that appeared so commonly in guidebooks of the early Anglo settlement period. Redlands is

an example of an environmental term, once in widespread use, that has suffered a decline in recent decades. Coined in the 1820s or 1830s, Redlands described a belt of thinly forested, fertile, reddish soil in East Texas, centered on the town and county of San Augustine. In San Augustine, a newspaper called the *Red-Lander* began publication as early as 1838, and the Redlands became famous as the best cotton producing region of East Texas. Apparently the replacement of cotton by pasture and commercial woodland after about 1930 caused the name Redlands to give way slowly to Piney Woods as the preferred regional term. Even in San Augustine County, question-

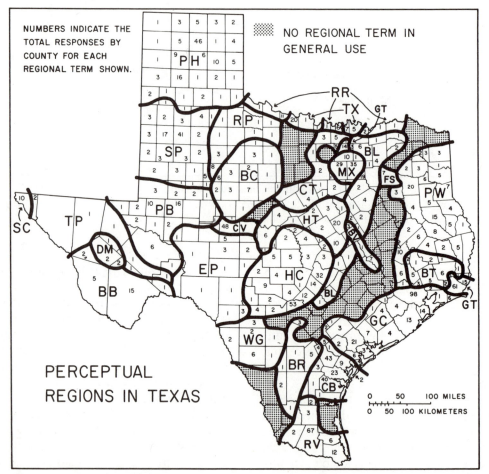

Figure 12.3. For an explanation of the abbreviations used, see Table 12.1. (Reprinted from Terry G. Jordan, "Perceptual Regions in Texas," *Geographical Review* 68 [1978], 295, with the permission of the American Geographical Society.)

naire respondents listed Piney Woods more often than Redlands (Figure 12.4).

Political terms account for some 14 percent of the Texas vernacular names. One of these, Panhandle, refers to a peculiarity of the Texas border, and a second, Heart of Texas, more or less defines the geographic center of the state (Figure 12.5). Tex(h)oma combines the names of Texas and Oklahoma but, curiously, is used only on the Texas side of the Red River. Free State, like Panhandle, is a nineteenth-century po-

litical term. It refers to Van Zandt County in East Texas, where local tradition holds that a planter seeking safety from the battle zone of the South during the Civil War brought his slaves there. He found, to his disgust, that almost none of the local Van Zandt farmers, most of whom were sand-flat poor whites, owned slaves. The planter soon left the county, saying he would as soon take his blacks to a free state as to Van Zandt. To this day the area remains the Free State of Van Zandt, a title com-

Table 12.1. Popular Regions of Texas, 1977

Region	Abbreviation (used on Fig. 12.3)	% of Respondents (in counties wholly or largely within the region) Using Name	Type of Name
Big Bend	BB	56	Environmental
Big Country	BC	38	Promotional
Big Thicket	BT	44	Environmental
Blacklands	BL	26	Environmental
Brazos Valley	BV	27	Environmental
Brush Country	BR	14	Environmental
Coastal Bend	CB	32	Environmental
Concho Valley	CV	63	Environmental
Cross Timbers	CT	18	Environmental
Davis Mountains	DM	33	Environmental
Edwards Plateau	EP	42	Environmental
Free State	FS	88	Political-historical
Golden Triangle, No. 1[a]	GT	81	Promotional
Golden Triangle, No. 2[a]	GT	20	Promotional
Gulf Coast	GC	32	Environmental
Heart of Texas	HT	59	Political
Hill Country	HC	71	Environmental
Metroplex	MX	22	Promotional, political
Panhandle	PH	70	Political
Permian Basin	PB	59	Environmental
Piney Woods	PW	44	Environmental
Red River (Valley)	RR	27	Environmental
(Lower) Rio Grande Valley	RV	76	Environmental
Rolling Plains	RP	50	Environmental
South Plains	SP	51	Environmental
Sun Country	SC	11	Promotional
Tex(h)oma(land)	TX	39	Political
Trans-Pecos	TP	20	Environmental
Winter Garden	WG	67	Promotional

[a]No. 1 lies in Southeast Texas; No. 2, in North Texas.

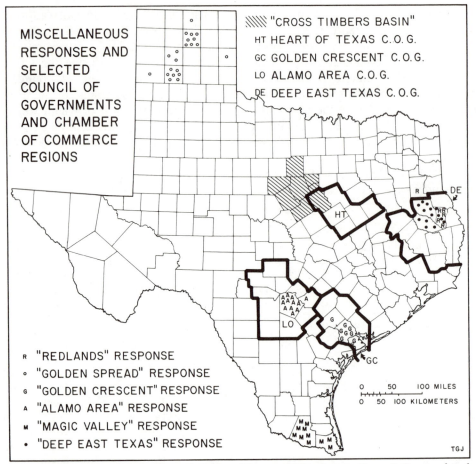

MISCELLANEOUS
RESPONSES AND
SELECTED
COUNCIL OF
GOVERNMENTS
AND CHAMBER
OF COMMERCE
REGIONS

▨ "CROSS TIMBERS BASIN"
HT HEART OF TEXAS C.O.G.
GC GOLDEN CRESCENT C.O.G.
LO ALAMO AREA C.O.G.
DE DEEP EAST TEXAS C.O.G.

R "REDLANDS" RESPONSE
○ "GOLDEN SPREAD" RESPONSE
G "GOLDEN CRESCENT" RESPONSE
A "ALAMO AREA" RESPONSE
M "MAGIC VALLEY" RESPONSE
• "DEEP EAST TEXAS" RESPONSE

0   50   100 MILES
0   50   100 KILOMETERS

Figure 12.4. Reprinted from Terry G. Jordan, "Perceptual Regions in Texas," *Geographical Review* 68 [1978], 297, with the permission of the American Geographical Society.

memorated by the name of a local news-paper. In South Texas, a Free State of McMullen was mentioned by one of the three respondents, and a hand-painted sign at the northern line of McMullen County conveys this vernacular message to highway travelers. Occasionally one also finds ref-erence to a Free State of Menard. Perhaps it is some measure of the strength of Texan regionalism, frontier individualism, and distrust of central government that these three different counties should bear the vernacular prefix Free State.

The wave of the future seems to be to give promotional names to vernacular re-gions. With few exceptions, existing pro-motional names appeared on the Texas scene after World War II, some even during the 1970s. Typically, promotional names are launched by local booster groups, such as the chambers of commerce or regional councils of governments, and then spread to the general public via the news media. These names speak to us of pure Texan boosterism and pride: Big Country, Golden Triangle, Sun Country. Metroplex was coined after the politically motivated de-cision to combine the Dallas and Fort Worth SMSAs. It is daily drummed into the consciousness of local residents by news-papers, radio and television announcers, and business owners who incorporate Met-roplex into the name of their firms.

A host of other promotional names have

Figure 12.5. The Heart of Texas popular region, enshrined for the ages in granite on the courthouse square in Brady, McCulloch County. The names of the twenty-nine popular regions often appear in the cultural landscape, providing daily visual reinforcement for them. (Reprinted from Terry G. Jordan, "Perceptual Regions in Texas," *Geographical Review* 68 [1978], 298, with the permission of the American Geographical Society.)

arisen but as yet have not displaced older, nonpromotional terms (Figure 12.4). Thus we see the venerable Panhandle endangered by Golden Spread, a name, according to one respondent, "coined by an Amarillo newsman to encouage tourism and business." Although Golden Spread sounds more like oleomargarine than a region, it is variously said to have been inspired by the expanses of golden wheat fields in the Panhandle or to typify "the golden opportunities of the area." As early as 1972, the Amarillo telephone directory contained nine Golden Spread entries, compared to fifty for Panhandle. Questionnaire respondents in the region listed Panhandle 133 times and Golden Spread 21 times. Similarly, the seam between the Gulf Coast and Coastal Bend regions seems to be parting and the two regions drifting apart, like a sort of perceptual plate tectonics, to make room for the Golden Crescent, a name being promoted by the area's council of governments. Elsewhere, a Golden Circle has surfaced in the Blackland Prairie south of Dallas, according to one Navarro County respondent.

Texans are so enamored of the adjective "golden" that the state boasts not just one, but two Golden Triangles. The older and better established of these, recognized by over 80 percent of the local population, lies in Southeast Texas, bounded by the cities of Beaumont, Port Arthur, and Orange. Blissfully ignorant of this prototypical Golden Triangle, boosters of the small city of Denton in North Texas began promoting the Denton-Dallas–Fort Worth triangle as "golden." Denton, naturally, was the Top of the Golden Triangle. The Denton campaign has never entered the consciousness of the Dallas or Fort Worth residents, but small-town people in nearby communities have been converted (Figure 12.6).

Figure 12.6. Typical Anglo-Texas boosterism in support of a popular region, the North Texas Golden Triangle. Billboard proclamations such as this one in Denton County are common in Texas, particularly for promotional regional names. (Reprinted from Terry G. Jordan, "Perceptual Regions in Texas," *Geographical Review* 68 [1978], 299, with the permission of the American Geographical Society.)

Promotional names generally are coined in an urban nucleus and spread outward into the surrounding rural and small-town districts. In this sense, they approximate nodal regions. The node of Big Country, for example, is the city of Abilene, and the name of the region is promoted by the Abilene news media and appears in the names of local business establishments. By contrast, environmental names are typically based in rural areas and often describe the distribution of some physical feature. As such, they are formal regions that have been popularized. The increased urbanization of the state suggests that nodal promotional regions will continue to proliferate and expand at the expense of environmental ones. In this sense, it is interesting to watch the spread of the name Magic Valley, a promotional variant of the Valley or Rio Grande Valley (Figure 12.4).

The role of councils of governments in fostering regional names varies from one part of Texas to another. The first of these councils was established only in the mid-1960s, encouraged by supporting legislation. Some of these councils adopted existing vernacular terms—such as Panhandle, South Plains, Brazos Valley, Coastal Bend, and Permian Basin—lending further support to the established names. Others, however, created new names that may eventually attain the status of vernacular regions. The Alamo Area Council of Governments, based in San Antonio, could give its name to much of the Brush Country and Hill Country, as well as part of a region that presently has no popular name. According to the survey, Alamo Area is already perceived as the regional name by 4 percent of the Bexar County respondents (Figure 12.4). The previously mentioned Golden Crescent Council of Governments has a name that can hardly fail in the long run, and the Texoma Regional Planning Commission bears a name that is already in the process of displacing part of the traditional "Red River Valley."

It is noteworthy, however, that territorially, the council of governments regions sometimes correspond only very weakly to the perceptual regions of the same name. For example, the Heart of Texas Council of Governments area lies east of the perceptual region, with an overlap of only three counties (compare Figure 12.3 and 12.4).

Reinforcement for dominantly rural perceptual regions often comes from district agencies of the Texas Agricultural Service, whose crop-reporting districts perpetuate names such as Panhandle, Coastal Bend, South Plains, and Rolling Plains. Similarly, the use of names such as Blacklands by farm-news columnists and correspondents for newspapers and radio stations helps preserve the traditional rural vernacular regions.

A REGION ABORNING

Geographer Wilbur Zelinsky once recounted his personal remembrance of "surfing" along the innovation wave of hula hoops across the United States. We cannot equal that experience, but we were present at the birth of a perceptual region. "Chamber of Commerce Holds Contest to Name Our Area" proclaimed a headline in the Stephenville, Texas, (Erath County) newspaper in the spring of 1977. "Names submitted for the contest should reflect the character, heritage, and geography, or similar identifying feature of the area centered in Erath, Comanche, Eastland, Palo Pinto, Hood, Hamilton, and Bosque counties." The chamber of commerce noted that "many other areas of the state already have an identifying name—such as Dallas–Fort Worth's Metroplex, Abilene's Big Country, and Waco's Heart of Texas."

Perhaps the Stephenville Chamber of Commerce was aware that the traditional environmental term *Cross Timbers* was still weakly perceived as the vernacular name of this largely rural region; in any case, the winning selection was Cross Timbers Basin, a familiar name with a slightly new twist. Rural tradition had overcome flashy boosterism, causing the rejection of entries such as Centroplex, Eye of Texas, Inland Empire, Agri-Plex, and Clearwater Country. The newspaper promised that "Cross Timbers Basin will be used by the Chamber of Commerce and the *Empire-Tribune* in the future in referring to this area, and other groups, businesses, and organizations have been urged to do the same." Since

the area in question is not a topographic basin, it is possible that the suffix will eventually be dropped, leaving the venerable name of Cross Timbers unaltered. What we witnessed was not so much the birth of a new vernacular region as the phoenixlike revival of an old, dying one.

PERCEPTION OF REGIONAL BORDERS

Many answers to the questionnaire indicated that the boundaries of perceptual regions are often seen as being rather sharp. Thus it was felt by some people that Bexar County lies on the "border of the Hill Country and Brush Country" and Jim Wells County "on the edge of the Rio Grande Valley; people often refer to it as being in the Valley anyway." Another respondent described Bexar County as "near the Hill Country but not really in it"; still another remarked that "north of San Antonio is referred to as the Hill Country." A Palo Pinto resident placed that county "west of the Metroplex," and Mitchell County was described as part of the "Permian Basin, although we are east of that." Scurry County is situated at the "bottom of the South Plains, at the northwest end of the Rolling Plains." Numerous respondents listed more than one vernacular name for their area.

A curiosity of the map is the belt running north and south across Texas in which no popular names are in common use (Figure 12.3). This fuzzy boundary zone stretches from the northeastern corner of the state southwest beyond San Antonio. Some rural respondents attempted to fill this vacuum with a traditional, almost vanished environmental name, the Post Oak Belt. The large majority, however, reported no name. In the near future, this long, narrow strip is likely to be filled by Alamo Area, Brazos Valley, Ark-La-Tex, and other council of governments names, as well as Metroplex and perhaps Golden Circle. Civic pride abhors a popular regional vacuum. We find it noteworthy, however, that this belt runs almost exactly along the old border zone between cultural impulses received from the Lower South and the Middle Atlantic areas. To the east of this zone, the traditional culture, society, and economy are those of the Deep South. To the west, the influence of Missouri, Arkansas, Tennessee, and Appalachia prevails. Also, much of the border zone falls within Geographer Donald W. Meinig's "Central Texas," an area of thorough mixing of the various Texas cultures, suggesting that the diversity of peoples has hindered the rise of a widely accepted nickname for the area.

THE BIBLE BELT AND ETHNICITY

Much has been written about the Bible Belt in the United States and its location has variously been placed in the Deep South and the Lower Midwest. To our knowledge, nobody has attempted to map the Bible Belt as a vernacular region on the basis of questionnaire responses. Although not designed to do so, the Texas survey revealed that there unquestionably is a vernacular Bible Belt and that part of Texas is in it (Figure 12.7).

In Texas, *Bible Belt* is not a derogatory term in the mind of most residents. Quite the contrary, it is a positive statement that many Anglo-Texans proudly make about their home counties. Roughly the northern half of the state seems to belong in the perceptual Bible Belt.

Ethnicity was also evident in many of the perceptions of the questionnaire respondents, most commonly as slurs but occasionally reflective of positive self-image among minority groups. Slurs ranged from such anti-Hispanic names as Grease Belt, Brown Bend, Wetback's Towel, and Tortilla Flat, to Redneck Holler, the Valley of the Krauts, and KKK Kountry. The South Texas zone of tension between Anglo and Mexican is neatly outlined by the distri-

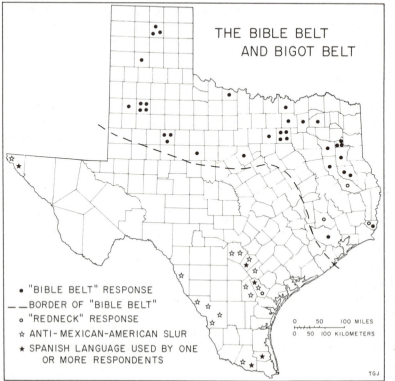

THE BIBLE BELT AND BIGOT BELT

- • "BIBLE BELT" RESPONSE
- — —BORDER OF "BIBLE BELT"
- ○ "REDNECK" RESPONSE
- ☆ ANTI-MEXICAN-AMERICAN SLUR
- ★ SPANISH LANGUAGE USED BY ONE OR MORE RESPONDENTS

0   50   100 MILES
0   50   100 KILOMETERS

Figure 12.7. Reprinted from Terry G. Jordan, "Perceptual Regions in Texas," *Geographical Review* 68 [1978], 304, with the permission of the American Geographical Society.

bution of anti-Hispanic slurs. The rising Mexican-American cultural and political awareness was revealed in the consistent usage of El Valle (del Rio Grande) instead of Rio Grande Valley; in the description of El Paso County as Baja Nuevo Mexico; and in the use of Sur Tejas, a possible reference to the desire of separatists to create a Mexican-dominated state in South Texas.

COMPASS DIRECTIONAL REGIONS

Quite aside from the popular names discussed above, compass direction terms and "central" are used by most Texans to describe various parts of the state. A second query on the questionnaire was designed to reveal such terms. The question read:

Residents of most parts of Texas identify their home counties by using one of the compass directions. Which, if any, of the following terms is used locally to identify the location of your county? . . . Check only the term(s) you have heard used by the inhabitants of the county: East Texas; North Texas; South Texas; West Texas; Central Texas; Northeast Texas; Southeast Texas; Northwest Texas; Southwest Texas; none of these; other (specify).

To be included in a directional-term popular region, a county had to (1) have a uniform response from at least 51 percent of the respondents and (2) be contiguous with the bulk of the counties in the region. The results, based on these criteria, were surprising in some areas and predictable in others (Figure 12.8).

West Texas was revealed to be the largest region, composed of a wedge-shaped territory that broadened to the west. Fort Worth, which has long claimed to be "where the West begins," is, in fact, three counties

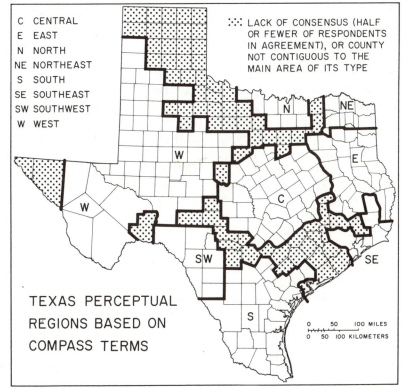

Figure 12.8. Reprinted from Terry G. Jordan, "Perceptual Regions in Texas," *Geographical Review* 68 [1978], 305, with the permission of the American Geographical Society.

removed from the easternmost reaches of West Texas, and more of the respondents from Tarrant County, the site of Fort Worth, identify with East, Northeast, and North than with West Texas. Abilene in Taylor County, long touted as "out where the West is at," lies instead in the eastern part of vernacular West Texas.

Southeast, Northeast, Southwest, and North Texas were perceived as rather confined border regions. Only one of these, Southeast Texas, enjoys council of governments support, in the form of the South East Texas Regional Planning Commission. There is, however, a Nortex Regional Planning Commission centered on Wichita Falls.

Of all the compass regions, East Texas receives the highest overall degree of identification and has the sharpest borders. The Trinity River marks most of its western boundary. Loaded with connotations of the Old South and the defeated Confederacy, East Texas is seemingly the most potent popular region of any in the state. An interesting variant detected was Deep East Texas (Figure 12.4). To some respondents, this traditional term means the area immediately adjacent to Louisiana, but the majority perceive it as the southern half of East Texas. The Deep East Texas Council of Governments adheres to this latter, more inclusive definition, as did many of the questionnaire respondents.

A second spatial definition of East and West Texas was achieved by looking at the responses for East, Southeast, and Northeast and those for West, Southwest, and Northwest. The resultant border of greater West Texas seldom ranges far from the 100th meridian, but that for the expanded East Texas region runs roughly from Dallas to Houston.

Central Texas, increasingly referred to as the Centex, occupies a sizable block of counties positioned to the east of center in the state. The perceptual Central Texas corresponds very closely to Meinig's region of this name. South Texas is a sizable region with rather blurred borders, defining spa-

tially the major Hispanic stronghold in the state. It carries definite ethnic connotations in the minds of most Texans.

In some "lack of consensus counties," especially in the far western part of Texas and the Panhandle, half or more of the respondents indicated that no directional terms were in use locally. These narrow transition zones serve as buffers between most of the regions. An exception is the Panhandle area, where a sizable undecided block of counties is found. Interestingly, this area corresponds very closely to the part of Texas belonging to the perceptual Midwest according to geographer Joseph Brownell. Curiously, some of Texas's largest cities—including Dallas, Fort Worth, El Paso, and San Antonio—lie in the transition areas.

Unlikely as it may seem, the majority of home county students at East Texas State University, in Hunt County, did not place their county in East Texas, nor were those at West Texas State or Southwest Texas State universities swayed by the names of their institutions. Only North Texas State students voted in a predictable manner, and even there the majority was rather small.

*   *   *

The Texas population at large, then, seems to share our view of the state as a diverse, balkanized province. Intricate and overlapping popular regions partition the state in the public mind, further justifying our similar view achieved through scholarly means. Texas is geographically many diverse areas, not one, and we strongly suspect that the majority of Texans identify more closely with some portion of the state than with Texas as a whole.

SOURCES AND SUGGESTED READINGS

Brownell, Joseph. "The Cultural Midwest." *Journal of Geography* 59 (1960), 81–85.
Gould, Peter, and White, Rodney. *Mental Maps.*

Baltimore: Penguin Books, 1974.

Hale, Ruth F. "A Map of Vernacular Regions in America." Ph.D. dissertation, Department of Geography, University of Minnesota, Minneapolis, 1971.

Jordan, Terry G. "Perceptual Regions in Texas." *Geographical Review* 68 (1978), 293–307.

———. "The Texan Appalachia." *Annals of the Association of American Geographers* 60 (1970), 409–427.

———. "Traditional Culture Patterns in Rural Texas." Map in Stanley A. Arbingast et al., *Atlas of Texas*, 5th ed., p. 31. Austin:

University of Texas, Bureau of Business Research, 1976.

Lewis, Oscar. *On the Edge of the Black Waxy: A Cultural Survey of Bell County, Texas.* Washington University Studies, New Series, Social and Philosophical Sciences, no. 7. St. Louis: Washington University, 1948.

Meinig, Donald W. *Imperial Texas: An Interpretive Essay in Cultural Geography.* Austin: University of Texas Press, 1969.

Zelinsky, Wilbur. "North America's Vernacular Regions." *Annals of the Association of American Geographers* 70 (1980), 1–16.

INDEX